The Edwardian Age

Conflict and Stability 1900–1914

The Edwardian Age: Conflict and Stability 1900-1914

EDITED BY
ALAN O'DAY

ARCHON BOOKS
Hamden, Connecticut

First published 1979 in England by
THE MACMILLAN PRESS LTD
London and Basingstoke
and in the U.S.A. as an Archon Book
an imprint of
THE SHOE STRING PRESS, INC.
995 Sherman Avenue,
Hamden, Connecticut 06514

Library of Congress Cataloging in Publication Data

Main entry under title:

The Edwardian age.

    Includes bibliographical references and index.
    1.   Great Britain—Politics and government—1901–1936.
2.   Great Britain—Social life and customs—20th century.
I.   O'Day, Alan.
DA570.E34   1979   309.1'41'0823   79–11809
ISBN 0–208–01823–9

Printed in Great Britain

Contents

Preface vi

Introduction 1
ALAN O'DAY

1   The Standard of Living, 1890–1914 13
T. R. GOURVISH

2   Political Economy in Edwardian England: The Tariff-Reform Controversy 34
PETER CAIN

3   Edwardian Politics: Turbulent Spring or Indian Summer? 60
WALTER L. ARNSTEIN

4   Critics of Edwardian Society: The Case of the Radical Right 79
G. R. SEARLE

5   The Character of the Early Labour Party, 1900–14 97
DENNIS DEAN

6   Irish Home Rule and Liberalism 113
ALAN O'DAY

7   The Family and the Role of Women 133
SUZANN BUCKLEY

8   Edwardian England and the Coming of the First World War 144
COLIN NICOLSON

List of Abbreviations 169

Bibliographical Notes 170

Notes and References 178

Notes on Contributors 191

Index 193

Preface

The Edwardian Age is similar to other volumes in the 'Problems in Focus' series in examining a limited number of important themes concerned with a specific problem or period. The volume does not pretend to treat all the issues of the Edwardian age or to present a unified view of the age. In one way or another each contributor has stressed the elements of stability and conflict discernible in his or her topic of discussion; hence the subtitle of the volume. But the various contributors do not always reach identical conclusions and occasionally the essays offer conflicting interpretations of the same theme.
theme.

The series attempts to treat given problems, summing up recent literature in the area and providing, where appropriate, a fresh interpretation or approach. This balance between summary and originality varies between contributions according to the nature of the topic discussed and to the intention of the author. All of the essays, however, are intended to be valuable to the student, teacher and researcher using the volume.

I have been extremely fortunate in having a group of contributors who not only submitted their essays on schedule but also tried to conform to the house rules without complaint. I am indebted to them: I could not have hoped for a more helpful 'team' and my task as editor has been greatly alleviated by their co-operativeness. I am especially grateful to Dennis Dean and Terry Gourvish, with whom I discussed the volume frequently and fruitfully; to Robert Skidelsky for a number of stimulating insights; and to Rosemary O'Day, whose expertise (both editorial and historical) has been invaluable on this occasion. Finally, I should like to thank both Derick Mirfin and Sarah Mahaffy of Macmillan for their encouragement and guidance at various points in the emergence of the volume.

ALAN O'DAY

Introduction

ALAN O'DAY

THE dominant theme of this volume is the question of whether there
was or was not a substantial crisis in Edwardian society. Hence the
book is subtitled *Conflict and Stability*. Naturally every age contains elements of both but the Edwardian period merits special attention. Sir
Edward Grey's declaration in 1914 that the 'lights are going out all
over Europe' has been seen as especially pertinent to Britain. After
1918, as A. J. P. Taylor has noted in *The Struggle for the Mastery of
Europe, 1848–1918*, Europe was subordinate, even irrelevant, in the
world. But Grey's comment reflects the nostalgia common amongst
Englishmen for the time when their country was, or at least seemed to
be, supreme. Today neither Europeans nor Americans have been
quite so pessimistic about the post-Edwardian years in their respective countries as contemporary observers were. The idea that the
Edwardian years represented a final golden age in society is largely a
parochial British concept, although such aspects as the attacks on liberal values; the attempts to pep up an ill performing economy; the
quest of Irishmen and women for a different role in society and politics; and the steps towards the construction of the so-called welfare
state do have a much wider fascination and importance.

That 1914 forms a break in the continuity of modern British history
is widely accepted, although historians are vigorously debating the
nature and extent of the change. Of the many writings examining
the Edwardian years, George Dangerfield's interpretation, first published in the mid-1930s, remains the most prominent and telling
indictment of pre-World War I Britain. Dangerfield, then a young
historian, was, of course, writing from the vantage point of the economic crisis, the rise of fascism, and the growing militarism characteristic of the thirties. Like other young men of his time, he was deeply
distressed by what he saw around him. The apparent serenity and
rationality of inter-war Europe was gone and the slow but steady
movement towards a better world seemed not merely to have stopped
but to have been reversed. Where did the fault lie? Many in the inter-
war period had ascribed the roots of their own difficulties to the war

and its aftermath. To them the Edwardian days had assumed the halo
of a 'golden age', perhaps now the last for Britain. They were quite
shaken by Dangerfield's contrasting argument that the erosion of
those values that had made Britain pre-eminent – the importance of
discussion, compromise and the willingness to abide by the 'rules of
the game' – rapidly took place in the years prior to the war, in that
very 'golden age'. His villains were trade union militancy and syndi-
calism, the Pankhurst feminists, and those Conservatives and Ulster
Unionists who encouraged and abetted armed resistance to Irish
home rule. Britain, he argued, was speedily transformed from a
rational society where fundamental decisions took place in the civilised forum of Parliament into an irrational nation where militancy on
the streets prevailed and forced decisions. For him, liberal England
had thereby been slain.

Few accept Dangerfield's portrait as more than an arresting and
highly personalised impression of the age. It is easy enough to demonstrate flaws in his analysis. Yet the influence of *The Strange Death of Liberal England, 1910–14* cannot be overestimated. It remains the most
widely read book on the period and the bulk of historical controversy
continues to centre on the issues he raised directly and by implication.
Of what did liberal Britain consist? To what extent did this Britain
remain intact after 1918? Was the Edwardian period merely the conclusion of Victorian Britain or did it generate an ethos, a style of its
own? Is it an age of transition or was the war the villain? Hence
Dangerfield's argument has retained its vitality. Although no-one
agrees with the precise details of the Dangerfield picture, the majority
of contributors do provide substantial support for his brushwork – the
central thesis that the Edwardian age was one of severe testing and
crisis for liberalism (with a small 'l'). Much recent literature has
stressed the stability and continuity of Edwardian ideals and institutions, while here reassessment of traditional themes and the inclu-
sion of new material has led the majority of contributors to points of
view which stress conflict and which are more congenial to the Dangerfield thesis.

Significantly, there is no attempt to amend Dangerfield's definition
of the core values of the supposedly liberal society. Even accepting the
caveats of some writers about how genuinely liberal Britain was, it is
clear that the Edwardians themselves had a reasonably coherent view
of what was meant and of themselves as a liberal society. The essence
of liberal Britain lay for them, as we have noted, in discussion, compromise, rationality, and the acceptance of decisions arrived at by

legally (not democratically) constituted authority. Dissent was openly condoned but any political battle was to be waged in newspaper columns, on platforms, and in Parliament – not on the streets. Englishmen boast of their ancient freedoms but liberal Britain was a quite recent concoction in fact. It emerged only in the later Victorian period. Its main characteristic was the ability of majorities to make decisions. Participation in the creation of those majorities was being democratised. The critical test was whether Britain could successfully retain her tolerant, discussion-orientated society in the face of democratic passions and appetites. Pessimistic observers wagered that she could not but, until the later Edwardian years at least, they seemed to be proved wrong by events.

The volume begins with T. R. Gourvish's discussion of the standard of living. His theme brings many of the issues of the age into perspective. The implication of his analysis is that the liberal state rested on an élite being able to convince the ruled that Britain was a freer, richer and happier country than any other. Even so, the Government promised that via hard work and merit life would be made even better and that men would reach their true level in the world. This doctrine was preached in the churches and chapels, in the press and popular literature, and by politicians. The élite would not be able to trust the masses, however, unless it succeeded in controlling and satisfying their greed. What made it all possible was Britain's enormous wealth. A wealthy nation could afford to be generous; it could risk being 'liberal'.

The liberal state, then, was built upon a foundation of growth economics. But after the early 1870s Britain was no longer to enjoy ceaseless prosperity. The problems of the economy have been debated by a bevy of distinguished historians. Disagreement over particulars, though, does not detract from their almost universal agreement that Britain's economic performance had slowed markedly. In agriculture some sectors and regions enjoyed post-1873 prosperity, but the large capital and labour-intensive grain sector suffered a contraction in size and profitability. In aggregate, agriculturalists experienced a relative and absolute decline from the 1870s until near the end of the century. Agricultural employment diminished and many tenants and labourers were forced to migrate to the cities or to emigrate. Landowners, who traditionally provided the governors of society, lost much of their economic and social creditability. Industry had a more varied fortune. In aggregate again, though, industry did not fare well; it was simply a case of hard-times and contraction for many businesses. The several Royal Commissions on agriculture and trade bore ample testimony to the intense concern of contemporaries about the economy.

Late Victorian Britain, Gourvish suggests, averted the degree of social conflict that might have been anticipated because for most employed workers the actual standard of living rose. Present-day economic recession in Britain has been accompanied by rapid inflation and stagnation of or falling standards of living. In contrast the economic slowdown after 1870 was accompanied by falling prices for food and basic commodities. Hence the unfavourable implications of Britain's economic difficulties were masked from a large section of the population. Indeed, the symptoms of the disease may even have been agreeable. However, during the Edwardian years, prices began to climb faster than wages, with a consequent rise in social and economic frustration. While this shift has for long been commented upon by historians, Gourvish reminds us that at heart the crisis was one of rising working-class expectations induced by a long generation of improvement in conditions. The psychological shock administered to workers was perhaps more injurious than the actual economic effects of stagnant and declining living standards. By the beginning of the Edwardian age the economic foundations of the liberal state were already insecure: Edwardians were made to pay for Victorian failures and the bill they received was both high and shocking. One might almost be tempted to retitle Dangerfield's book, *The Delayed Death of Liberal England*.

Whatever the Edwardians were they were not complacent. A significant group made a determined effort to preserve the fabric of the Britain they knew. A socially committed few conducted social surveys, most pertinently of poverty, and advocated reforms that would guarantee minimum living standards to all subjects. Poverty was certainly not discovered by the Edwardians but it was studied by them. The remarkable and careful work of Charles Booth in London and Seebohm Rowntree in York both defined poverty more systematically than had been the case previously, and demonstrated that much of it owed nothing to laziness, improvidence or intemperance. It was the old, the young, the disabled and the widowed who suffered most. The findings of Booth, Rowntree and their contemporaries fuelled public interest and political initiative. The Liberal Government between 1906 and 1914 fathered many important measures that have been seen as pioneering the development of the modern welfare state. Not surprisingly, these welfare proposals – notably national insurance, school meals and so on – have been discussed extensively by historians. Bentley Gilbert, for instance, has written a distinguished study of the evolution of the national insurance legislation and, very recently, Jose Harris has published a heroic biography of the *eminence grise* of welfare, William Beveridge. The origins of the welfare state have seemed of exceptional importance for the present generation of historians. This volume of essays deliberately does not contain a discussion of the development of the welfare state and its legislation – which is well covered in easily accessible works.* Rather it features discussions by T. R. Gourvish and Peter Cain of the motives behind such legislation and alternatives to welfare proposals.

T. R. Gourvish argues impressively that welfare legislation, no matter how well intended or how useful to its recipients, was essentially merely a palliative for the fundamental problems of the Edwardian economy and society. He suggests that historians' fascination with the distribution of income has been matched unfortunately by a neglect of the more crucial issue of wealth generation. Whatever the value of welfare to defenceless groups in society, it could not provide a real answer to the problems of the employed wage earner or of the nation as a whole. Politicians, by stressing reform, he implies, avoided the fundamental and larger question. Hence, following the Gourvish analysis, one can see that the issue of the economy's slowing down and the attendant consequences was central to the character of the Edwardian period – a point which contemporaries neglected (or could not see) and which historians are in danger of ignoring if they concentrate exclusively on welfare legislation.

Peter Cain follows with an analysis of the industrial economy. He focuses on the tariff reform movement which sought to change the direction of Britain's economic fortunes. Advocates of protective tariffs believed that the restoration of industrial prosperity was the first order of the day. This movement had many aspects and attracted a mixed, often confused, following. Some saw in it a force for imperial unity as well as a domestic rescue operation. In Joseph Chamberlain, Cain observes, the protectionists had a gifted spokesman and, overall, they displayed a notable talent for diagnosing industrial malaise and attributing the disease to particular causes. As he argues, however, problem identification and vigorous advocacy of a solution proved easier for them than providing an economically and politically con-

---

* Derek Fraser, *The Evolution of the British Welfare State* (Macmillan, 1973). and J. R. Hay, *The Origins of the Liberal Welfare Reforms 1906–1914* (Macmillan, 1975).

vincing programme of reform. Failure to do this was due partly to the complexity of the issue itself; partly to divided and frequently muddled thinking within the protectionist ranks; partly to fortuitous improvements in the economy which undermined support for protection at crucial moments; and perhaps most of all to the grip enjoyed by free trade economics. In Britain, unlike in the United States or Germany, free trade was identified closely with prosperity in the minds of people from all classes. Workers, in particular, feared more expensive food.

Paradoxically, Cain's essay shows how industrial hard times were eroding the stability of society and the consensus of support for Victorian liberal doctrine while at the same time the Tariff reform movement's failure revealed the hold of stability in Edwardian Britain. Whatever the momentary problems of the economy, a majority of Britons remained suspicious of any protectionist panacea. Some may attribute this seeming stability to rigidity and a lack of imagination. For whatever reasons, frustration certainly did not lead to an easy or hasty change of attitude on the part of the people. Tariff reformers were not necessarily ideologically opposed to welfare proposals but they did, as Cain demonstrates, offer a distinctive view of the problems which Britain had to face. Tariff reformers tended to argue that their pet scheme would provide a fundamental resolution of Britain's primary economic problems. They tried to convince people that a more prosperous country would require less welfare provision or at least be in a position to finance it; that Liberal concentration on welfare represented an incorrect analysis of the problem; and that welfare legislation put the cart before the horse.

A number of social critics on both the political left and the right were concerned about the direction in which Edwardian society was moving. The political left has received the bulk of historical attention but here G. R. Searle, in an original study, looks at the sources of support, the strengths and weaknesses, and the ultimate failure of right-wing critics. These men, he argues, had simply lost confidence in the ability of the liberal state to meet the problems of the age. Indeed, what held the far right together was a growing hatred of liberal democracy and a tendency to identify it as the true enemy of British revival. Their views were perhaps not so far distant from those of the Marxist left. A similar vein of militant authoritarianism ran through the thinking of the left and the Radical Right. Searle implies that although the left has been the primary interest of historians, the far right was more prominent and more dangerous to the liberal state. Where the Marxist left had the benefit of a coherent ideology, the right often built upon

a collection of hatreds and frustrations. Yet the latter negative qualities reflected more accurately the inner mood of the British people.
Moreover, the radical right had superior access to the ruling class and
the ideas of some right-wing leaders seemed to be permeating some
sectors of the Conservative Party. Yet the Radical Right had
ambivalent feelings towards the Tory Party – some hoped to convert
or infiltrate it while others thought it a major obstacle to fundamental
change.

In several respects the strengths and deficiencies of Radical Right
critics of the liberal state serve to highlight the twin themes of stability
and conflict. These men had a tenable and sometimes appealing case
against the liberal state, but they were neither united nor coherent
about what might be substituted for it. The Radical Right resembled
the tariff reformers (with whom many overlapped) in being abler critics than doctors. The most coherent group on the right were the
advocates of national efficiency, a movement discussed at length in
Searle's, *The Quest for National Efficiency* (1971), but this was wider than
the radical right itself and was at heart traditional in its aims and
methods. The potential of the far right, then, although much greater
than that of its opposite number on the far left, was never close to realisation. These critics were in themselves both a symptom of and a
force for instability in Edwardian society. Yet many of these men were
more inclined to extreme talk than radical action and were reluctant
to break with either the Conservative Party or (fully) liberal democratic ideology. Although the Radical Right's activity was motivated by
many of the same frustrations that would fuel Oswald Moseley's fas-
cist movement in the 1930s, it was a good deal less prepared to break
with the liberal heritage. Dangerfield's assertion that Conservatives
contributed to the break-down of the values of the age is partly
confirmed and partly gainsaid by Searle's treatment.

The inability of Liberalism to respond to the problems of the
period is the principal theme explored by Alan O'Day's analysis of
the Edwardian approach to Ireland. For long Irish home rule has
seemed to most historians to be the tragic example *par excellence* of
the good cause thwarted by irrational militant resistance. Many,
like Dangerfield, looking backward have seen in the 1916–21
bloodshed the consequences of the failure to implement home rule
before the war. Liberals have been made to bear a portion of the
blame, but mainly for their lack of resolve and good faith in
making home rule a reality. O'Day takes exception to this line of
argument, insisting that by the Edwardian years home rule was

dead as a viable policy alternative although it continued to have importance as a symbol for Irishmen. By 1905 neither Irishmen nor Liberals were primarily concerned with it and Conservatives, who showed a remarkable reforming impulse in Ireland, used it merely as a stick with which to beat opponents. He argues, however, that when the Liberals' Irish reforms began to encounter resistance (and specifically when a further local government bill failed in 1907) Irish nationalism found it expedient to revert to the orthodox demand for home rule. The Liberal majority then lost its initiative and also its ability to build an alternative constructive policy. Home rule became a vital issue once again simply because Liberal Party leaders were unwilling or unable to formulate a new line of approach to the Irish problem and because Irish nationalists wanted it that way. For the first half of the Edwardian period, Ireland was something of a source of stability in the state as a consensus based on reform emerged. In the second half the basis of common action was shattered and Ireland became a chief factor in the disintegration of the stable, cohesive British state. But O'Day is quite clear that responsibility for the course of the Irish crisis rested with the Liberals. He would side, in a sense, with Dangerfield concerning the disruption of liberal England but his cast of villains is very different. When the Liberals failed to provide the necessary initiative and leadership, the way was clear for the disruption of the liberal state by other forces. Had the Liberal leadership been innovative where Irish policy was concerned, home rule would never have been revived. Similarly O'Day joins Gourvish, Cain and Searle in suggesting that the weakness of Britain's economic situation further exacerbated existing problems.

Colin Nicolson, too, examines the relative weakness of liberal ideology but from the perspective of foreign policy. Traditional, conservative (with a small 'c') ideas enjoyed a resurgence during the Edwardian age. Nicolson argues that those ideals usually associated with Gladstonian foreign policy had a limited appeal only for either the governing classes or the public at large. National strength through a well-supported military and through decisive action in line with British self-interest were the hall-marks of the growing conservative mood in foreign relations. Simply put, British interests would be served best by using a mailed glove. Nicolson believes that the Gladstonian alternative, which at its peak commanded only minority allegiance, was faltering. The illusion of a Britain subscribing to Gladstonian principles was maintained for much of the period of Liberal government, but only because Gladstone's ideals were held in reverence by some at the centre of affairs and possibly also because the language of liberalism changed less quickly than did the reality of its attitudes. Nicolson finds that the preference for 'realism' in foreign policy now had an especially strong grip on the popular imagination. Even the few remaining Gladstonians were slowly adapting to the new mood and modifying their old tradition, especially as competition with Germany became more intense. The implication of Nicolson's point is that the ideological roots of Liberals were under attack; that the chief supporters of Gladstonian policy were seeking to re-define their position; and that the move towards war was neither sudden nor unpopular, as has sometimes been imagined. He does appear to confirm Dangerfield's view that some important change was taking place in liberal Britain and that what was emerging was a tougher-minded, more militant and self-interested ideology. Where he departs from Dangerfield, however, is in his emphasis on the essential weakness of liberal ideals in the first place and on the rationality of the new conservatism.

Indeed, Cain, O'Day and, to some extent, Searle confirm the Nicolson view of conservatism. In total in this volume it appears as a far more rational and constructive force than historians have usually allowed. Typically, the right has been pictured as a confused, retrogressive element in the body politic. Here quite clearly the impression of a constructive, developing body of conservative thought is emphasised. Where Liberals, as proposers of welfare, as supporters of home rule and of the womens' franchise (with notorious exceptions) have always seemed the force for positive, forward-looking change, Conservatives have always appeared the reverse. Their manipulation of the House of Lords to prevent the passage of reform legislation has always appeared to epitomise this negativism of the Conservative party. To date even the semi-official Tory historians, like Lord Blake, have been at least apologetic for their party's past attitudes and practices. The essays in this volume, however, reveal a different, and often more impressive, side to some sectors of Conservatism. Foreign policy, Nicolson demonstrates, was a stabilising factor in Edwardian society but only in the sense that it was part of something resembling a palace revolution against the very foundations of liberal ideals.

Perhaps the final irony of liberalism is captured by Suzann Buckley's reassessment of the suffragette movement. Most writers have concentrated on the politics and tactics of the struggle. Recently, historians have begun to interest themselves in how the feminist movement is related to the wider economic and social context in which it functioned. This interest owes much to the preoccupations of the present-day feminist movement, especially in America, where such issues are daily being explored. A good deal of this literature is frankly as militant and committed in a literary context as was Mrs Pankhurst in a physical way. Political emancipation of women has come to be seen as a symbolic struggle over the validity of liberal doctrine. For long it has seemed clear that supporters of votes for women were upholders of the liberal doctrine of widening governmental participation and of 'trusting' the people. Opponents, in contrast, have seemed to be anti-liberal in their rejection of these doctrines. Dangerfield's main concern was with the militancy of the feminist struggle and the fact that the contest was fought in the streets rather than in the political arena, and not with the political issue of women voters. The Prime Minister, Asquith, certainly no feminist, was primarily concerned with the impact of womens' votes on his party's fortunes at the polls. He thought that middle-class female enfranchisement boded ill: he wanted either something wide enough to help the Liberal party or nothing at all. Suzann Buckley develops a quite distinctive argument. She insists that what many women sought in the ballot was not an extension of such liberal values as compromise and toleration but their curtailment. Women objected to the breakdown of the traditional family and the sexual freedom which the liberal ethos appeared to encourage. The ballot was essential and was to be used to implement not freedom from family ties but a restoration of sexual purity, enforced by the power and authority of the state. In many cases militant feminist radicalism masked an essentially conservative, almost authoritarian attitude. The tools and rhetoric of liberalism were effectively being used against liberalism itself. It might be fair to conclude from her analysis that Dangerfield was correct in stressing the role of militant feminism in undermining the liberal state but that he misread the signs somewhat when describing the nature of the attack.

Taken together, six of the essays provide general support for Dangerfield's point that liberal Britain was in crisis during these years and emphasise the forces for instability in Edwardian Britain. But the historians who stress elements of stability in that society do not go unrepresented. Most of the six essays which emphasise conflict in that society do not deny the presence of many stable elements. Indeed the main point is that there was a sufficiently strong attachment to the old liberal ideology to make movement into a new ideology a matter of struggle, of tension. Our colleagues, Walter Arnstein and Dennis Dean, are more traditionalist and do not share this view of Edwardian Britain as a society drawn in opposing directions by contrary winds. Both urge the vital stability of Edwardian Britain. Arnstein's survey of Edwardian politics is primarily directed to providing an up-to-date assessment of a now vast and confusing literature. His conclusion, however, is that, despite change (something common to all ages), Britain was recognisably the same politically in 1914 as it had been in 1900. He does not find any convincing evidence that politically speaking liberal Britain has died or was on the verge of death or that the Liberal Party was on the slope of inevitable decline. He reminds us that when one looks beyond the bounds of Britain, particularly across the Atlantic to the United States, similar developments did not lead to the collapse of either liberal ideas or the Democratic party. Arnstein, an American, subtly asserts that too much British history has been written from a narrow, parochial and restricting British viewpoint.

Likewise, Dennis Dean surveys the trends in historical writing on the development of the Labour movement. The chief debates he discusses are those concerning the motivation for separate Labour representation in the House of Commons and whether the rise of Labour inevitably meant the decline of the Liberals. Though Dean sees some shifts in the mood of labour in the years immediately prior to 1914, his overall conclusion is that Labour was little more than a scion of Liberalism and posed little threat to the parent. A fuller defence of the alternative view can be found by reading Ross McKibbin's recent, *The Evolution of the Labour Party, 1910–1922*. Dean believes that labour leaders were more interested in questions of recognition and respect of workers than in income distribution; the ownership of the means of production; or social welfare. Leaders who sought more radical or different ends generally lost their influence within the Labour movement. The movement was progressive rather than militant or disruptive: its leaders never sought to break with the liberal ethos of discussion and compromise. Together Dean and Arnstein suggest that there was a great deal in Labour and the so-called 'new liberalism' that was distinctly reminiscent of Gladstonianism.

Clearly, whichever view is preferred, conflict and stability coexisted in the Edwardian age. The dispute at issue is the extent to which one prevailed over the other. The period was not isolated from its Victorian forebear or from the post 1918 years. But it did bring problems to the fore which were distinct from those of either its predecessor or its successor. To some extent the Edwardians were victims of the Victorians' policies; the events of 1914 cut short abruptly the brief attempt at regeneration and solution of inherited problems made by the vigorous Edwardian generation. The lively historical debate about aspects of the age will continue to fascinate and instruct us.

1. The Standard of Living, 1890-1914

T. R. GOURVISH

AT the aggregate level there appears to be little doubt about Britain's continuing progress in the Edwardian age. Recent calculations indicate a steady rise in the principal indicators – Gross National Product, consumers' expenditure, and income from employment. In *per capita* terms, net national income (at current prices) increased from £36 in 1890 to £43 in 1900 and £51 in 1914, while consumers' expenditure (at 1913 prices), £37 in 1890, was £43 in 1900 and £45 in 1914.[1] But the distribution of this increased wealth, which had obsessed the late Victorians, continued to haunt Edwardians. The existence of widespread poverty in the midst of plenty, revealed in the path-breaking investigations of Charles Booth and Seebohm Rowntree in London and York, was reaffirmed in studies of a number of towns, including Middlesbrough, Northampton and Warrington.[2] There was also a veritable explosion of popular publications, notably Chiozza Money's *Riches and Poverty*, Masterman's *The Condition of England*, Reeves's *Round About a Pound a Week*, and Ponsonby's *The Camel and the Needle's Eye*.

Most of these efforts, however, were directed at the dispersion of wealth rather than its movement over time. Measurement of the trend of real earnings was a matter for more sober reflection, and it attracted relatively few writers. The principal contributors, A. L. Bowley and G. H. Wood, who took advantage of the increased volume of official data on wages, unemployment, and retail prices to produce estimates of average real wages, were always anxious to emphasise the conceptual and statistical problems surrounding their work. Bowley, for example, eschewed the term 'real wages', referring instead to a wages cost-of-living 'quotient', 'because of the numerous qualifications with which it must be used'.[3] Nevertheless, the Bowley–Wood estimates were sufficiently impressive to create a historical consensus for the period, and this has been cemented by the recent study by Phelps Brown and Browne, *A Century of Pay*. Average real wages, it is now commonly agreed, proceeded as shown in Figure 1.

After a fairly sharp rise in the early 1890s, amounting to 8 per cent in 1892–5 (Bowley; Phelps Brown and Browne) and 11 per cent in 1892–6 (Wood), stabilisation was a characteristic of the next two decades. And, since falling real wages were a feature of two comparatively long sub-periods – 1899–1905 and 1908–13 – the overall picture for 1899–1913 is of a decrease of 0.4–0.5 per cent a year. Edwardian Britain, then, must be associated with the first serious interruption to the upward movement of real wages for at least a quarter of a century, and the years of regression were far more numerous than the years of advance.

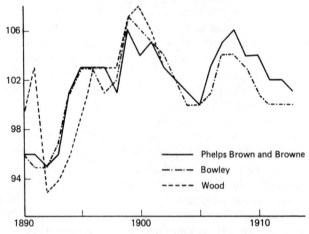

FIGURE 1   Average real wages 1890–1913 (1890–9 = 100)
SOURCES. Average real wages, allowing for unemployment: G. H. Wood, 'Real Wages and the Standard of Comfort Since 1850', *JRSS*, LXXIII (1909) 102–3; wages/cost-of-living quotient: A. L. Bowley, *Wages and Income in the United Kingdom since 1860* (Cambridge, 1937) p. 30; wage earnings 'in composite units of consumables': E. H. Phelps Brown and M. Browne, *A Century of Pay* (1968) pp. 444–5.

Explanations for this hiatus in real wages naturally centre on price inflation. While money wages were about 19–20 per cent higher in 1913 than in 1890–6 (Bowley; Phelps Brown and Browne), prices more than matched this rise. Over the period 1896–1913, the Board of Trade's wholesale-price index rose by 32 per cent, its food and drink component by 21 per cent. The other price indexes suggest a higher rate of growth, the Sauerbeck–*Statist* index producing an increase of 39 per cent, and Rousseaux's overall index one of no less than 45 per cent. Our knowledge of the cost of living, based as it is on Bowley's rather speculative work, suggests we should think in terms of a 20 rather than a 40 per cent rise (23 per cent from 1896 to 1913), but this was sufficient to outpace money-wage increases for much of the period. Here, we should note that money wages actually fell at the turn of the century (1900–4, Bowley; 1901–2, Phelps Brown and Browne) and again around 1908 (1907–8, Bowley; 1907–9, Phelps Brown and Browne). Undoubtedly, the widespread industrial discontent of the period was fuelled by the conjunction of price inflation, an entirely new experience for a whole generation of workers, and the first general assault on increasing money wages since the late 1870s. The situation soon became clear to contemporaries. Philip Snowden, for example, writing in 1912, observed that the trend of wages, 'if at all marked, has been rather backward than forward', while 'since 1900 there has been a steady and continuous increase in the price of . . . necessary commodities'. At the same time, G. R. Askwith's Cabinet paper on labour unrest of 1911 showed that the Government was well aware of the potentially explosive effects of the lag of wages behind prices.[4]

The concurrence of, at best, stationary real wages and rising income per head quite obviously indicates an income redistribution against wage-earners in Edwardian Britain. The available evidence bears this out. As industrial production increased, by 58 per cent between 1890 and 1913, the wage-earner's share of value added declined relative to profits. Phelps Brown and Browne's 'wage–income ratio' – that is, money-wage earnings divided by income generated per occupied person in industry – averaged 72 per cent in the 1880s and 71 per cent in 1890–3. But it fell to 64 per cent in 1896–9, remaining more or less at that level until the First World War.[5] In addition, investors, particularly those who participated in the shift to profitable foreign ventures after 1905, were able to smile again after a bleak period.[6] Thus, although income from employment expressed as a percentage of GNP remained fairly constant – the mean for 1890–1913 was 50.8 with a standard deviation of only 0.8 – the share of wages alone (using Bowley's estimates) drifted downwards, from 42 per cent in 1890–6 to 36 per cent in 1910–13.[7] Part of this variation is to be explained by the growth of salaried occupations. The salary–wage ratio increased from 21 per cent in 1890 to 33 per cent in 1913 and 36 per cent in 1914.[8] None the less, a redistribution in favour of property-owners was in evidence. Chiozza Money, for example, in the 1910 edition of *Riches and Poverty*, was able to show that 'the wealthy classes have increased their share of the national dividend both actually and relatively' since the first edition five years earlier. His top 3 per cent of income-earners, with incomes of over £700 a year, raised their share of national income from 33.3 per cent in 1903-4 to 34.4 per cent in 1908-9.[9] Admittedly, rough and ready calculations such as these are subject to fairly wide margins of error. But the contemporary concern with the gap between rich and poor occurred at a time when that gap could be shown to be widening, when the strength of capital was reasserting itself.

At present, it seems unlikely that there will be a serious challenge to this rather gloomy picture of the standard of living of the majority of Edwardians. Nevertheless, the more obvious criticisms of our 'received view' must be fully recognised. First of all, Bowley and Wood remain the origin of most subsequent historical analysis. Quite simply, it is the widespread use of their results that explains the existing similarities in computation and interpretation. The most recent statistical works only follow a well established trend. Thus, for the period after 1860, Phelps Brown and Browne take Wood's series of average money wages, adding data from Bowley for 1911–14, while Feinstein, in his *National Income* volume of 1972, uses Bowley's wage-earnings index. Both of them adopt Bowley's cost-of-living index, without modification. This dependence on Bowley and Wood has obviously perpetuated the deficiencies inherent in their data. Taking wages first, while coverage is reasonably adequate, the problems multiply when we try to use the series to answer questions about overall living standards. Both indexes rely on wage *rates*, not on earnings. Bowley's index makes no allowance for short time, overtime and unemployment, while Wood's efforts to adjust for the last on the basis of the statistics of unemployment in certain trade unions can only be highly approximate given the 'formidable defects' (Feinstein's phrase) of this source. Not only is there no provision for short-time working, strikes, and lock-outs, but the sample is also far too small and unrepresentative to facilitate its use as a proxy for general unemployment levels. Neither series makes any allowance for the welfare effects of shorter hours or changing levels of social-service provision. Turning to prices, our material is even less satisfactory. Bowley's index is generally preferred to Wood's 'frankly experimental' series, but it is by no means free from criticism. Information on food prices comes from London alone, the clothing series is grossly inadequate, and wholesale prices are used wherever retail-price information is scanty.

The sub-index of working-class rents must also be examined. Here again, Bowley's calculations rest on insecure foundations. The Board of Trade provided estimates for only five years in our period – 1890, 1895, 1900, 1905 and 1912 – and the first three observations were derived from house-valuation returns, a source which may well underestimate the extent of rent increases. Information for October 1905 and May 1912 is much more complete, but, given the wide parameters of the rental payments cited for each type of accommodation, we should not accept the Board of Trade's conclusion that rent levels were stationary between 1905 and 1912 simply because these parameters remained more or less unchanged. Nor is it certain that rents were static between 1900 and 1905. Bowley rightly accepted that his series was subject to considerable margins of error, but contended that the possibility of serious distortion was lessened by allocating a weight of only 16 per cent to rent in his cost-of-living index. This is undoubtedly true, but such a weight is at variance with the budgetary experience of the majority of working-class families. If we accept the view of the Board of Trade, in its *Report* of 1908, that the predominant type of rented accommodation in 1905 was four- or five-roomed, we may use the unweighted mean of rental parameters for such properties in the principal cities – London, Birmingham, Liverpool, Manchester, Newcastle and Edinburgh – to produce an 'average rent' of 7s. 6d. (37½p) a week. This represents no less than 34 per cent of the 'average wage' in that year (£1.08 according to Phelps Brown) and 25 per cent of a wage of 30s. (£1.50). Even if we exclude London and Edinburgh, where rents were particularly high, the revised 'average rent' of 6s. 6d. (32½p) produces percentages of 30 and 21 respectively. Clearly, a weighting of 25–30 per cent is a more accurate reflection of working-class rent burdens.[10] Two additional features serve to bias the sub-index in a downward direction. First, no adjustment is made for the increase in average rents consequent upon the declining importance of rural rents in the national picture. Secondly, part of the observed increase in rents is excluded because it represents rates payments for improvements in urban amenities. This deduction may be justified, but quality adjustments are not attempted for the other variables. Taken singly, the procedures criticised may have minimal effects on the final calculations. Taken together, however, they suggest that the rent series may be some distance from working-class reality in the period.

The validity of the established picture of average real wages may be criticised further by referring to occupations. If, for example, we are concerned with the experience of those who remained in the same occupation in the same industry, then the Bowley–Wood average,

which adjusts wage earnings to allow for changes in the relative numbers employed in the different industries, has less relevance than an
unadjusted series. In this context, Wood's alternative calculations are
instructive. His *unweighted* money-wage series – for a 'workman of
unchanged grade' – exhibits for 1890–1910 a rise of only 6 per cent, as
compared with an increase of 14 per cent for the 'average worker'.
Clearly, the real wage experience of a generation of immobile workers
was worse than that of the working community as a whole, where
some of the pressure was alleviated by a shift in favour of higher-wage
industries.[11] On the other hand, if we wish to measure the full extent
of the improvement created by occupational mobility, we should not
be satisfied with a procedure which allows for changes within manual
occupations alone. Reference should also be made to the increasing
opportunities for white-collar employment. Between 1891 and 1911,
for example, the numbers employed in government, defence, the pro-
fessions and commerce grew by 63 per cent, while the total occupied
workforce increased by only 22 per cent.[12]

Given the above criticisms it would be highly desirable to replace
the Bowley–Wood schema with an approach which included all the
necessary components and discarded rough approximations. But we
should be quite clear about the dangers inherent in attempting such a
revision. Since only a small adjustment would be needed to produce a
different trend – a 6 per cent correction of either wages or prices in
1913 would be sufficient to reverse our perceived downward trend in
real wages over the period 1899–1913 – it would be foolish to try to
replace one crude assessment of the national picture with one based
on equally shaky foundations. This is not to say that the effects of
short-time working, unemployment, welfare provision, occupational
mobility and so on are unimportant; but the quality of the available
evidence is not sufficient to permit us to assign the exactitude of index
numbers to hypotheses concerning them. At this stage it is important
to observe that the absence or poor handling of certain variables does
not necessarily invalidate our picture of the period.

Support for a cautious position may be drawn from the work of the
Marxist scholar Jürgen Kuczynski. In his brief survey of the experience of labour under capitalism he is highly critical of the
Bowley–Wood indexes, arguing that they 'tend to convey the impression of a more favourable development of labour conditions than
has actually taken place'. An attempt is made to correct part of this
'bias' by modifying Wood's cost-of-living index, incorporating *all*,
instead of *half*, of the observed rise in rents. But it is significant that

Kuczynski is not tempted to make further adjustments for the other deficiencies he finds. Consequently, his series of real wages, allowing for unemployment, reveals trends which are practically identical to those already outlined – namely, a 9 per cent rise in 1892–6, and a 7 per cent fall (0.5 per cent a year) in 1899–1913.[13]

Accepting that there are limitations in the Bowley–Wood approach, is there any comfort to be derived from regional and local data, the customary refuge of the historian faced with inadequate national evidence? It is certainly clear that the wide variations in local earnings and rents characteristic of the 1850s persisted into the twentieth century. E. H. Hunt's recent study of regional wage variations leaves us in no doubt as to the 'extraordinarily slow reduction of differentials before 1914'.[14] Nor do these wage differences appear to have been offset by variations in local price levels. On the contrary, Hunt suggests that there was a surprising similarity in the cost of living (excluding rent) in the different regions, although his evidence is rather limited, especially for urban areas.[15] Thus, we can be quite sure that Edwardian Britain, like Victorian Britain, was a country of marked contrasts in real earnings. The most striking examples are well known, of course. It is almost platitudinous to refer to the gulf between agricultural workers' earnings in poor counties such as Norfolk and Suffolk and those in relatively prosperous Lancashire and Durham, or that between industrial workers' earnings in high-wage centres such as Birmingham and Manchester and those in country towns in East Anglia and the West Country. By the early twentieth century these differentials were gradually narrowing, it is true, but more subtle variations were appearing, the result of contrasting industrial experience as foreign competition intensified. But it is one thing to establish that there were substantial regional differences in levels of real earnings, another to measure with any accuracy the *trend* of regional standards of living in our period. Here, unfortunately, we must concede that detailed evidence is just as elusive as it is in the search for national averages.

The most complete evidence we have relates to real wages in London, where there is both Frances Wood's contemporary study for 1900–12 and Rufus Tucker's two-century survey of the London artisan, published in 1936. Both produce results which conform closely to the national picture. Wood suggests that real wages fell by 6 per cent from 1900 to 1912, while Tucker's artisan, after experiencing a rise of 11 per cent from 1892 to 1897, suffered a fall of 6 per cent (0.4 per cent a year) between 1899 and 1913.[16] Elsewhere, results are more difficult to obtain. For Sheffield, Sidney Pollard has produced a detailed analysis of money earnings from 1851 to 1914. His combined index of two distinct groups of industries – the 'light' and 'heavy' metal trades – is particularly important because it indicates a far greater degree of fluctuation in earnings from year to year than is suggested by either the national or the London studies. Not only did earnings in Sheffield change direction more often, but the amplitude of change was greater. Using a common base of 1890–9 = 100, for example, Sheffield earnings ranged from 87 in 1893 to 124 in 1913, while the Phelps Brown and Browne series ranged from 99 (1890–6) to 119 (1913). For the 'heavy trades' considered separately, the fluctuations were even more extreme, the range being 81 (1893) to 140 (1913).[17] This instability in earnings was obviously translated into instability in real wage levels, and it is a little dangerous, perhaps, to seek to isolate trends over a relatively short time period. Pollard, in fact, did not present any estimate of real wage movements. Presumably, he was unable to find local price data of suitable quality over the comparatively long period with which he was concerned. Certainly, he resisted the temptation to deflate his earnings series by London or national data. However, unless Sheffield's prices diverged markedly from the national pattern, there must have been a considerable rise in real earnings in the mid-1890s which was not cancelled subsequently by inflation. A very rough approximation – produced by deflating Pollard's combined index by Bowley's cost-of-living index – suggests a real wage gain of over 30 per cent in 1893–7, and a fall of under 10 per cent in 1899–1913, a much brigher picture than that offered by the Bowley–Wood data.

Recently, further efforts have been made to augment our knowledge of regional real wage movements, notably by Barnsby and Hopkins for the Black Country, and by Roberts for north-west Lancashire.[18] Unfortunately, these studies are not particularly illuminating for our period, since none of them provides what is really wanted – namely, an index of earnings for several trades (duly weighted), deflated by an adequate series of local retail prices. The work on the Black Country is concerned with broad changes in the standard of living from the mid nineteenth century, and, consequently, detailed evidence for 1890–1914 is not presented. Price data are nearly always inadequate over long time periods, and here the authors have to rely on the contract prices of institutions to produce cost-of-living indexes which exclude rent. For earnings, annual evidence is offered only for selected occupations, and, particularly, miners in the Wolverhampton area (to 1900) and glass-makers in Stourbridge. It is difficult to extract anything of significance from this information, but another rough calculation may be made by deflating Hopkin's earnings data for a Stourbridge glass-maker (top grade) by an amended version of his cost-of-living index (adding observations for milk in an unweighted index of price relatives). The results suggest that, for this labour aristocrat, at least, a gain in real wages in the mid 1890s, 15 per cent over the period 1892–6, was cancelled out by the fall from 1899 to 1913: 13 per cent.[19]

In contrast, Elizabeth Roberts is concerned solely with the period 1890–1914. However, her examination of conditions in Lancaster and Barrow deals, in the main, with the insights to be derived from oral evidence. While she presents some valuable information on the less easily quantifiable aspects of working-class standards of living, her evidence on wages and prices is disappointingly thin, and therefore no attempt is made to produce a general estimate of local trends in real earnings.[20] Similar problems doubtless await local historians of other areas. We are certainly a long way from establishing with any precision the extent to which regional experience differed from the national picture.

It would be rather churlish, however, to leave our survey of regional work without referring to its more general application in the standard of living debate. In fact, the strength of such studies lies as much in the doubt they cast upon crude methods of obtaining estimates of average real earnings as in their own 'necessarily tentative and provisional' results. Barnsby, for example, was able to show the importance of making adjustments for unemployment *and* short-time working, although his calculations were based on somewhat subjective evaluations of the 'state of trade'. Nevertheless, the dangers of relying upon estimates of earnings which assume full employment are clearly indicated. If we do so with the Black Country coal-miner, for instance, we find a 4 per cent drop in earnings over the period 1893–7, and an 8 per cent increase to 1899; but, when an adjustment is made for short time, the figures become 24 and 62 per cent respectively.[21] Similar insights may be derived from the other studies. Frances Wood produced a retail price index for London which exhibited a rise of only 8 per cent in 1900–12 – half that shown by the Board of Trade index for London used by Bowley.[22] Indeed, all the studies emphasise the necessity of obtaining adequate price information, especially on rents, even if some of their efforts are disappointing. Finally, Roberts makes good use of the oral record to challenge the validity of a number of assumptions about working-class earnings and expenditure patterns. Family earnings, she stresses, were influenced by methods of payment, migration in search of work, and the casual wages of women. We may also have been far too critical of working-class food prejudices and cooking skills.[23] Comments such as these certainly point the way to further research.

In conclusion, it is clear that Britain in the Edwardian period was still a country whose economy was characterised by regional diversities, and we should therefore heed Hunt's caveat that 'generalizations about the standard of living can easily be meaningless unless qualified by regional accounts'.[24] The studies we have examined confirm that variations existed, and we may hope for more complete studies in the future. In the meantime, however, we must make the important observation that, while the amplitude of the basic trends can be shown to have varied from place to place, no regional scholar has yet challenged the broad hypothesis offered by the national data: namely, that real wages *rose* in the mid 1890s and *tended to fall* after about 1900.

Our hypothesis becomes a little more fragile when it is applied to both occupational groups and particular industries. First of all, we should expect the fortunes of workers to vary with their relative levels of skill, scarcity value, and the nature of technological and organisational change in each industry. Certainly, differentials between the skilled, semi-skilled and unskilled do not seem to have been eroded in our period. Indeed, Bowley's work suggests that the gulf between skilled and unskilled actually widened to the mid 1900s, when the former's earnings were nearly double those of the latter. On the other hand, the attack on real wages after 1900 probably worked more against the higher-paid, where the margin for cuts was greater, than against the unskilled. Evidence in support of these propositions is rather elusive, but we do have Kuczynski's analysis of the respective experiences of the 'labour aristocracy' and the 'great mass of workers'. The labour aristocracy, it seems, after enjoying a marginally higher increase in real earnings from 1887–95 to 1895–1903, were hit twice as hard as the rest of the workforce to 1909–14, their 'net real wages' falling by 8 per cent, compared with a 4 per cent reduction for the 'great mass'.[25] However, at this level of analysis, there can be no suggestion that skilled or unskilled workers as a whole experienced trends in their standard of living which were markedly at odds with those delineated by our general hypothesis. It must be left to further research, on a more limited basis, to isolate greater differences, between grades of labour.

The distinction between white-collar and blue-collar workers must also be examined. Edwardian Britain, with its growing army of clerks, petty bureaucrats and lower professionals,was very much the age of the lower middle class. How did their experience compare with that of wage labour? First, it must be admitted that white-collar workers were as heterogeneous a body as their wage-earning counterparts. There was more than a world of difference, for example, between the office boys and humble pen-pushers engaged on routine work on fixed salaries in small firms, and the 'executives' working for large companies and institutions which granted regular pay increments and ample opportunities for promotion. The former were often earning less than skilled or even semi-skilled manual workers in high-wage industries such as engineering, while the latter were always very clearly differentiated from the whole of the working class. This in itself suggests that trends in real earnings varied considerably. For the clerk on a fixed salary or with a very narrow pay band, the rise in prices after 1896 quite obviously brought with it a substantial cut in real earnings: applying Bowley's cost-of-living index, a reduction of up to 20 per cent is implied. There must have been a great many in this position. Indeed, Gregory Anderson has gone so far as to assert that 'there is strong evidence that clerks' money wages between 1870 and 1914 were stagnating'.[26] More statistical evidence would be welcome, to establish this point beyond doubt, but it is certainly true that the security of employment for clerks, particularly at the lower end of the market, was deteriorating in the late nineteenth century, the result of an abundant supply of labour coupled with a pressure on jobs, encouraged by increased foreign competition and moves towards rationalisation.[27] On the other hand, it is equally clear that many clerical workers enjoyed a considerable increase in real earnings throughout our period as a consequence of favourable conditions of employment. Banking and insurance, for example, were noted for their high salaries and regular increments. Ten clerks working for the Sea Insurance Co. at an average salary of £121 in 1890 were earning £423 in 1914, while those with the Royal Exchange could look forward to raising their initial pay of £90 in 1890 to about £400 within twenty-five years.[28] But, even in the railway industry, which from the 1880s was experiencing considerable financial difficulties, and which was the subject of numerous complaints about its treatment of clerks, it was still possible to prosper. A study of eighty London clerks employed by the South Eastern and London, Chatham and Dover railways (the 'South Eastern and Chatham') – by no means the most generous of employers in the industry – provides a clear illustration of this (Figure 2).

Thanks to regular salary increments, from 1890 to 1913 the men experienced an average rise of no less than 190 per cent in their real earnings. For 1899–1913 the increase was 54 per cent, or 3.1 per cent a year. Admittedly, some of this improvement may be attributed to the fact that the cohort includes a number of young recruits, who were taken on at very low starting salaries – £15–60 a year – and whose position was bound to change substantially as they matured. But, even if we exclude all those earning less than £65 in 1890, we are left with forty-eight clerks whose real earnings increased by 161 per cent from 1890 and by 48 per cent (2.9 per cent a year) from 1899. Moreover, in only one year – 1900 – did prices outrun salaries. Otherwise, living standards improved steadily, in marked contrast with the situation facing the majority of wage-earners.

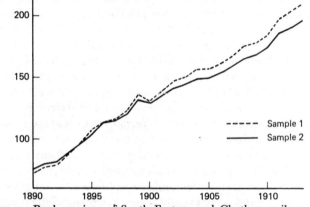

FIGURE 2   Real earnings of South Eastern and Chatham railway clerks, 1890–1913 (1890–9 = 100)

Sample 1: 80 clerks (1890–9: £102 per annum)

Sample 2: 48 clerks (excludes those with 1890 salary below £65 per annum) (1890–9: £126.50 per annum)

SOURCE: South Eastern and Chatham Railway Staff Register, RAIL 633/346, Public Record Office. From 1899 the South Eastern and the London, Chatham and Dover railways were worked as one concern.

Turning to the experience of blue-collar workers, variations from industry to industry are clearly of interest. However, before we explore the available evidence, a further note of caution must be sounded. Not only is there a general paucity of information on earnings, which limits the value of comparisons, but in addition the quality of the data on wage rates is very variable. Researchers are thus forced to grapple with the several problems raised by differing methods of payment (principally piece rates and time rates), variations in hours of work, and changes in industrial organisation, with their implications for a multiplicity of work grades. All this must cast some doubt, at least, upon the comparisons which have been attempted. The most readily accessible information – Bowley's 'wages or earnings' data for seven industries – gives a very clear indication of the difficulties. Three of Bowley's series are incomplete, one (for coal-mining) is a series of piece rates, and another (for agriculture) is admitted to be very uncertain indeed. As Keith Burgess has pointed out with reference to cotton textiles, although his remark could apply equally to most if not all of the other major industries, 'the diversity of labour utilization . . . especially as this relates to methods of wage payments, makes it difficult to generalize about the trend of wages, except in terms of notional averages'.[29]

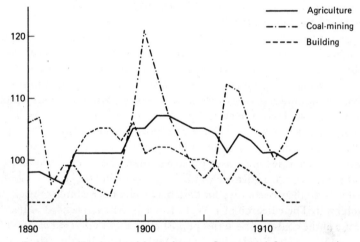

FIGURE 3   'Real wages' by industry, 1890–1913 (1890–9 = 100)
SOURCE: Bowley, *Wages and Income in the United Kingdom since 1860*, pp. 8 and 30.

Nevertheless, Bowley's work may still offer some useful insights, despite the obvious difficulties of interpretation. In Figure 3, the wage data for agriculture, building and coal-mining are combined with Bowley's cost-of-living index to produce notional estimates of 'real wage' movements. Allowing for the uncertainty of the results, it does seem that both building and agriculture followed the 'national' pattern in exhibiting a rise in the mid 1890s and a fall from the turn of the century. But building workers experienced a more severe threat to their real earnings position as house-building activity slackened. The data here suggest a fall of 12 per cent over the period 1899–1913.

One thing is clear. Coal-mining retained its traditional reputation as an industry subject to extreme fluctuations in earnings. Here, for example, a rise of 29 per cent in 'real wages' from 1897 to 1900 was followed by a fall of 20 per cent from 1900 to 1905, and instability was again a characteristic of the period 1905–11. Fluctuations of a similar order of magnitude can also be found in Rhodri Walters's data for South Wales miners.[30] In such a situation, it is naturally more difficult to establish the existence of underlying trends. The matter must be pursued, however, since the miners have been singled out as a group which, unlike the majority of industrial workers, was 'appreciably better placed in 1914 than . . . twenty years earlier'.[31] At first sight, this seems to be a rather fragile hypothesis, especially if we confine ourselves to the period 1890–1913. Contrary to the experience of most of his fellow workers, the miner actually suffered a fall in real wages in the mid 1890s – 5 per cent, in the period 1894–7 – and, although a rising trend might be suggested for the period from 1897, very different results are obtained with other base years. Thus, while a 15 per cent rise is indicated for 1897–1913, an 11 per cent *fall* is shown for 1900–13. On closer inspection, however, the miner's lot can be shown to have improved considerably. First, the overall position becomes much clearer if we take a broader perspective. Piece rates rose sharply between 1888 and 1890 and did not return to pre-1888 levels thereafter. As a result the miner's 'real wage' increased by no less than 44 per cent from 1886 to 1913, although this advance was principally owing to the steep rise in rates *before* 1890. Secondly, our data may well underestimate the gains achieved. The research of J. W. F. Rowe is instructive here. A harsh critic of the coal-mining series published in the *Abstract of Labour Statistics* and used by Bowley, he convincingly argued that the 'true' wage rates of face-workers increased by 80 per cent rather than 50 per cent from 1888 to 1914.[32]

One final, but important, observation must be made. All that we have been measuring so far is the change in the purchasing power of the face-worker's piece rate, and this is some distance from an estimate of the movement of average real earnings in the industry as a whole. Whether such an average – were we able to calculate it – would challenge our optimistic hypothesis is a matter for debate. The increasing presence of 'on-cost' (i.e. non-productive) workers, whose pay was not only lower than that of face-workers but also less subject to fluctuation, suggests that a more stable but more pessimistic picture of real earnings is feasible.[33] Face-workers' earnings may also have been less volatile than piece rates, owing to the effects of voluntary absenteeism in periods of prosperity. On the other hand, earnings fell more sharply than rates where short-time working was enforced by employers.[34] Whatever our speculations, the only firm evidence we have is clearly optimistic. Tony Slaven's detailed study of the Govan Collieries indicates that the earnings of face-workers improved considerably, and the improvement was not limited to the years before 1890. 'Real earnings', obtained by using Bowley's cost-of-living index, rose by 81 per cent over the period 1886–91, fell back in the 1890s (by 28 per cent, 1891–1900), then increased by no less than 101 per cent from 1900 to 1913.[35] It is true that the Govan colliers were particularly well placed in a company where industrial relations were comparatively good and there were opportunities to increase productivity at the coalface. But in lieu of other evidence we must conclude that face-workers, at least, enjoyed a substantial rise in real earnings at a time when the majority of workers were under pressure. However, we must also accept that this was accompanied by a continuation of the instability which had bedevilled the industry. The insecurity of earnings was a potent factor in labour relations, and it deserves almost equal emphasis.

Engineering and textiles, like building and agriculture, appear to conform to the 'national' picture, in that notional estimates of 'real wages', based on the wage-rate data of the *Annual Abstract of Labour Statistics*, show a rise in the mid 1890s and a fall from 1899. While the customary caveats apply to these estimates, it is worth pointing out that the data for engineering produce a very similar pattern to that for building, suggesting that for both industries the gains of the mid 1890s were more or less cancelled out by the subsequent fall to 1913. The increasing use of piece rates in engineering may mean that our findings, which are based on time rates, are unduly pessimistic. But here, at least, there is no indication that engineering workers were particularly well favoured in the period, as is asserted in the literature.[36] Some industries, however, witnessed steady gains in money-wage levels. The Board of Trade's Department of Labour Statistics, in its *Report* for 1913, observed that workers in printing and the food and tobacco trades, and employees of public authorities 'have not had a year of falling wages during the 20 years [from 1894] covered by these statistics'.[37]

Railwaymen, it is commonly agreed, did not do well in Edwardian

Britain, although the evidence is not as clear-cut as might be expected. Wage rates tended to be fixed for relatively long periods of time,
and this produced a serious threat to the standard of living of many
employees in the years of inflation which followed 1896. The rates in
use in 1890 for South Eastern enginemen, for example, were not
altered until 1919.[38] At a more general level, Rowe's estimates of
money-wage rates in the building, engineering, cotton, coal-mining
and railway industries from 1886 show the last to have obtained by far
the smallest increase. For 1891–1913 this amounted to only 9 per cent,
representing a reduction in 'real terms' of 5 per cent. On the other
hand, railwaymen's earnings probably performed more satisfactorily
than rates, owing to increasing opportunities for paid overtime. Certainly, the Board of Trade's series of average earnings from 1896 to
1913 is not particularly pessimistic. 'Real earnings', employing
Bowley's cost-of-living index, fell by 7 per cent from 1899 to 1900, but
remained stationary thereafter. Only if average earnings in other industries increased more substantially than their respective wage rates
could we be sure that the railway picture was exceptionally gloomy.
But this is distinctly a matter for argument, and, given the extreme
difficulty of making inter-industry comparisons, we should be wise to
reserve judgement.[39]

Cyclical fluctuations in wage levels varied markedly from industry
to industry. Coal-mining has already been cited as an example of particularly severe instability. But it was not the only one. Earnings in the
Sheffield trades, for instance, were also highly volatile: in the 'heavy
trades' – engineering, iron and steel, and so on – a 25 per cent fall in
real earnings in 1890–3, was followed by a 54 per cent rise to 1899.
Some occupations, however, were scarcely affected by the trade cycle.
Railwaymen, for example, were virtually insulated from fluctuations.
In the period 1900–13, mean earnings (at 1900 prices) were 24s. 10½d.
(£1.24), with a standard deviation of only 2¾d. (1p).[40] Clearly, inter-
industrial variations of this kind deserve emphasis also. For many
families predictability of income was as vital to economic security as
higher but more erratic gains in wages unprotected from the vicissi-
tudes of unemployment and short time.

Undoubtedly, then, real-wage trends varied from industry to industry, although it is difficult to measure these accurately enough to
permit firm comparisons. We can say, however, that with the exception of coal-mining these variations do not appear to have been sufficiently large to produce a dramatic divergence from our general
picture. The severity of the attack on real wages after 1899 certainly

varied. Sometimes it was enough to wipe out the gains of the 1890s; sometimes it was not. But most blue-collar workers in the major industries were able to associate the Edwardian period with some kind of pressure on their economic position.

We must conclude with some observations on the working and living environment in which real-wage movements were set. If living standards were a question of average real wages or earnings alone, we could let the matter rest. But the term 'standard of living' has been applied in a more general sense to embrace both tangible and less tangible elements, and many historians have tempered their analysis of real wage trends by referring to factors making for an improved 'quality of life' before 1914. Here, it is asserted that the gloom of stagnating or falling real wages was greatly relieved by improvements in working conditions – a gradual reduction in the length of the working week, government measures to control the worst abuses of factory and workshop, concessions won by a larger and more powerful union movement, and greater opportunities for white-collar work. In addition, there was an intensification of both voluntary and state effort in the field of welfare, while life in the cities was enhanced by a more varied diet, cheap transport, and a range of leisure facilities.[41] However, by no means all historians share this interpretation. There is evidence to support the contention that work was becoming more, rather than less, demanding, and that skilled workers faced a growing risk of displacement by the semi-skilled. The general insecurity of the period is amply demonstrated by the rash of serious industrial disputes, nowhere more visible than in the years 1910–14. Welfare measures seem to have done little to reduce the poverty of the unskilled; parks, trams, and music halls little to relieve the squalor and misery of the inner-city areas for those unable to escape them.[42]

As we have already suggested, the patchiness of the evidence available to historians precludes an authoritative judgement on the extent of changes in the level of living before 1914. But although our verdict is necessarily intuitive, it does seem that in the short run much of the Edwardian effort was more potential than real. Many of the advances promised by Liberal Government legislation – health and unemployment insurance, for example – came too late to have a serious impact before the First World War. The significance of measures dealing with workmen's compensation, conciliation, and the sweated trades lay more in the change in social policy they represented than in the immediate results achieved, which were limited. Working hours may have been reduced in some industries, but there was no substantial general reduction until 1919–20. And, if work was becoming safer, there was certainly no reduction in the number of fatal accidents. The union movement grew in strength and influence, but it was everywhere challenged by a more organised employing class, blackleg labour, typified by William Collison's National Free Labour Association, and a hostile legal environment. Given these circumstances, it is difficult to suggest that the attack on real-wage levels was offset by improvements in working conditions.[43]

What were the immediate effects of the Edwardians' undoubted interest in welfare? Certainly, the range of their activities was impressive. For the first time there was legislation dealing with school meals and medical inspection, old-age pensions, and health and unemployment insurance. Government spending on social services increased from under 2 per cent of GNP in 1890 to over 4 per cent in 1913. There was also a very considerable voluntary effort. This was very much an age of experiment in social work: the health visitor and hospital almoner, and the crèche, playground, and school for mothers were all new developments. It is difficult to deny that these activities, however they may have been resented or misunderstood by the recipient working class, did not have some ameliorative influence.

Maternal and infant mortality was a special concern in the early twentieth century, and here success was immediate. For the first time the infant mortality rate began to fall: in England and Wales the rate for infants up to twelve months old fell from 163 per 1000 live births in 1899 to 105 in 1914. It is true that mortality among the children of the unskilled remained much higher than for other groups, but even in the poorer districts reductions were achieved whenever a concerted effort was made by local government and voluntary bodies. In the London borough of St Pancras, for example, with its enlightened medical officer of health, settlements, health visitors and schools for mothers, the rate was cut from 152 in 1904 to 92 in 1914.[44] Doubtless, a good deal of the reduction in mortality could be attributed to safer and more plentiful urban milk supplies and to better sewerage. But there can be no disagreement that the decline was a substantial one.[45]

In general, however, Edwardian welfare activity tended to be palliative rather than preventive, and budgets often were small. Old-age pensions were too niggardly and came too late to make much of an inroad into the poverty of the elderly before 1914, while the fall in infant mortality only created more problems for the family on the poverty line. The urban working class may have had an opportunity to enjoy an improved diet, and the consumption of alcohol certainly fell after 1899: of beer by 18 per cent, and of spirits by 37 per cent, to 1914.[46] But tobacco consumption continued to rise, and the price of many staple items in working-class budgets rose faster than the over-all cost of living. Moreover, bread, margarine and jam – the mainstay of low-income families – were losing nutritive value as a result of more efficient production by the food-processing industry.[47] There is little to suggest a significant fall in the incidence of debilitating disease in the population as a whole. The rejection rate of would-be recruits in the First World War was no better than that during the Boer War a decade and a half earlier.[48] Welfare measures and dietary improve-ments may have compensated some groups for the interruption to real-wage increases, but it would be unwise to claim that these effects were in any way substantial.

There may have been a new vitality about urban life. Certainly, the middle and upper-middle classes were more disposed to parade the advantages of wealth, particularly in the capital. But urban poverty remained a vast and intractable problem. Over 30 per cent of the population failed to meet contemporary notions of an acceptable minimum, and these were hardly generous. For the unskilled worker, especially in the casual trades, any pressure on wage levels or changes in the cost of basic items brought the danger of falling into society's penurious 'residuum'. There was little comfort in the Edwardian period for the 60 per cent of railway employees earning less than 25s. (£1.25) a week, and none at all for men such as John Heaseman, a shunter at Bricklayers' Arms, London, whose real wage (with a wage reduction in 1902) fell by 32 per cent from 1899 to 1913.[49] To talk of an expanded range of opportunities for this section of Britain's workforce was clearly an obscenity.

The disparity between the fortunes of capital and labour naturally bred resentment, and fed by stagnating or declining real earnings this sometimes bordered on open revolt. The strikers and rioters of Tony-pandy and Liverpool in 1910 and 1911 were hitting out not only at their own economic insecurity but also at the visible signs of an export boom with its concomitant prosperity for more favoured sections of the population. The palliatives offered by Edwardian governments and charity workers were too little and too late to prevent a serious display of protest in the years immediately before the First World War. Indications of an improving quality of life were insufficient to disturb the impression that the early twentieth century represented a serious challenge to the gains made by the working population in the latter part of Victoria's reign.

Statistical Appendix
'Real Wage' Index, 1890–1913 (1890–9 = 100)
TABLE A
'National' estimates

Year	Wood	Bowley	Phelps Brown and Browne	Kuczynski
1890	99	96	96	100
1891	103	95	96	98
1892	93	95	95	95
1893	94	97	96	95
1894	96	101	101	97
1895	99	103	103	100
1896	103	103	103	104
1897	103	101	103	103
1898	103	102	101	103
1899	107	107	106	107
1900	108	106	104	105
1901	106	105	105	111
1902	103	104	103	102
1903		102	102	100
1904		100	101	98
1905		100	100	99
1906		101	103	102
1907		104	105	102
1908		104	106	97
1909		103	104	95
1910		101	104	98
1911		100	102	99
1912		100	102	97
1913		100	101	100

TABLE B

'*Regional*' *estimates*

Year	London (Tucker)	Sheffield (Pollard)	Stourbridge glass-maker (Hopkins)
1890	95	99	93
1891	96	98	94
1892	95	88	95
1893	97	84	99
1894	101	92	102
1895	103	99	104
1896	103	108	109
1897	105	111	99
1898	102	107	106
1899	104	113	98
1900	101	106	91
1901	101	102	81
1902	100	96	88
1903	99	95	89
1904	98	91	99
1905	98	91	87
1906	100	97	101
1907	101	96	94
1908	99	91	91
1909	97	91	91
1910	96	98	88
1911	96	103	91
1912	96	105	86
1913	98	105	85

Table C
Occupational-industrial estimates

Year	South Eastern and Chatham railway clerks (Sample 1)	(Sample 2)	Agriculture (Bowley)	Building (Bowley)	Coal-mining (Bowley)	Govan colliers (Slaven)	Engineering (AALS)	Textiles (AALS)
1890	72	75	98	93	106	109	94	96
1891	77	79	98	93	107	114	95	98
1892	79	81	97	93	96	101	94	96
1893	87	88	96	96	99	95	94	96
1894	96	96	101	101	99	96	99	101
1895	107	104	101	104	96	98	102	103
1896	114	113	101	105	95	91	106	103
1897	116	115	101	105	94	101	105	101
1898	123	120	101	103	99	104	103	98
1899	136	132	105	106	107	90	106	104
1900	131	129	105	101	121	82	100	100
1901	138	135	107	102	114	88	101	101
1902	147	141	107	102	107	92	101	101
1903	150	144	106	101	103	98	100	100
1904	156	148	105	100	99	98	99	99
1905	157	149	105	100	97	108	99	101
1906	161	153	104	99	99	120	99	104
1907	167	159	101	96	112	143	97	104
1908	175	165	104	99	111	154	100	107
1909	178	168	103	98	105	135	99	104
1910	184	174	101	96	104	145	97	102
1911	197	186	101	95	100	135	97	100
1912	203	190	100	93	103	138	96	101
1913	209	196	101	93	108	165	93	99

AALS = Annual Abstract of Labour Statistics.

2. Political Economy in Edwardian England: The Tariff-Reform Controversy*

PETER CAIN

IN the course of giving his working-class audience at Chatham in 1909 an excellent review of the case for tariff reform, F. E. Smith, the rising young Unionist MP, put his finger on the difficulties which the 'fiscal question' presented as an issue of public debate:

> It is a question which demands a study of economics; but it is none the less, one upon which an economist, whose mind is unillumined by political intuition or business training, may go far astray. It is a question of politics, but one upon which a politician, whose policy is divorced from the science of economics, would hardly be a trustworthy guide.[1]

The many-faceted nature of the tariff problem probably explains why so many contemporaries were baffled by it and why modern historians have shied away from tackling it in depth. What follows is a review of some of the most accessible evidence on both the economics and the politics of tariff reform. The essay will try to show why the tariff campaign took off after 1903, what the economic arguments of both the fiscal reformers and their orthodox opponents were, and whose 'solution' was most realistic in view of Britain's economic difficulties at that time. Finally, there is a brief review of the electoral and party history of tariff reform, to emphasise and underline the fact that the reasons for the political successes and failures of tariff reform before 1914 often had very little to do with any objective assessment of Britain's needs as a great industrial power.

* I should like to thank Dr W. R. Garside for his advice and criticism, which was a great help to me at all stages in the preparation of this essay.

I

At the turn of the century, the alarm felt at Britain's relative decline as an industrial power, and the strategic and political ramifications of this decline, reached a peak of intensity. That the problem was a serious one can be appreciated by a brief look at Great Britain's economic performance in the late nineteenth century in relation to her closest national competitors. (See Table I.)

TABLE I

Percentage share of world manufacturing production

Year(s)	UK	Germany	USA
1870	31·8	13·2	23·3
1881–5	26·6	13·9	28·6
1896–1900	19·5	16·6	30·1
1913	14·0	15·7	35·8

SOURCE: League of Nations, *Industrialization and World Trade* (New York, 1945) p. 13.

After 1870, Britain fell from first to third place as a manufacturing nation in terms of total output. The United States overtook Britain in the early 1880s and Germany passed her around 1900. What underlines the severity of this change in the balance of economic power is the way in which Britain was overtaken as a producer of iron and steel (see Table II), a sector the output and efficiency of which was vital both to economic welfare and to naval strength.

The slump in Britain's position as a steel producer in the 1890s was particularly startling. Steel was an area of rapid innovation and Britain lagged technologically by 1900, highlighting, amongst other things, her tardy acceptance of new methods and new industries. Some part of the more rapid growth of output of iron and steel in the United States and Germany could be accounted for by their later start and the enormous size of their own tariff-protected domestic markets; but some of it was also owing to their ready adoption of more modern industrial processes with greater growth potential.

Britain's relative decline as a manufacturing power was also reflected to a large degree in her changing position as a foreign trader. Her share of world trade in manufacturing fell slightly from 37 per cent in 1883 to 35·8 per cent in 1890, and then more precipitately, to

TABLE II
Percentage shares of world output of pig iron and steel

Years	Pig iron			Steel		
	UK	Germany (+ Saar)	USA	UK	Germany (+ Saar)	USA
1875–9	46·0	12·7	15·6	35·9	16·6	26·0
1885–9	34·7	15·8	27·4	31·8	17·8	31·4
1895–9	26·1	17·7	32·1	19·8	22·5	35·4
1900–4	20·4	18·4	38·6	15·1	22·3	41·0
1905–9	17·5	18·9	41·7	12·4	22·1	43·5
1910–13	13·9	21·0	40·2	10·3	22·7	42·3

SOURCE: P. L. Payne, 'Iron and Steel Manufactures', in D. H. Aldcroft (ed.), *The Development of British Industry and Foreign Competition, 1875–1914* (1968) p. 72.

28·4 per cent by 1900.[2] Textiles remained by far the most important export, accounting for 55 per cent of the total of all commodity exports by value in 1870 and 38 per cent in 1913.[3] The significance of this was that textiles had a declining rate of growth in world trade by 1900 and the fastest-growing sectors – such as steel, transport equipment, metal manufacture, chemicals – were areas in which Britain was relatively backward. Moreover, the United States and industrialising countries in Europe, aided by their tariffs, were excluding many British-manufactured exports from their markets. Only 7 per cent of Britain's cotton piece-good exports were sold in Europe or the United States in 1900[4] and this vividly illustrates the tendency for Britain, as 1914 approached, to find more and more of her major export markets for manufactured commodities in the underdeveloped or semi-developed parts of the world. The rate of growth of exports by value, which had been 2·8 per cent per annum in the 1870s and 2·9 per cent per annum in the 1880s, fell suddenly to 0·4 per cent per annum between 1890 and 1900.[5] Meanwhile import values continued to rise inexorably and at a faster rate than exports. This was partly owing to new raw-material needs and rising demands for foodstuffs as living standards slowly improved. But the most alarming feature of this growth was the rapid increase in manufactured imports. Only 5·5 per cent of imports by value were manufactured goods in 1860, rising to 17·3 per cent in 1880 and to 25 per cent in 1900.[6] The fate of the steel industry provides a dramatic example of this trend. Imports of steel in

1875 represented only 8 per cent of Britain's exports; by 1913 they were equivalent to 45 per cent of her sales abroad.[7] Not surprisingly, the iron and steel interests were in the van of the attack on free trade at the turn of the century; and there was strong support in other industries, such as sections of the woollen industry, which had been badly battered by American and European protection.

The balance-of-trade deficit, which had always been a feature of Britain's pattern of overseas commerce, widened quite sharply towards the end of the century. Whereas in the 1870s and 1880s the visible trade gap was, on average, about 30 per cent of British domestic exports and re-exports by value, between 1891 and 1900 it rose to nearly half. The gap would have widened even more but for the rapid increase in the export of coal, mainly to Europe. Coal represented only 3 per cent of total domestic exports by value in 1870 and had risen to 9 per cent by 1900.[8]

That the widening deficit on trade did not bring the balance-of-payments crisis with which we are now so familiar was owing to the steady rise in 'invisible' income from exports of services such as shipping and insurance and the returns on the accummulating mass of British capital placed abroad. The importance of this invisible income can be gauged from Table III.

II

By the time of Queen Victoria's death the competition of other industrial powers was causing deep anxiety amongst business leaders and the political élite. Fears of German penetration of the British domestic market and of markets abroad was particularly acute at this time and resulted in a complex reaction made up of part admiration and the desire to imitate, and part xenophobic resentment.[9] The rise of German power in particular raised questions about Britain's future international security, her ability in the longer term to feed and house her growing population adequately, and the value of the pragmatism and amateurism which played such a large role in Britain's business and political life. Britain's isolation during the Boer War, the revelations about the physical unfitness of aspiring army recruits, her embarrassing inability to defeat the small Transvaal Republic swiftly: all served to underline Britain's weaknesses and to prompt a widespread search for the means to improve what was called at the time 'national efficiency'.[10] When, in 1903, Chamberlain set off on his mission to convert the electorate to tariff reform, he did so in the confident

TABLE III

Balance of payments on current account, £m (quinquennial averages)

Years	(1) Balance of trade	(2) Shipping income	(3) Profits dividends, etc.	(4) Insurance	(5) Miscellaneous	(6) Balance of invisible trade (2+3+4+5)	(7) Balance of payments on current account (1+6)
1871–5	−64	+51	+83	+16	−12	+139	+75
1896–1900	−159	+62	+132	+16	−11	+199	+40
1901–5	−177	+71	+149	+18	−13	+226	+49

SOURCE: P. Deane and W. A. Cole, *British Economic Growth, 1688–1959* (Cambridge, 1964) p. 36.

belief that the abandonment of free trade and closer economic unity between the geographically far-flung territories of the British Empire would result in a new framework of economic activity within which industrial regeneration, the creation of an 'imperial' race fit to rule an empire, and the maintenance of world-power status would all become feasible objectives.

Protection for British industry and preferential arrangements between Empire countries had been extensively discussed in Britain since the late 1870s, but it was only when these ideas were taken up by so eminent a statesman as Chamberlain that they moved to the forefront of politics. As Colonial Secretary after 1895 he had been increasingly impressed by the growth of the United States and Germany behind their tariff barriers and determined to try to weld the Empire together to produce an integrated unit large enough in population and resources to take Britain into the twentieth century as a great power. He had pioneered state involvement in the economic development of Britain's dependent empire and tried to encourage closer trading links with the white settled colonies. He was particularly worried about the latter, which he felt might soon drift off into the economic orbit of faster-growing powers and be lost to the British connection if some deliberate attempt to forestall natural economic forces were not made. Canada, whose export trade was already dominated by the United States (see Table IV) and which seemed fated eventually to be absorbed by her enormous southern neighbour, was Chamberlain's most anxious concern.

TABLE IV

Percentage shares of Canadian imports for consumption by value

	1870	1890	1900	1910
UK	57·1	37·5	24·2	24·3
USA	32·2	46·4	60·1	60·9
Others	10·7	16·1	15·7	14·8

SOURCE: O. J. Firestone, *Canada's Economic Development, 1867–1953* (1958) p. 162.

In 1896 Chamberlain floated the idea of an imperial *Zollverein* – free trade within the Empire and a tariff against foreign goods – but this not only offended free-trade sentiment in Britain but also did not suit the white colonies either, since they were determined to protect their small but promising industrial sector from British competition. What the colonies wanted, and what they pressed on Chamberlain at the

Colonial Conference of 1897, was a system of mutual preferences which would give them a securer foothold in the British market for their foodstuffs while in return they discriminated in favour of British exports in their own markets. Chamberlain became convinced that this was the only politically feasible method of beginning the long trek towards imperial unity. He repudiated certain treaties with foreign powers in 1897 in order to allow the Canadians – who were anxious to forestall American dominance of their import trade – to grant Britain preferences on some manufactured commodities. In return the Canadians awaited some reciprocal concession and the other white colonies also looked to some gesture from Britain to convince them that closer economic unity with the mother country was possible and desirable. In 1902–3 Chamberlain tried to begin this process of discrimination in favour of the white colonies by urging his Conservative Cabinet colleagues to retain the 2s. (10p) per bushel duty on grain imports, imposed temporarily during the Boer War, on foreign imports while allowing colonial produce in free. His defeat on this issue convinced him that the time had come to try to convert his own party and, he hoped, the electorate to a programme of tariff reform. The campaign, which began in Birmingham in May 1903 as a plea for imperial economic unity, gradually developed into a more broadly based demand for protection and preference as Chamberlain toured the country to muster support. From then until the outbreak of war the tariff question and the issue of economic relations with the Empire played a central part in the political battle.[11]

In the course of the argument over fiscal policy, some defenders of the existing system, including learned ones, did show an alarming propensity to assume that free trade was a kind of natural law to question which implied either crassness or blasphemy. On their side, some of the political supporters of tariff reform, whose economic opinions were robust rather than carefully thought out, cheerfully argued that their policies were an instant and unfailing remedy for every known economic ailment now and in the future. And there were propagandists and politicians on both sides who, from calculation rather than conviction, deliberately adopted these or similarly outlandish opinions on the platform and in Parliament.[12] None the less, although the public debate was not carried on at a particularly high level over all, there was on both sides a reasonable degree of intelligent and open-minded argument, which we can now attempt, briefly, to present.

Chamberlain, and the tariff-reformers who supported him, were much impressed by what they took to be the important role played by protection in encouraging the growth of Britain's competitors and in reducing her own.[13] They pointed to the tariff barriers of the United States and Europe as a means of ensuring the home market for domestic producers and building up strength for onslaughts abroad. They were particularly impressed and alarmed by the evident fact that the protectionist barriers behind which the iron and steel industries had grown abroad gave them the means to dump cheap exports on the open British market when times were slack, undermining prices, output and investment in the British industry. The overall result of the policy of protectionism by other industrial powers was, they argued, the slowdown in the growth of British exports, investment and employment opportunities. Manufacturing exports accounted for a declining percentage of total overseas earnings, and coal and foreign investments, two of their replacements, were in themselves stimulants to the growth of competitors. The tariff-reformers feared that, in the long term, many of Britain's staple industries would be slowly eroded, worsening the employment problem, reducing living standards and undermining Britain's position as a great power, which position ultimately depended upon her manufacturing strength. They offered a gloomy prospectus for a future free-trade Britain, denuded of her industries of technological and strategic significance, importing not only food and raw materials but also manufactured goods, and paying for them with financial and other services, coal and the products of such cheap sweated labour as could still compete internationally. Such a free-trading nation might conceivably be wealthy. But the wealth would be badly distributed and, in power terms, Britain would have descended to the status of a Holland or a Portugal, unable to sustain an economic relationship of any significance with her Empire, which would be pulled away from her by the centripetal force of the dominant American and European economies.

Protection for British industry was, therefore, felt to be of the first importance, but many tariff-reformers went a great deal further than this. They were determined to counteract the cosmopolitanism which was characteristic of a free-trade economy, and which they felt militated against Britain's future security, by turning as much of Britain's trade as possible into imperial channels. In the opinion of the Empire-minded among the tariff-reformers, a system of mutual preferences between Britain and her white Empire especially, was the key to future industrial survival. The white settled colonies already did a very large amount of trade *per capita* and cultural bias did give the British a competitive edge in their markets. They were also expected to grow rapidly in both population and wealth in the new century. Many tariff-reformers were determined to capitalise on these favourable trends and tendencies. Preferences for colonial foodstuffs in the British market would, it was hoped, stimulate colonial economic growth, while reciprocal concessions on industrial imports in the colonies would increase the demand for British goods and promote domestic manufacturing investment and employment at good wages. It was believed that in this system, capital and labour, in so far as they were attracted abroad, were more likely to go to other Empire countries than to feed the growth process of foreign rivals. An important group of tariff-reform supporters expected that the long-run effect of a preferential system would be the growth of an economic unit on the same scale as the United States. The economic bonds between the now scattered parts of the British race would also provide the basis for military and political union and future joint control over the dependent Empire. Some preferentialists still assumed that Britain would remain the manufacturing centre of any imperial union; but there were others who applauded the idea of spreading industry, complementary to Britain's, throughout the white colonies. They looked forward to the day when the economic unity of the Empire was so complete that free trade would be accepted within its confines and when it would be a matter of indifference as to whether the political and economic centre of the Empire were in London, Sydney or Ottawa. In projecting this grand imperial vision, the most committed and intelligent of the economic imperialists argued that the whole tariff package, including protection, might reduce income in the short run but would ensure steady growth and great-power status in the future. But they always insisted that the initial grant of small preferences to colonial food-producers would not raise prices in Britain. Competition between the colonists themselves would keep down prices: the benefit they foresaw from preferences was a steadier and enlarged demand for colonial food, leading to improved supply and lower costs. It was also argued that increased costs from tariffs in general could be offset to some degree by remissions in existing revenue duties; and that the consumer would receive benefits from welfare measures such as old-age pensions, which could be more easily financed if tariff revenue were raised. What they did not sufficiently explain was how a tariff designed as a revenue-raising device could at the same time act effectively to protect British industry from foreign competition.

By no means all of the opponents of free trade were Empire preferentialists. Some were interested in protection for particular industries and ignored the question of improved trade with the colonies. And British agriculturalists objected just as much to imperial preferences as they did to free trade in general, and wished to be protected against both foreigner and colonialist. Another and more interesting group argued for tariffs as a means of retaliation and were uneasy with the imperial and social-reform side of the Chamberlain programme. They agreed with Chamberlain about the economic and political consequences of 'one-sided free trade' but wished to use tariffs as bargaining counters with the ultimate aim of increasing the amount of free trade in the world. Balfour, the leading retaliationist, in his *Economic Notes on Insular Free Trade* (1903), declared himself to be 'in harmony with the true spirit of free trade when I plead for freedom to negotiate that freedom of exchange may be increased' (paragraph 63).[14] In a more-free-trade world, the retaliationists expected that Britain could maintain her position as an international trader without special recourse to imperial markets through preferences.

On their side,[15] most free-traders agreed that particular industries might obtain some benefit from protection, but they were firm in their belief that the overall effect of a protectionist policy would be to raise costs, succour the inefficient and lower output and employment. They poured scorn on the idea that the growth of the United States and Germany had been helped by tariffs. Their economic strength, it was claimed, reflected the extent of their natural resources, the size of their markets and their growing entrepreneurial and artisan skills, and, if anything, protection had hindered their progress. Tariff protection had been adopted in these countries, they asserted, at the behest of particular value, stressed by the preferentialists, of Empire markets of political corruption. The general body of consumers and wage-earners were the losers. Free-traders were particularly severe about the proposals for preferences, which they were sure would raise food prices and reduce real wages. They were also sceptical about the particular value, stressed by the preferentialists. of Empire markets in the future. Both protection and preference were expected to provoke harmful retaliation from important customers and the idea of using tariffs as negotiating weapons, as Balfour proposed, was usually dismissed as likely to have the opposite effect to that intended. In so far as Britain did need some defence against the tariff barriers of other nations, it was felt that the most-favoured-nation treaties Britain had signed with many powers – which saved Britain from being discriminated against – were a sufficient safeguard.

Believers in free trade often remained undisturbed by claims of industrial decadence and deaf to the argument that the relative decline in Britain's economic power might have awful political and economic consequences. Provided that they were assured that the national income was rising absolutely, many free-traders were satisfied that all was well. They denied that unemployment could ever be a consequence of free imports, arguing that, if any industry did decline under the stress of competition, the labour and capital resources released would find employment elsewhere. Much was made of the fact that many leading industries, such as cotton and shipbuilding, were internationally competitive and would suffer from increased costs if tariffs were introduced. The export of capital seemed, to the free-traders, only to indicate that there were surplus savings, unwanted by industry, which went abroad and benefited Britain by cheapening her imports and boosting the demand for her exports. When faced with the problem of dumping, many free-traders, while admitting that steel might be badly affected, pointed to the fillip which cheap steel imports gave to the rapidly expanding shipbuilding trades. Also, some of the more radical supporters of free trade accepted all these arguments and added their own: namely, that free trade was essential to promote the maximum international economic co-operation and, therefore, furthered the cause of peace.

There were free-traders who did agree with the tariff-reformers that British industry was ailing and needed regeneration. Like many of the tariff-reformers, they looked to vigorous state action in social reform, technical education and other fields to help the regeneration forward. But they could not accept protection as a part of this process, because, for the reasons adduced above, they felt that it promoted corruption and inefficiency. And, although there were 'Little Englanders' amongst them, some free-traders were sympathetic to closer unity of the countries of the Empire, while maintaining that preferences, besides failing to make economic sense to a cosmopolitan economy such as Britain's, were more likely than not to provoke dissension and bitterness between the colonies and the mother country.

III

At first sight, the remarkable revival which took place in Britain's export trade in the Edwardian period may seem to undermine entirely the arguments upon which the tariff-reform campaign rested.

Exports, after growing at an average rate of only 9·4 per cent per annum between 1890 and 1900, rose dramatically to 5·4 per cent per annum between 1900 and 1913. The balance-of-trade gap narrowed and fell from 50·2 per cent of exports in 1896–1900 to only 23·5 per cent in 1911–13. Invisible income also increased very sharply, with the result that the balance-of-payments surplus grew to giant proportions just before the First World War. (See Table v.)

The previous steady rise in the percentage of imports accounted for by manufactured goods was also arrested. The item 'manufactures and miscellaneous' goods accounted for 25 per cent of imports in 1900 but only 23·5 per cent in 1910; and, although Britain's share of world trade declined from 28 to 25 per cent between 1900 and 1913, this was a much less precipitate fall than in the previous decade.

It can be argued, however, that this upsurge in exports was more in the nature of the final flourish of the traditional export economy than an indication that the fundamental difficulties of the economy had been overcome. The single most important component of the export boom was the rapid increase in the export of textiles to Empire markets, especially India, whose market was grossly overstocked at the outbreak of war. The buoyant factor in trade with Europe still continued to be the export of coal rather than the export of manufactured commodities, and the tendency for Britain to rely on finding openings for her manufactured exports in less-developed areas of the world was not checked in this period. The export boom also took place against a background of a sluggish rate of increase of industrial production, stagnant productivity and, as prices rose, a fall in real wages and in the share of wages and salaries in national income. This latter phenomenon was closely connected with the fact that investment income from foreign sources – which was badly distributed – contributed a growing share of total income in the years before 1914. Besides this, Britain's relative performance in the vitally important iron and steel industries was as discouraging in the Edwardian period as previously. (See Table II.)

The export boom of the Edwardian period, far from aiding any industrial reconstruction in Britain, probably hindered it by maintaining the profitability of many of the older staple industries, such as textiles, for a longer period.

Britain's main economic problem in the Edwardian age might be characterised in this way:[16] she was a relatively declining manufacturing centre with low profitability, as compared with the rates of return available in other industrial centres and other areas of rapid

TABLE V

Balance of payments, £m (quinquennial and triennial averages)

Years	Balance of trade	Shipping income	Interest, dividends, etc.	Insurance	Government expenditure	Balance of invisible trade	Balance of payments current account
1896–1900	− 159	62	132	16	− 11	+ 199	+ 40
1911–13	− 140	100	241	27	− 22	+ 346	+ 206

SOURCE: Deane and Cole, *British Economic Growth, 1688–1959.*

economic development. Hence the tendency, particularly marked after 1870, for her to invest so much of her capital abroad. This investment could, like United States overseas investment since 1945, have been direct investments in industrial concerns and, as such, highly profitable. In Britain, though, there was a great gulf fixed between the industrial sector, which was largely self-financing, and the financial sector, largely centred on the City of London, which was geared to the needs of a rentier class with an interest in low-risk securities offering a steady, if unspectacular, income. Between 1909 and 1913, for example, only 14 per cent of Britain's overseas loans went directly into mining and manufacturing industry, where the largest returns were possible, and nearly 47 per cent of it went into transport undertakings, which usually offered a low, fixed-interest return.[17] This tendency to invest in the infrastructural foundations of developing primary producing countries, such as Australia, Canada and the Latin American states, certainly helped to cheapen the cost of primary imports, as the free-traders claimed, but they were wrong to suggest that it was significant in creating much of a demand for British manufactured exports in the Edwardian period. One major function of Britain's massive loans to Canada after 1900, for example, was to allow the Canadians to import large quantities of consumption goods from the United States.

Since the British failed to gain the benefits of direct investment in the industrial growth of her rivals, it could be argued that she would better have insured her own long-run economic growth prospects by channelling much of her overseas investment into domestic industry, especially into those commodities which were growing most rapidly in world trade. This was made even more important in that, given the capital-intensive nature of many of the newer industries, the time was passing when industrial self-finance would be sufficient to ensure optimal growth. Unfortunately, this possibility was also inhibited by the disjunction between industrial and financial wealth in Britain. But, we may ask, in what ways, if any, could the adoption of policies of protection and preference have encouraged an increased level of domestic investment, helped Britain to shift resources out of the older basic industries, and encouraged the adoption of the newest technology?

We should consider, first, the simplest case – that of using tariffs as retaliatory weapons: had this worked the result would have been a liberalisation of trade with other industrial countries. This would have suited cotton, shipbuilding, and certain sectors of the woollen trades which had been excluded from industrial markets abroad by tariff barriers, but it would probably not have been of much help to, say, the iron trades or chemicals, whose major problem was lack of competitiveness in the domestic market and in third markets.[18] The stimulus which this would have given to industrial change is not very obvious either. It is also true, as the free-traders claimed, that the result of the use of tariffs as diplomatic weapons might well have been escalating tariff wars, which could have disastrously destabilised international trade in general.

The effects of permanent tariffs on imports of manufactured commodities would have been more complex. The free-trade claim that imports of manufactures could not cause unemployment is a dubious one. There is something to be said for the idea that free imports in areas such as steel did lower profitability, output and employment opportunities. A protective tariff here might have encouraged growth and innovation by securing the domestic market. The strategic necessity for a strong and growing steel industry might also have justified a protective policy. On the other hand, as the free-traders warned, the pressure for protection was also likely to come from those powerful older sectors of industry which were losing their competitive edge and which, in the interests of long-term efficiency, it might be best to leave to their fate. A protectionist policy would have made sense only if it had been part of a wider government plan designed to encourage the growth of newer sectors of industry, sheltering them from competition in the early stages of their growth. Since this degree of state involvement in the economy was practically out of the question in Edwardian times, the presumption is a strong one that protection was more likely to be forthcoming for those industries which were in decline, arresting the tendency to shift resources into newer areas of enterprise.

Similarly, the effect of preferential arrangements with Empire countries would have been to provide bolt holes for traditional industries rather than to promote dynamic economic growth. The preferences granted by the Canadians to Britain in the 1890s and subsequently did have some effect – as Table IV shows, the share of Britain in Canada's consumption imports stabilised at about 24 per cent between 1900 and 1910 – but the tariff-reformers grossly exaggerated the future growth potential of both white colonial and dependent Empire markets, and the extent to which the Empire could have absorbed an increasing share of Britain's exports was very limited. In so far as the Empire did become more important as a market for certain manufactured commodities over time, it tended to act as a brake on the need for industrial change. The share of the Empire in Britain's commodity exports as a whole did not increase between the 1880s and 1913, always being in the region of 33–35 per cent of the total.[19] If coal – which mainly went to Europe – is excluded from consideration, though, it is clear that the Empire was becoming more important for a number of extremely significant exports.

TABLE VI

Empire share of British exports (percentage by value)

	1870	1890	1900	1913
Cotton goods	34·7	44·1	45·8	51·7
Woollen goods	14·0	20·8	29·4	33·5
All manufactured textiles	26·6	37·2	39·7	43·9
Pig iron and iron goods	21·7	33·5	36·7	48·2

SOURCE: W. Scholte, *British Foreign Trade From 1700 to the 1930s* (Oxford, 1952) pp. 166–7.

The exports mentioned in Table VI are from the traditional industrial sectors of Britain, and the Empire's ability to take an increasing share of them meant that they were cushioned to some extent against the effects of changes in the world economy.[20] Given this, and the fact that the growth of Empire markets was to be slower than many tariff-reformers anticipated, it is hard to argue that preferences would have been of great value to an economy in need of diversification.

There is a further point of a more general kind which undermines the protectionist case. The tariff-reformers claimed that Britain's free-trade system exposed her to too much competition and that protection and preference would mitigate this. However, there was an important sense in which the free-trade system itself reduced the severity of foreign competition in overseas markets. In the multilateral system of international payments based on Britain, the United States and Europe, in exporting to Britain, could earn the surpluses which allowed them to import from many primary producing countries, including Empire ones, without the necessity of exporting directly to them. If Britain had gone protectionist, the fall in the surpluses that the United States and Europe could earn there would have made it necessary for them to compete more abroad in order to maintain their level of imports from the primary producers. And, if preferences in Britain's favour had been granted in the Empire, this would have stimulated American and European competition in other markets important to Britain, such as those in Latin America or the Far East.[21]

On the whole then, protection and preference would not have done much to revive the fortunes of British industry or to ensure rapid growth in the future. In so far as they were successful they would have been likely temporarily to inoculate Britain against the need for change, with drastic long-term consequences. They would probably also have provoked damaging retaliation against the two-thirds of British exports which did not go to the Empire, as well as have obliged Britain to levy some small duties on a large percentage of her imports. Finally, they may have helped to increase competition in overseas markets and to destabilise the system of international trade and finance. In an ideal world Britain would have done best to try to revitalise her industrial structure through economic planning, in which protectionism might have had some part. Given that that was out of the question at the time, the most obvious conclusion to be drawn is that the problem was an intractable one which no tariff-reform prescription alone could have overcome. It is true that some tariff-reformers were aware of the need for protection to run concomitantly with a degree of social and educational reform, but what they proposed was very limited and was just as firmly supported by some stern free-traders, such as Haldane and other members of the Liberal imperialist circle.

There may also be something to be said for the belief of many of the proponents of orthodoxy that free trade helped to lower international tension. This view received support in diplomatic circles. Eyre Crowe, the senior clerk at the Foreign Office, argued in 1907 that 'in proportion as England champions the principle of the largest general freedom of commerce she undoubtedly strengthens her hold on the interested friendship of other nations'.[22] Certainly, many of the rank-and-file tariff-reform supporters were bitterly anti-German and fiscal reform was often seen as a means of undermining Germany's burgeoning prosperity by attacking her trade with Britain and the British Empire. The Germans, for their part, were extremely apprehensive about the possibility of British protection, which, they were inclined to believe, would be used principally to attack their commerce. Hoffman has gone so far as to say that 'the pressure of German business on British markets drove Britain towards protection and imperial preference, while the drift towards Tariff Reform stimulated German navalism and imperialism'.[23] Although this overstates the case, it is probably worth keeping in mind that a Unionist victory on a tariff-reform platform before 1914 might have made relations with Germany worse than they were, by provoking tariff warfare. The export boom,

the consequent softening of commercial competition and the maintenance of free trade may have removed from relations between
Britain and her great European neighbour at least one source of conflict.

IV

With the benefit of hindsight, it is possible, then, to argue that the
tariff-reform strategy would have been an inappropriate one for
Britain to adopt. Tariff reform was, in fact, rejected by the electorate,
but not precisely for the kind of reasons enumerated above, as can be
seen by briefly examining the complicated political fortunes of the
Chamberlainite cause before the outbreak of the First World War.

Chamberlain's decision to campaign for a policy of tariff protection
and imperial unity in 1903 marks another turning point in his restless
search for a party structure which could properly house the particular
combination of social radicalism and imperialism which animated
him and his supporters. The Liberal Party would have been a better
outlet for his social reforming zeal, but he had abandoned it in 1886
over Gladstone's Irish policy, which offended his ideal of imperial
unity. The conjunction of Conservatives and Liberal Unionists in the
Unionist Party thereafter did not answer exactly to his needs either.
The Unionists were dominated by the landed interest and the commercial and financial power of Southern England, and, although they
attracted some urban middle-class votes, Chamberlain's more democratically based industrial support in the west Midlands did not
fit easily into the whole. As an associate of the Conservatives,
Chamberlain's social-reforming activities were muted; and, although
they were more imperially minded than the Liberals, his Conservative
colleagues often looked with either distrust or indifference on his
schemes for imperial economic development when he was Colonial
Secretary. By 1903 Chamberlain had decided that he could rescue the
declining electoral fortunes of the Unionists by offering the new cry of
imperial economic unity and social reform. The policy was intended
to create a new mass base of support amongst the industrial working
class, who he hoped would be attracted by the mixture of economic
benefits and patriotism. It was also expected to have the advantage of
wresting the power of the Unionist Party away from the older interests
and making it a more democratic organisation. Chamberlain hardly
expected to win the next election with his new 'Tory democracy', but
he felt that he could eventually reshape the party to meet the modern

challenge of industrial efficiency, social welfare and Britain's future as a great power. There is little doubt that the centre of Chamberlain's proposals was those concerning imperial economic unity and social reform. The protectionist part of the programme meant less to him and was adopted partly because of the need to broaden the base of his support amongst the voters.[24]

From 1903 onwards, the party was split between Chamberlain's group and those who stood firmly for free trade, with the party leader and Prime Minister, Balfour, uneasily poised with his supporters between the two opposed groups. Chamberlain's faction was squarely based on the Midlands iron trades, which were loud in their demands for protection against German competition but had a great deal of support amongst 'non-industrial' MPs. The Unionist free-traders, a much smaller group, comprising eighty-three of the 392 Conservative and Liberal Unionist members who sat in the House of Commons between 1903 and 1906,[25] had connections with industry and commerce. Their strength lay in industries such as cotton and shipbuilding and the City and overseas trade, all of which had flourished hitherto under a regime of free trade. Many of these free-trade MPs, though by no means all of them, were also alarmed at the prospects of Chamberlainite social reform. Between these two bitterly divided sets of interests Balfour vainly endeavoured to mediate. Balfour was more sympathetic to Chamberlain's ideas than to those of the Unionist free-traders, though he was lukewarm on social-reform questions. His adoption of the retaliationist position was partly tactical, an attempt to find some common ground between Chamberlain and his opponents which would prevent a party split and electoral disaster. Another reason for Balfour's refusal to plump for the tariff-reform cause was that he was frightened of Chamberlain's determination to democratise the party, perhaps placing in jeopardy many of the institutions and ideals which the party had hitherto defended. It was for this reason that the support of the landed interest was largely behind Balfour before 1906. Precise figures are difficult to obtain, but the Chamberlain and Balfourite groups were probably reasonably similar in size, while the Unionist free-traders were in a minority. The latter were put under intense pressure by Chamberlain's supporters and their Tariff Reform League in an attempt to drive them out of the party or to force them to recant their free-trade beliefs. Some did drift over to the Liberals, but most could not stomach even the mild form of social radicalism then espoused by the Liberals or their connection with the movement for Irish home rule. They remained as a bitter and discontented rump within the Unionist Party, slowly diminishing in numbers in the face of the relentless determination of the Chamberlainites to expel them from the ranks.[26]

It was in this state of civil war and internal confusion that the Unionists went into the election of 1906. Only 3 per cent of the Unionist candidates could be said to be out-and-out free-traders by this stage. The largest group, about 55 per cent of the total candidates, could be categorised as Balfourite or retaliationist in sympathy. Some of them were adamant that there should be no 'food taxes'; most were lukewarm about the whole idea of closer unity with the Empire, tending to stand by Balfour's position, which was that, although preferences could not be dismissed entirely from consideration, they should be accepted only after a conference with the colonies and, perhaps, a further election. Besides this, although 40 per cent of the candidates gave general support to Chamberlain's plea for a tariff on manufactures, plus imperial preference, very few would make any specific commitment. Many remained studiously vague on the details and often pledged themselves to adjust tariffs in such a way as to ensure no increases in the cost of living. The Chamberlainite concern for social reforms such as old-age pensions was almost entirely engulfed during the election by the grand claim that tariffs would, somehow, solve the problem of low wages and unemployment.

For their part, the Liberals found the defence of free trade an admirable issue on which to reunite their forces scattered since the Irish crisis of the 1880s. Free trade, together with the nonconformist revival over the education issue, the 'Chinese slavery' question and an increasing commitment to social reform, helped them to one of the biggest electoral triumphs of modern times. Despite their strenuous attempts to convert trade unions and the urban working man to tariff reform, the Chamberlainites were defeated by the overwhelming determination to avoid imperial preference and the 'dear loaf'. The emergent Labour Party, like the Liberals, also stood firmly for fiscal orthodoxy and benefited by it. Besides failing to attract the mass urban vote, the Unionists also lost the allegiance of many urban business interests on the question of tariffs and even alienated a considerable portion of the agricultural vote, which favoured protection but was scornful of preferences. No doubt many erstwhile Unionist supporters voted Liberal or stayed at home, because the evident disunity of their party on the fiscal issue confused and disheartened them.[27]

The unresolved conflict over tariff reform and in particular the widespread apprehension that preferences would increase the price of food and lower real wages, played a large part in reducing the number of Unionist MPs from 374 in 1905 to 157 at the general election of 1906. None the less, Chamberlain could console himself with the fact that the relative strength of what was called by contemporaries the 'Whole Hogger' faction within the party had increased to such an extent that it accounted for about one-half of all Unionist MPs after the election. The Whole Hoggers tended to be the younger members of the party and their main areas of strength lay in the west Midlands, Merseyside and parts of London. They were dedicated both to fiscal reform and to the modernisation of the party. This did not, however, guarantee the complete acceptance of Chamberlain's plans, since, although they were all solidly protectionist, a commitment to imperial preference was still a matter of some dispute among them.[28]

Balfour did begin to shift his position, albeit hesitantly, towards that of the Whole Hoggers after 1906. In so doing, he was influenced not only by the protectionists' power within the party, but also by what seemed to be cavalier treatment that the Liberals meted out to the colonies, at the Colonial Conference of 1907, over the question of preferences. In November 1907 he went so far as to commit himself to a policy of small, widespread duties on imports, with the proviso that there should be no additional burden on the working class as a result of these duties and that raw materials should be exempt.

In the following years, Whole Hogger strength within the party continued to grow. The industrial depression and unemployment of 1908–9 prompted interest in protection amongst the electorate and won the Unionists some by-elections. More important in shifting the party's interest in the direction of protection was the Liberal Party's own movement to the left at this time. As their commitment to welfare reforms increased and the naval rearmament programme also got under way, the Liberals were more inclined to listen to the likes of Lloyd George and Churchill, who demanded increases in direct taxes, super-tax and land duties to pay for it. Alarmed by the attack on property, the landed interest and those of the commercial and financial classes who had often been opposed to tariffs or inclined to agree with Balfour's original *via media*, turned to support for tariff reform as an alternative means of raising revenue. Some of the new-found interest in tariff reform at the time of Lloyd George's famous 1909 budget came from those who had hitherto had a direct economic interest in free trade through their business affairs, but who regarded tariff reform as a small price to pay for containing a 'socialism' which they felt threatened the very basis of their social existence. While the Liberals warmed to their theme that the rich should pay for welfare and defence, the Unionists voiced their fear that Liberals were wantonly attacking those savings of the propertied which formed the basis of investment and further economic growth. Tariff reform, it was now argued, would help to spread the growing burden of public finance more equitably and prevent a decline of industry and finance and the flight of capital abroad.[29] This increasing enthusiasm throughout the party for tariffs left the remaining Unionist free-traders in a fairly hopeless position. A few more crossed the floor of the House, but most of them were terrified of the coming of the welfare state and could not join the Liberals. Some of them were converted to tariff reform and some of the obdurate ones simply retired when Parliament dissolved for the elections in 1910.

When the Lloyd George budget was rejected by the House of Lords, precipitating a constitutional crisis and an election in January 1910, Tariff Reform played a leading part in the Unionist election campaign. Protection was presented as the panacea for the industrial problem, a viable alternative to socialistic extravagance and revolutionary constitutionalism. Nearly all Unionist candidates at the election supported tariffs as a means of increasing wages and employment. Half of all the candidates emphasised their importance as a way of raising revenue and substantial numbers of candidates supported protection because it would increase Britain's international economic negotiating power, or emphasised its importance as an anti-dumping device. The precise degree of protection involved was, however, rarely stated, and the commitment to preferences, although greater than in 1906, was also vague. Although half of all Unionist candidates at the first election of 1910 claimed to support imperial preferences, only 17 per cent of the total actually admitted that this would mean a tax on food imports; and only 2 per cent went so far as to state that imperial preference might involve duties on both foreign and colonial foodstuffs.[30]

At the 1910 election, the Unionists recovered somewhat from the traumatic defeat of 1906, making many gains in their old strongholds in south-eastern England and further inroads into the west Midlands. On the other hand, they made very little impression on the 'Celtic fringe' or, more importantly, on the industrial north of England. The net result was that the Liberals lost their overall majority but retained power with the support of Labour and the Irish Nationalists. After the election, the constitutional crisis over the House of Lords' powers dragged on and another election became inevitable. At this point many of the Whole Hoggers wanted to increase the emphasis on tariff reform. True to their Chamberlainite inheritance, they would have been willing to compromise on the Lords question, to support a substantial degree of social reform and even to consider a degree of Irish independence if only they could come to power with a mandate to get rid of free trade. The trend of opinion within the party as a whole was somewhat different. Many Unionists were deeply worried by the attack on the House of Lords and convinced that, now the Liberals were dependent on the Irish and Labour, the assault on their privileges and institutional power would be renewed with interest. To forestall the attack and win the next election, many Unionists felt that it would be essential to calm the fears of the electorate, particularly over the question of preferences and duties on food imports. Increasing commercial prosperity in 1910 also undermined some of the interest amongst the electorate in protectionist strategies. So, before the second election of 1910, in December that year, Balfour, after much hesitation, decided to agree that the whole question of tariff reform should be put to a referendum should the Unionists win. But the strategy failed and the December election confirmed in essentials the verdict of January. The referendum pledge may, however, have played a part in encouraging a few Lancashire constituencies to return to Unionism.[31]

The election of 1910 indicated, as is evident from a study of the electoral map, something of a polarisation, on class lines, of political attitudes. No fewer than 78 per cent of Unionist seats were won in an area south of a line drawn from the Humber to the Dee, while areas north of that line and Wales accounted for 64 per cent of the seats of the other parties, mainly the Liberals.[32] The Unionist heartland was that part of England dominated by commercial and financial power – much of it centred on overseas trade and foreign investment – and the still-powerful remnants of the landed interests. They, together with their dependent flocks of clerks, distributive traders, small businessmen, farmers and agricultural labourers, had rallied in 1910 to the defence of property and traditional institutions. Protection had become a part of this defence, as the antithesis of progressive taxation, despite the fact that many southern interests – such as those in the City – did benefit from free trade in their straightforward business dealings. In the northern industrial areas the working men were, for their part, dedicated to social reform and to cheap food, which held them firmly to the Liberal or Labour plan of increased taxation of the rich, and free trade. And, in 1910, the industrial business class were still aligned with them, because they felt that protection and preference would harm their economic interests.

By 1910 the dilemma of the Unionists was acute. Defence of traditional institutions inclined them to protectionism. But in order to win elections and ensure that these institutions should be properly defended they had to attract some support from industrial Britain and this tempted them to modify their stance on tariff reform. In 1910, Balfour was prepared to weaken the whole protectionist case so as to attract additional votes. None the less, given the escalating demands on the public purse, not only for social reform but also for increased defence expenditure (which the Unionists supported vigorously), protectionism as a revenue device was increasingly difficult to avoid. Besides this, there is some evidence to suggest that tariff reform was beginning to frighten the industrial middle class less than Liberal budgets, and that by 1914 they were moving back to the Unionism they had abandoned in 1906.[33] In these circumstances, the tendency within Unionism was to cleave to protection in general but to modify the preferentialist part of the programme in order to attract industrial working-class votes in addition to those in the west Midlands. It is not surprising that Bonar Law, Balfour's successor as leader of the Unionist Party, should have agreed in 1913 that, in the event of Unionist victory, preferences on food would not be imposed without a further election.[34]

V

The tariff-reform movement suffered a complex fate before 1914. The leading academic and political proponents of fiscal reform had a powerful case to argue. If it now appears that they placed far too much emphasis on the abandonment of free trade as a remedy for Britain's industrial crisis, it remains true that they were calling attention to a real problem, as Britain's subsequent decline as a great economic and political power in the world amply illustrates. Closer attention to their diagnosis of Britain's economy might have led to a more realistic appraisal of the problems it presented, even if their main remedies had only a limited applicability.

The fact is, none the less, that the admittedly complicated question of the merits and demerits of protection did not get the attention it probably deserved. The majority of politicians and businessmen, and the mass of the electorate, tended to praise or damn tariff reform for reasons which were either partial or purely self-interested or even misleading and confused. Industrial voters, for example, were prejudiced against tariff reform because of the possibility of preferences, often forgetting the wider issue of protection in general and the arguments for it and ignoring the plausible claim that preferences would have little or no effect on the cost of living in the immediate future. Many of the supporters of fiscal reform, on the other hand, were merely trying to protect a vested interest or escape from the consequences of industrial change and failed themselves to put the question in the wider context which Chamberlain and his allies vainly pressed them to consider.

Besides this, the straight question of the plausibility of claims of the tariff-reformers in relation to Britain's economic and industrial performance and prospects was obscured in that the controversy became enmeshed in the more fundamental political and ideological battle between the main parties, as opinions and attitudes polarised on class lines. As the industrial working class became more conscious of their desire for social and economic change, protection came to be viewed as a rich man's device for avoiding income redistribution, and there is no doubt that the Unionists, as the defenders of privilege, saw tariffs first and foremost as a means of socialism and confiscatory taxation. As the tariff controversy became part of the struggle for surpremacy between contending political philosophies, its chances of being considered objectively as an economic weapon diminished accordingly.

Finally, it must be emphasised that, although protection was firmly embedded in the Unionist programme by 1914, this did not mean that Chamberlain's original strategy had been entirely successful. As the social crisis developed, many of the groups who gathered around the tariff-reform standard turned out to be just those older interests which Chamberlain had wished to bypass or contain as he tried to transform Unionism into a mass-based movement. Even worse, the Unionists had clearly decided by 1914 that, if they were to woo some of the industrial vote away from the Liberals and Labour (and they could not otherwise win an election), they would have to drop the preferential policy which was at the centre of Chamberlain's own plans for a revitalised imperial Britain. When war broke out, the 'social imperialist' group within the Unionists, who had taken up the inheritance after Chamberlain's illness in 1906, had reached, it seems, a dead end in their fight for an Empire-based economic programme. It was to take a long, debilitating war and much political and social upheaval to create the conditions which would allow a government successfully to put into practice a policy of protection and closer economic unity with the Empire.

3. Edwardian Politics: Turbulent Spring or Indian Summer?*

WALTER L. ARNSTEIN

I

Was Labour's Keir Hardie prescient or premature in 1906 when he declared that it was 'obvious to everyone who took the slightest interest in public affairs that the old two-party system is breaking up'? Alternatively, in keeping with the editorial policy of the quarterly *Victorian Studies* (for which Victorian England ends in 1914), ought we to look upon the Edwardian political world as constituting the 'Indian summer' chapter of a volume that had opened with the Reform Bill of 1832? Should stress be placed upon the 'classical' manner in which aristocrats (and occasional plutocrats) still loomed above the parliamentary arena, with the Right Honourable H. H. Asquith, 'the last of the Romans', and that scion of the house of Cecil, the Right Honourable A. J. Balfour, yet walking arm-in-arm out of the Palace of Westminster after an evening of verbal swordplay? Did the battle over the budget of 1909 and its aftermath mark, as Kenneth Morgan has recently suggested, 'a glorious high noon' of liberalism rather than the onset of a 'strange death'?[1] To sum such questions up, are Edwardian politics more appropriately assessed in the framework of a 'turbulent spring' or in that of an 'Indian summer'?

It is not the purpose of this brief essay to provide a chronological account of either the Conservative ministries of 1895–1905 or of the Liberal ministries of 1905–15. Its purpose, rather, will be to find at least a provisional answer to the questions posed in the preceding paragraph by utilising some of the major scholarly books and articles of the past two decades that have focused on Edwardian politics. In the process the essay will touch upon the electoral setting, upon the issues and pressures that apparently determined the outcome of by-

* I am grateful to Dr Esther Simon Shkolnik for her assistance

elections and general elections, and upon the changes and continu-
ities of political practice during the fourteen years that preceded the
assassination at Sarajevo, that shot truly heard round the world – and
not least of all in the British Isles.

When the era opened in 1900, Lord Salisbury was ensconced at
10 Downing Street for life – or so it seemed – at the head of a Conservative–Liberal Unionist Government to whom the electorate had
just granted a new, and apparently overwhelming, lease of political
life in the general election.

A Government majority of 402 (334 Conservatives and sixty-eight
Liberal Unionists) faced a dispirited minority of 184 Liberals, eighty-
two Irish Nationalists and two independents in the House of Commons chamber. The Liberals remained dominant in Wales, but – for
the first time since 1832 – the Conservatives and their allies had gained
a bare majority in Scotland; in England proper the Government had
won a majority of seats not merely in the counties but in every major
city as well. Many of these triumphs had been narrow, to be sure, and
some Liberals drew comfort from the realisation that the cumulative
popular-vote margin was far from overwhelming:

Unionists	1,676,020	51·1 per cent
Liberals	1,503,652	45·9 per cent

Such comfort was dissipated considerably, however, by the awareness
that, since 163 of the Unionist seats had been uncontested (as con-
trasted with only twenty of the Liberal seats), the Government had
found it unnecessary to entice their full complement of supporters to
the polls.[2] Liberal comfort was dissipated yet further by consciousness of the divisions that had racked the party since the resignation of Gladstone in 1894 – over imperialism, the Boer War, social
reform, the place of Irish home rule in the party's programme, and
over who should lead the party. Analysts are agreed that the Liberals
remained the political voice of the religious nonconformists and of the
majority of politically conscious skilled workers, but, as the century
opened, such support was apparently far from sufficient.[3]

The electorate of 1900, the product of the Reform Act of 1884, is
often loosely described as one involving virtually all adult males. As
has recently been demonstrated, the reality is far more complex.
Some classes of adult males that were then left off the electoral regis-
ters still are: namely, lunatics, criminals, aliens and peers. A yet
larger number were left off as recipients of poor relief. Still more were

omitted because, as domestic servants residing with their employers or as sons living with their parents or as soldiers living in barracks, they were not eligible for any of the franchises (householder, occupier, or £10 lodger) under which most males qualified for the vote. Approximately 12 per cent of adult males fell into the above excluded categories. In the words of one frustrated Liberal MP, 'The intricacy of our franchise laws is without parallel in the history of the civilized world.'[4]

Equally intricate and even more influential in keeping voters off the electoral rolls were the registration rules, which insisted that to qualify for registration a person should have lived at the address for which he claimed the franchise for at least twelve months. Since each register came into effect six months after it was compiled, the practical effect was to impose a residence requirement of at least eighteen months. This mattered relatively less in the county seats (where a change often left the voter in the same constituency). It mattered a great deal in the larger cities and, most of all, in metropolitan London, where, on average, more than one family in five moved each year, and where each move into a different constituency represented effective (if not necessarily permanent) disenfranchisement. The result was 'democracy tempered by registration', and (once apathy is also taken into account) an electorate in which only 58 or 59 per cent of men over twenty-one were eligible to vote.[5]

If two adult males in five were ineligible to exercise the franchise at any given general election, then one in fourteen (they cast between 500,000 and 620,000 additional votes) might vote twice, three times, or even twenty times. The more extreme examples constituted a staple of Radical outrage. A majority of plural voters owned a home in one constituency and a business in another. Both their precise number and their specific political impact are matters of speculation rather than of established fact, but it seems clear that, while during the mid nineteenth century plural voting aided the Liberals more than the Conservatives, between 1886 and 1918 it aided the Conservatives more than the Liberals – by a ratio of perhaps 65 : 35. The nine university seats, an additional form of plural voting open to all graduates who had received MA degrees, were admittedly Conservative or Liberal Unionist strongholds throughout this latter period. Annoying and anachronistic as plural voting appeared to most reformers, it apparently did not determine the outcome of any general election.

Despite numerous attempts at piecemeal reform, the franchise and registration rules of 1884–5 remained intact until 1918. So did a seat Redistribution Act (1885), which permitted large divergences in the population size of constituencies: by 1910, one-third of the electorates diverged from the average by 50 per cent or more, and Ireland was over-represented by forty seats.[6]

While the national government still played a much smaller role in the day-to-day life of the populace than it does today, political leaders played a larger role. The football heroes and popular music and screen stars who were to rival, and often to overshadow, cabinet ministers and party leaders in later years lay yet in embryo. More newspaper headlines were devoted to politics than to sex or crime. Edwardian elections, though more honest and less costly than their mid-Victorian counterparts, retained a carnival atmosphere involving flags, songs and processions. The period of polling still stretched over three or four weeks, and political meetings attracting 10,000 or even 20,000 people were far from unknown.[7]

Less than six years after winning one of its most overwhelming triumphs, the Conservative Party was to suffer its most stinging defeat. The explanation for this turnabout, it will be argued here, lies less in any positive reform programme that the Liberal Party or its new Labour ally was to offer the electorate in 1906 than in the errors of commission of the Conservative ministry. The Conservative–Liberal Unionist Government was to be punished by the voters not for its inaction but for its accomplishments.

The first of these accomplishments was the winning of the war in South Africa. The triumph that had, on balance, attracted popular support in October 1900 turned out thereafter to be an electoral liability. Not only did the war drag on for yet another year and a half, but in addition it came to involve the wholesale burning of farms and the internment of Boer families in concentration camps, practices that the Liberal Party leader, Sir Henry Campbell-Bannerman, denounced as 'methods of barbarism'. Less often was the Boer War interpreted as an example of a benevolent mother country coming to the assistance of its citizens oppressed in distant South Africa by autocratic Afrikaaners. More often was the conflict portrayed as one for which Britain had tripled its military budget and sacrificed domestic reform for the sake of an international congeries of mine-owners. The war was kept alive as a political issue by the Elgin Commission of 1903, which indicted ministerial as well as military incompetence, and by the Government-supported programme of importing Asian contract labourers to work the South African mines, a plan condemned as 'Chinese slavery' by the Liberal Opposition.

Even those Britons who had strongly favoured the South African

War agreed privately that the conflict had demonstrated an unfortunate degree of ineptitude on the párt of the Army and an unduly low level of physical vitality on the part of the military recruits. In the great-power rivalry in which their country found itself engaged, they might usefully learn a few lessons from dynamic imperial Germany. The 'quest for national efficiency' that resulted transcended party lines,[8] but while supporters of such a quest – Lord Rosebery, R. B. Haldane, and Sydney and Beatrice Webb among them – stood on the sidelines, Arthur James Balfour was very much in a position to give concrete application to often amorphous desires. In July 1902 he succeeded his uncle the third Marquess of Salisbury as Prime Minister.

There followed three of the most significant years in British history. The alliance with Japan in 1902 and the Entente with France in 1904 drew Britain out of the diplomatic isolation that the Boer War had revealed, while the Committee on Imperial Defence sought to make the Empire a more unified military entity. Major reforms were launched in the areas of education, the sale of alcoholic beverages, immigration and unemployment. Balfour was a skilful parliamentarian and a witty conversationalist, but he completely lacked the ability to mould his programme so as to mobilise his party and so as to make himself thereby the symbol of popular aspirations. As the *Quarterly Review* observed in 1906, 'The "man in the street" would probably say that Mr. Balfour did not possess the qualities which go to make up statesmanship, but that he was a clever, resourceful, dexterous party leader. This seems to us almost the contrary of the truth.'[9]

Every major reform that Balfour put forward increased the number of his political enemies. The Education Act of 1902, which launched a national system of secondary education, also reawakened the slumbering Nonconformist conscience to the virtues of political Liberalism; the 'Free Churches' were less impressed by what the measure did for 'national efficiency' than by the manner in which it compelled local ratepayers to subsidise certain Church of England schools and by the fact that in some areas such institutions became the only secondary schools available to the children of Nonconformist parents. An analogous fate befell the Licensing Act of 1904. It reduced the number of public houses, a step that ought to have won the applause of temperance forces; but the pubkeepers were compensated for the loss of their property from a fund levied on the trade in beer and spirits. It was consequently denounced as a 'brewers' Bill', and won or rewon the Liberal Party yet further recruits. The Wyndham Land Act may have done more than any other single measure to transform the tenant farmers of Ireland into peasant proprietors but – like the Government's diplomatic accomplishments abroad – it too was as likely to alienate as to attract electoral strength.

The step that ultimately did most to injure the Balfour Government's electoral prospects was yet another positive proposal, Joseph Chamberlain's 1903 recommendation that the British return to a policy of protection – in order to weld the Empire into an imperial tariff union, in order to protect British industries and their workers from subsidised foreign competition, and in order to obtain new sources of revenue with which to pay for such social reforms as old-age pensions. Balfour was not so wedded to 'free trade' as a theoretical principle to object to using retaliatory tariffs to force down foreign imposts, but he objected to tariffs on imported food as politically disastrous – as indeed the proposal proved to be. With extraordinary skill, Balfour imposed for two and a half years a façade of unity over a party and a party organisation now split three ways – into Chamberlainite tariff-reformers, free-traders, and Balfourite champions of an elusive *via media*.

Both 'free trade' and 'protection' could – and did – become passionate political slogans, but which British organisation was likely to man the electoral barricades on behalf of 'negotiation with retaliation'? With the most rational of intentions, Balfour permitted his party and its programme to fall between the proverbial two stools, the butt of satirists and wits, and even of Opposition leaders noted more for their good sense than for their cleverness. Balfour, explained Sir Henry Campbell-Bannerman, resembled a general who, having given the command to his men to attack, found them attacking one another; when informed of this he shrugged his shoulders and said that he could not help it if they insisted on misunderstanding his orders.[10]

Balfour's final ploy was to submit the resignation of his Cabinet in December 1905 without first asking for the dissolution of Parliament and the holding of a general election. His apparent hope was that the Liberal Opposition would, in the very creation of a Cabinet, so demonstrate its own disunity over Irish home rule and the Empire as to confirm its inability to govern. His hopes were foiled by the oft-underrated Campbell-Bannerman, who found a place in the Cabinet for the leader of every major party subdivision with the exception of Lord Rosebery, the idiosyncratic ex-Premier, who in effect excluded himself.

While the national organisation of the Unionist Party fell into disarray and his private secretary warned Balfour of 'a dearth of good candidates',[11] Herbert Gladstone, the Liberal Chief Whip, revitalised the Liberal organisation and did much to insure an opponent for just about every Unionist candidate. 156 Unionists had been elected without a contest in 1900, but only five were to have that advantage in January 1906. As A. K. Russell had demonstrated, there was a high degree of overlap in the occupational background of Unionist and Liberal candidates:

	Unionists	Liberals
Landed interests	40	15
Industry	30	30
Finance	55	35
Commerce	10	15
Transport and shipping	10	20
Working men	–	5
Lawyers	30	30
Armed services	25	5
Academics	5	10
Newspaper proprietors and journalists	5	15
Miscellaneous	15	15

Yet the table does illuminate significant differences as well; and in addition it may be noted that Liberal candidates tended to be younger, were more likely to have attended a state secondary school, and were far more likely to be affiliated to a church other than the Anglican (40 per cent, as against 15 per cent of Unionist candidates).[12]

The greatest apparent weakness of the Liberal Party candidates in facing an electorate a majority of which was clearly in some sense made up of members of the working class, and which included more than a million and a half trade-union members, was that so few of its own candidates were of working-class background. The paucity of such working-class candidates had (in part) inspired the formation in 1900 of the Labour Representation Committee (LRC), which in the general election of 1906 fielded fifty candidates. In the hope of averting triangular battles which would benefit the Unionists, Ramsay MacDonald, the LRC secretary, and Herbert Gladstone negotiated in 1903 a private pact which gave the Socialists a clear run against the Unionists in most constituencies in which they stood and encouraged their withdrawal in favour of Liberals in others. That pact has been much criticised by latter-day Liberals for permitting the Labour cuckoo into the Liberal nest, thereby giving the fledgling Labour Party an unfortunate and unnecessary boost.[13] Such a conclusion rests on the oft-unexamined premise that, in the course of the twentieth century, party polarisation on the basis of social class would both inevitably and entirely supersede party division on the basis of religion, nationality and occupational pressure group. As Henry Pelling has persuasively demonstrated, what discouraged Liberal constituencies from adopting candidates of working-class background was less the hostility of party leaders or significant differences of sociopolitical philosophy than the problem of providing financial support for the election and the maintenance of persons lacking an independent income in a Parliament that paid no salary to its members. Most of the future leaders of the Labour Party, men such as MacDonald, Arthur Henderson and Keir Hardie, had first sought adoption as Liberal candidates.[14] Until 1918, and perhaps even later, it remained theoretically possible that – even if class were to become the prime determinant of party affiliation – the Liberal Party would succeed in absorbing politically the burgeoning trade-union movement just as the Democratic Party was to do in the United States. Under such an assumption, Gladstone's pact with MacDonald may be interpreted not as unwittingly encouraging Labour independence but as deliberately tying a Labour tail to the Liberal dog.

II

The Liberal triumph of 1906 has often been interpreted as a triumph for social reform. In the words of Alfred Havighurst, 'the real significance of the election is in its impetus to social democracy: the rising demand for better standards of living for the workingmen, for greater equality of opportunity, for limitations of economic privilege and for security against sickness, unemployment, and old age.'[15] It is certainly a fact that, in the course of the previous thirty years, Liberal theorists had done much to transform political liberalism from a negative creed (emphasising the removal of chartered economic, political and religious privileges) to a positive 'constructive' ethos (seeking government protection for the less well-off members of society and sanctioning the use of the tax system to promote a modicum of wealth redistribution). Liberal candidates did mention certain social reforms in their election programmes (69 per cent referred to Poor Law reforms and pensions and 68 per cent to land reform) but they were even more likely to allude to free trade (98 per cent), education (86 per cent), Ireland (78 per cent) or temperance (78 per cent), and almost as likely to mention fiscal retrenchment (54 per cent).[16] The issue of old-age pensions was as often as not used as a stick with which to beat the Unionist Government: in the words of one Liberal Publications Department pamphlet, 'In 1895 the Tories promised *Old Age Pensions* and got a large majority in the House of Commons. WHERE ARE THOSE OLD AGE PENSIONS?'[17]

Whatever was promised in the electoral programmes of individual Liberal candidates, the party leadership carefully abstained from setting forth a social-reform programme pledging all Liberals. As James Bryce reminded Campbell-Bannerman, such a programme could be 'embarrassing'. Besides, as R. B. Haldane, the new Secretary of War, observed, the Liberals 'could not make great promises because they had . . . [first] to pay off a load of debt'. Once the election was safely over, the Liberal Prime Minister reminded Parliament that 'the policy upon which the Government has taken office and upon which they have been supported by their friends is the policy of retrenchment'.[18]

The key issues of the campaign were those issues that the Balfour Government had wittingly or unwittingly created, and all of the attempts by the Unionist campaigners to make Irish home rule the central issue or to portray the Liberals as 'a party of Imperial disintegration' were deftly turned aside by Campbell-Bannerman; he insisted on a 'step-by-step' approach that would burden the next Parliament with no measure comparable to Gladstone's home-rule bills of 1886 or 1893. Once the election was over, the Conservative *Quarterly Review* provided a surprisingly dispassionate and persuasive appraisal of the reasons for the outcome:

while it is true that many grievances co-operated to make the Unionist party unpopular, it is also true that most of these different grievances had some common elements, so that they appeared to the electorate like various accounts of a single indictment rather than a number of distinct charges. Thus the attack on Chinese labour, on Protection, and on the Taff Vale judgment, all formed part of an accusation of plutocratic conspiracy. Even the Education Act was presented as a victory for privilege, and so fell in with the general charge that the Unionists were the party of the rich and the selfish, who were ready to degrade the British conquests in South Africa by gathering gold through the labour of slaves, to build up a system of monopoly by taxing the food of the poor, to keep the public schools of the nation as a preserve for their friends, and to put workmen under the heel of the capitalist by overthrowing the trade-unions.[19]

What is most fascinating about all the political issues here cited (as well as that of temperance reform) is that they were all issues with which the nineteenth-century Liberal Party had been concerned ever since it had begun to emerge during the 1830s and 1840s from its Whig cocoon. And in every case the party apparently desired a return to the late Victorian *status quo*. Just so did the new Labour Party wish to restore the protection from legal challenge that trade-union funds had enjoyed before the Taff Vale case. The *Quarterly Review* was not oblivious to the irony of the situation:

> It is remarkable that the party cries which were most successful were negative. No Chinese labour, no taxes on food – these were the most generally destructive pieces of electioneering ordnance. Even the attacks on the Education Act and the Taff Vale judgment were in a sense conservative. The electorate was hostile, not to long-existing and venerable institutions, but to recent changes. . . . The wish was to get rid of vexatious innovations: there was no clamour for novelties. The instinct of the people was critical, not constructive. 'Anathema,' not 'credo' was the voice of the polls. . . .
>
> Most conspicuously was this the case in respect to the fiscal controversy. Mr. Chamberlain called his policy reform – tariff reform; and he used all the rhetoric of a reformer. . . . On the other hand free-traders argued in language typically conservative for the *status quo*. . . . Thus pitted against one another were the warm, hopeful, promising, discontented, fiscal reformers, and the cold, cautious, sceptical, complacent fiscal conservatives; and conservatism prevailed.[20]

Even if the *Quarterly Review* assessment is not accepted as the final word, it remains suggestive. For not only were the most frequently professed Liberal goals fundamentally Victorian, but so also were the tactics. Facsimiles of Anti-Corn Law League pamphlets of the 1840s were issued by the thousands, and the return of the Unionist Duke of Devonshire to the political allegiance he had severed over home rule in 1886 was hailed as a restoration of Victorian unity.[21] The National Free Church Council, theoretically above politics, sided openly with the Liberals, and temperance organisations, free-trade associations and the 100,000-woman-strong Women's Liberal Federation contributed greatly to the processes of registration and canvassing. 'When they told me our food would cost more', wrote one widow to Joseph Chamberlain 1909, 'I would not let [my husband] vote Conservative as he had always done.'[22] Among England's and Scotland's Irish voters, the cause of nationalism prevailed over that of religious education, and Jews were attracted anew to the Liberal cause by concern with the 1905 Aliens Act. Finally, the Liberals had on their side not the national press – it still sides with the Unionists by a ratio of almost two to one – but the most potent symbols (the 'big loaf' versus the 'little loaf'; the sausage; and the slant-eyed Chinaman) and the most effective stump orators. Balfour was no demagogue, and, as one Conservative journalist complained afterwards, 'What had we to set against Asquith, Grey, Haldane, Lloyd George, or even Winston [Churchill]?'[23]

In terms of parliamentary seats the Liberal victory of 1906 was the greatest in the party's history. 400 Liberals were elected as compared to 157 Conservatives (including twenty-four Liberal Unionists), thirty Labour, eighty-two Irish Nationalists, and two others. The Liberals completely dominated Welsh and Scottish constituencies, and, for the first time since 1885 and the last time ever, secured a majority of English seats as well. Only west Lancashire, Birmingham and Sheffield remained major islands of Conservative power. Even the by-elections they had won in 1904 and 1905 had not presaged so astonishing a turnabout, and in one significant respect it was not. The total popular vote margin (a more significant figure in 1906 than in 1900, because a total of only fifty Conservatives, Liberals or Socialists stood unopposed) did not represent a landslide:[24]

Conservatives	2,451,454	43·6 per cent
Liberals	2,757,883	49·0 per cent
Labour	329,748	5·9 per cent

III

Whatever popular-vote totals statisticians may compile, it was the votes in the House of Commons that counted, or so at least the jubilant Liberals of 1906 believed. And indeed the Campbell-Bannerman Government did in the course of 1906, 1907 and 1908 add to the statute book a measure reversing the Taff Vale judgement, a school-lunch programme, an eight-hour day for miners, and (with surprisingly little calculation of long-term financial implications[25]) a system of noncontributory old age pensions for most Britons aged seventy or older. Yet, when it came to the issues that had brought victory in 1906, such as education and alcohol licensing, and a measure to end the practice of plural voting, they found a rock-like House of Lords blocking one reform measure after another. At the request of Campbell-Bannerman, the House of Commons resolved in 1907 that 'it is necessary that the power of the other House to alter or reject Bills passed by this House should be so restricted by law as to secure that within the limits of a single Parliament the final decision of the Commons shall prevail', and in 1908 his successor, H. H. Asquith, invited the Liberal Party 'to treat the veto of the House of Lords as the dominating issue in politics'.[26]

Yet the House of Lords, with Balfour's complicity, had discriminated cleverly. Neither Campbell-Bannerman nor Asquith dared hold a general election on issues about which only a minority of their supporters felt passionately, especially not at a time when almost every by-election went badly. Between January 1908 and March 1909 eight successive by-election seats were lost to the Conservatives, and a sense of desperation was beginning to overtake the leadership of a party that had so recently exulted in triumph. The *Nation* sorrowfully reminded the party in November 1908 'that in a democracy nothing fails like failure'.[27] Although the conventional historical wisdom has insisted that the Liberals were fearful of being outflanked on the political left by the Labour Party, the electoral realities of 1908 suggest another answer. As Bentley Gilbert has emphasised, 'the Liberal enemy was not the ghost of Karl Marx, not even of Henry George, but of Joseph Chamberlain'.[28] In the aftermath of 1906, the champion of tariff reform had been felled by a stroke, but his ideas had captured the National Union of Conservative and Unionist Associations, and, with the economic downturn of 1907–8, they seemed to be making an increasing impact upon the electorate as well. The question of the hour was how to raise large new sums to pay for warships and pensions, and 'tariff reform' seemed to provide the most painless answer. 'I have realised from the first', Asquith privately conceded, 'that if it could not be proved that Social reform . . . can be financed on Free Trade lines, a return to Protection is a moral certainty'.[29]

With the budget of 1909, the Liberal Cabinet sought to make a virtue of necessity, to revivify party morale and to outwit the House of Lords and their other political enemies by *raising* taxes. Increased alcohol-licence fees and taxes on alcohol were designed to rally the nonconformists. Land taxes were designed to justify a national valuation of land, long one of the prime political goals of the new Chancellor of the Exchequer and Welsh agrarian Radical, David Lloyd George. Car and petrol taxes were designed to put the unemployed to work building highways. Super-taxes and higher death duties were designed to please the poor and hurt the rich.[30] Although the original purpose of the budget was to bypass the Lords – which had not turned back a finance bill since 1860 – rather than to madden them, by September 1909 the Unionists were 'spoiling for a fight'. So outraged were their adherents – landlords, brewers, bankers and others – and so outrageous did Lloyd George's revolutionary claims for the Liberal budget sound, that Balfour felt he had no choice but to force a general election. For Asquith the decision of the Lords to vote down the budget represented a 'breach of the Constitution' and a 'new-fangled Caesarism'. For the lofty peers the rights of the Commons had to give way to the rights of the nation; the House of Lords, they formally affirmed, 'is not justified in giving its consent to this Bill until it has been submitted to the judgement of the country'.[31]

IV

The House of Lords rejected the Budget on 30 November 1909, and Parliament was prorogued three days later. Since the Liberals wished to utilise the electoral register that became official in January, polling did not begin until 15 January, and the result was an unusually long formal political campaign, possibly too long to permit the Liberals to maintain the mood of passionate indignation on which they had launched it. 'Shall the People be Ruled by the Peers?' was the rhetorical question Asquith addressed to the 10,000 men who were crammed into the Albert Hall on 10 December. Although the Prime Minister was less active in the campaign thereafter, Lloyd George and Winston Churchill stumped the country in a manner reminiscent of Gladstone's 'Midlothian campaign' of 1879–80. With Balfour ill for much of the campaign and Joseph Chamberlain an invalid, the Unionists were no oratorical match for the Liberals; nor was the Conservative Central Office the equal of the Liberal Central Office headed by Sir Robert Hudson, that 'organiser of genius'. As a result the major parties were each able to spend some £900 to £1100 per candidate, with Labour spending only marginally less. Nor were the Liberals as much at a disadvantage in terms of press support as they had been in 1900 or even in 1906.[32]

Not merely the tactics but also the issues of the campaign were for the Liberals fundamentally Gladstonian, and on 29 December 1909, the centenary of the birth of their great Victorian leader, his spirit was summoned from the grave to do battle against the stubborn peers. He was recalled as the scornful critic of the upper house, as the champion of free trade, as the author of path-breaking budgets, as the enemy of entrenched privilege, and – in muted fashion – as the advocate of Irish home rule. (For Liberal candidates, the key issues were the House of Lords, free trade, and the budget; only 39 per cent mentioned the desirability of Irish home rule.)[33] The Liberal leaders had not yet decided precisely how the House of Lords should be curbed constitutionally,[34] but they were very much agreed that the veto had to be 'smashed' and the pre-1909 *status quo* reaffirmed; never again were the peers to be allowed to 'veto' a budget and thereby bring down a popularly elected government. Thousands of Liberal posters depicted a coroneted, decadent peer clutching bags of unearned wealth, while for the President of the Local Government Board, John Burns, the key issue was, 'Will present snobbery, past jobbery, ancient robbery unite with dogma and drink to fetter our hands and chloroform our minds again?'[35]

The Unionists portrayed themselves not as defenders of hereditary noblemen, however worthy, but as protectors of popular rights. According to the *Daily Mail*, the budget was 'an audacious attempt to force socialism upon the country without consulting the people'. Balfour mocked the Liberal effort to persuade the people that they were suffering 'some terrible indignity, by having their opinion asked about the Budget'. By the end of 1909, the Unionists were sufficiently united on the virtues of tariff reform to make the issue a focus of party unity rather than division. Despite the nation's recovery from the economic downturn of 1907–8, tariff reform was put forward as the sensible alternative to the vagaries of Lloyd George's budget, and thousands of Unionist posters depicted the iniquitous 'Herr Dumper', the *nouveau riche* foreigner who had filled his coffers at the expense of Britons still chained to a self-defeating free-trade policy. From now on, 'England expects that every foreigner will pay his duty.' The 'free-trade' budget, the Unionists were quick to remind the workingman, had not exactly kept down his costs:

Dearer Baccy, dearer Bread
Dearer Living, dearer Dead
Dearer Whiskey, Beer and Gin
Is what you get when the Rads are in.[36]

In the closing days of the campaign, the Unionists used with apparently increasing success one additional issue, the naval threat posed by Germany. In a series of sensational articles in the *Daily Mail*, Robert Blatchford, the former socialist, charged that Germany was 'deliberately preparing to destroy the British Empire' and that Liberal ineptitude had left the country unprepared to defend itself; Balfour's support gave the issue an importance it would otherwise have lacked.[37]

The outcome of the election made it clear almost from the start that the year 1910 would constitute one vast prelude to a second general election: Liberals, 275; Conservatives (including 31 Liberal Unionists), 273; Labour, 40; Irish Nationalists, 82. The pendulum had swung significantly, but not far enough to put the Unionists back in power – unless they could abandon their name and *raison d'être* and join forces with the Irish Nationalists. Sir Edward Grey's reaction was that of most detached observers: 'The moral [was] that neither party had succeeded in gaining the confidence of the country.'[38] After initial hesitation, Asquith became more confident that he could keep in office a Liberal–Labour–Irish coalition with an overall majority of 112; after all, Lord John Russell and Lord Palmerston had kept analogous coalitions in power a half century earlier. The necessary cost was a new commitment to Irish home rule, an issue that the prospective curbing of the House of Lords had once again transformed into practical politics.

V

Early in 1910, the budget passed with Conservative acquiescence, and Labour was made happy with a statute largely reversing the Osborne Judgement of 1909, which had outlawed the use of trade-union funds for political purposes. Ordinary politics then gave way, as a result of the death of King Edward VII and the succession of King George V, to an unprecedented confidential constitutional conference. Despite the protests of the Labour and Irish (and some Liberal and Unionist) backbenchers, the top four Liberals and the top four Conservatives met clandestinely more than fifteen times between June and November in order to attempt to resolve by consensus the issues – the future of the House of Lords, tariff reform, defence – that had just polarised the country. The break-up of the conference – probably as the result of Balfour's ultimate unwillingness to make any concession toward Irish home rule[39] – led immediately to the general election of December 1910.

The campaign was briefer than it had been eleven months earlier, and, since the voter register was a year old and eighty-six fewer seats were contested, the participating electorate was smaller; but recent students of the election have cast doubt upon the apathy that supposedly afflicted the voting population.[40] Nor were the issues absolutely identical.

The Liberals now possessed a specific House of Lords reform plan – measures that won the approval of three successive Houses of Commons over a two-year period were to become law even without the assent of the peers – and the Conservatives were hard put to come up with an agreed substitute. The lack of a substitute reform plan undermined their campaign, but Balfour eventually championed a national popular referendum as the proper solution if the two parliamentary chambers could not agree on a major question. Since January many Unionists had once again become discomfited that tariff reform would involve taxes on food, a clear electoral liability. Thus, when the Liberals challenged Balfour to state that tariff reform should be subject to such a referendum, he took up the challenge and agreed. The decision may have gained votes for the Unionists, but the Chamberlainite 'Whole Hoggers' viewed it as a stab in the back. The meaning of tariff reform once again became fuzzy rather than clear-cut. For 89 per cent of the Unionist but only 37 per cent of the Liberal candidates, national defence was an issue. Social reform was listed by 49 per cent of the Unionists and 44 per cent of the Liberals. For 88 per cent of the Unionists (but only 41 per cent of the Liberals) Irish home rule was a key, perhaps the key issue. Unionists did their very best to make John Redmond the electoral villain. The Irish nationalist leader had just returned from a fund-raising tour in the United States, and the *Observer* snarled, 'The Dollar Dictator has forced his marionette ministry to stampede the House of Commons.'[41] The Irish issue doubtless hurt the Liberals with some voters, but it also assured them the fervent support of Irishmen resident in England.

At first glance, the December 1910 election results bear a startling resemblance to those of January:[42]

January 1910	Seats	Total votes	Percentage of total	Unopposed
Unionists	273	3,127,887	46·9	19
Liberals	275	2,873,251	43·1	1
Labour	40	532,807	8·0	–
Nationalists	82	126,647	1·9	55
December 1910				
Unionists	272	2,426,635	46·4	72
Liberals	272	2,290,020	43·8	35
Labour	42	374,409	7·1	3
Nationalists	84	131,720	2·5	53

It is true that fifty-five seats had changed hands since January and that, in seats contested both times, a tiny (0·8 per cent) swing towards the Tories could be discerned. Yet the second election proved decisive in a fashion that the first had not. Tory frustrations notwithstanding, the second election restored the authority and spirit of the Liberal Government; assured of Irish and Labour support, it was to remain firmly in the political saddle until 1915. 'I think that our election here has cleared the air,' wrote Asquith, 'and made the way fairly plain, if not exactly smooth.'[43]

The election did several other things as well. It underlined the manner in which political divisions reflected significant degrees of both geographical and socio-economic polarisation. Liberal gains in 1906 in southern and western England had melted away, and the Tories were again firmly entrenched as the party representing agricultural and suburban England and, with the exception of portions of metropolitan London, most of the south and east. The 1906 gains the Liberals had made north of the Humber and the Dee had largely held, however, and the Liberals were confirmed as the party of Welshmen (seeking the disestablishment of the Anglican Church), of Scotsmen (seeking land-law reform), of the nonconformist remnant, and of working men in the industrial Midlands.[44]

What of the Labour Party? It had burst dramatically upon the scene with thirty MPs in 1906, and its fortunes had been given a boost in 1909 when the Miners Federation decided formally to align itself with the Labour Party. Thirteen Liberal–Labour MPs consequently joined the Labour ranks, and when Parliament dissolved in 1909 the parliamentary party could claim forty-five members. Yet the group was compelled to campaign 'as a part of the Radical wing of the Liberal Party', emphasising the budget and the curbing of the Lords' veto, and, when the polls had closed, Labour had gained three seats and lost eight, leaving a total of forty. Not one of its forty victors had faced Liberal opposition; it failed to win a single seat in a constituency in which both major parties fielded candidates.[45] In December the party gained five seats and lost three, but only two of those victories involved a Liberal opponent and none involved the opposition of both major parties. 'The big thing that has happened in the last two years', wrote Beatrice Webb late in 1910, 'is that Lloyd George and Winston Churchill have practically taken the *limelight*, not merely from their own colleagues, but from the Labour Party.'[46] Henry Pelling and Paul Thompson have independently concluded that the long-run prospects of the party were better than they seemed, and the expansion of trade-union membership from 2,513,000 in 1907 to 4,135,000 in 1913 ought to have helped;[47] yet the Labour Party of 1910–14 was a divided and oft-dispirited group. Between the general election of December 1910 and the outbreak of the war in August 1914, the Labour Party failed to win a single by-election (of twenty that took place) and lost four of its seats at by-elections (two to Liberals and two to Conservatives).[48] Without some kind of continuing *de facto* Liberal–Labour pact, Liberal electoral prospects looked poor and Labour prospects worse.

For every reader of George Dangerfield's *Strange Death of Liberal England*, the parliamentary and constituency politics of 1911–14 tend to be overshadowed by that 'unconscious turning from respectability ... which had twisted pre-war England into a maze of conflicting violence'.[49] It is a series of dramatic and apparently interlinked stories that Dangerfield tells: of obdurate peers who risked swamping rather than acquiescing (as a majority ultimately did) in the Parliament Act of 1911; of militant suffragettes for whom violent means – the throwing of bags of flour from House of Commons galleries, the slashing of pictures in art museums, the breaking of Oxford Street shop windows, the burning of empty houses – supplanted constitutional ends; of trade-union members who were prepared to lose over 40 million working days in strikes in 1912 (compared with 2 million in 1907); of Ulster Covenanters and their Unionist supporters who seemed ready to defy the Constitution and encourage military mutiny in order to block home rule for all of Ireland. That there was a note of rebellion in the air even more sober historians have conceded;[50] and yet the amount of actual bloodshed proved minimal, and by the spring of 1914 in England if not in Ireland the tide of militancy had already ebbed. What

Dangerfield has conveyed was a vague mood of leftist rebellion; but, as Pelling has shown, the average working man, though interested in legislation safeguarding his trade union, was sceptical of 'welfare state' measures such as the National Insurance Act of 1911, which hurt rather than aided the electoral prospects of the Liberal Party.[51] Both at the local-government level and in national by-elections in 1912 and 1913, what was at work was not so much 'The Strange Death of Liberal England' as 'The Strange Revival of Tory England'.[52] The most likely outcome, moreover, was not apocalyptic, merely a Conservative triumph in the general election scheduled for 1915. Ten years of Tory rule (1895–1905) would have been followed by ten years of Liberal rule (1905–1915), and they in turn would have been followed by a term of Tory rule once more.

The ultimate reason why the sense of imminent catastrophe that Dangerfield conveys is historically misleading is not that he was unduly selective in his use of quotations or that the note of passionate unease that he discerned in the pre-war atmosphere was not present. It was there, but it was soon to be transformed into the remarkably calm domestic centre of that hurricane we call World War I. The militant suffragettes took to rolling bandages and encouraging timid young men to don uniforms; they were subsequently to be handed the vote, as a polite afterthought to the all-encompassing Reform Bill of 1918. The syndicalists did not ultimately transform the labour movement or supplant the Labour Party. The despairing Unionists who were prepared to defy the Constitution in the name of the Constitution were to become Baldwinite Conservatives pledged to his precepts of 'Faith, Hope, Love, and Work'. Despite the war and the great depression, most of the inter-war era turned out to be politically more placid than the era about which Dangerfield wrote. Beneath the agitated surface of Edwardian England, as this brief survey has strongly suggested, the nuts and bolts of two-party politics, both at the parliamentary level and at the constituency level, remained in place. An occasional swing of the pendulum does not constitute the tolling out of an era, and, had it not been for an interruption of a quite different nature, the very gradual late Victorian and Edwardian adaptation of political parties and practices might well have continued. We do indeed find turbulence in Edwardian England, but we may not be altogether mistaken if we view Edwardian politics through the autumnal haze of an 'Indian summer'.

4. Critics of Edwardian Society: The Case of the Radical Right

G. R. SEARLE

Historians who have written about Edwardian politics have spent much time examining the state of Liberalism and of the Liberal Party in the hope of finding here some clue that will explain the misfortunes which befell that party during the First World War and the 1920s. Thus, the friction at constituency level between Liberals and the newly founded Labour Party has been seen as a harbinger of later events, when the Liberals found themselves reduced to irrelevance in a society more demonstrably polarised along class lines. Other historians, less concerned with the Liberal Party as an election-fighting organisation, have analysed Liberalism (in this sense, usually 'liberalism') as an ideology or a set of assumptions about how political life should be conducted, and an interesting debate has developed about whether or not it was 'in crisis' in the pre-war period. This emphasis in historical writing is entirely understandable, but it has somewhat obscured the self-evident fact that the Conservatives faced much greater difficulties in those years. Indeed, it would be easy to give an account of Edwardian politics in which the emphasis fell on 'the crisis of Conservatism' and on the parlous state of the Conservative Party on the eve of the War.

The fundamental weakness of the Conservative Party lay in its inability to win elections. At the end of the Edwardian decade the Conservatives were in opposition, having lost three general elections in a row. This disastrous performance compares starkly with an earlier period of Conservative hegemony which began in 1886, when Gladstone split the Liberal Party in taking up the cause of Irish home rule. Reinforced by the dissident Liberals (called Liberal Unionists), the Conservative Party dominated British politics for the next twenty years.[1] However, as early as 1902 there were signs of a revival in Liberal fortunes; indeed, it was partly a desire to prevent this revival from developing further momentum which encouraged Joseph Chamberlain, Colonial Secretary in Balfour's Conservative administration, to make his momentous speech at Birmingham in May 1903 which launched the tariff-reform campaign. But tariff reform, far from winning back the initiative for the Government, crippled the Conservative – Liberal Unionist Party for the following decade. The Liberals won a landslide victory in 1906, 400 of their candidates being elected; and their opponents proved incapable of ejecting them from office when the country again went to the polls, in 1910.

This sorry record of electoral failure forms, however, only one aspect of the 'crisis of Conservatism' in Edwardian Britain. For the Conservatives were the self-professed guardians of national and imperial interests and, as such, were understandably alarmed at continuing evidence of Britain's relative decline as a great power in the opening decade of the twentieth century. Indignant patriots on the right had already expressed dismay at the inability of the Conservative-led governments of Lord Salisbury and Arthur Balfour to arrest this trend, and the catastrophes of the Boer War had provoked violent attacks on the responsible ministers: Lord Lansdowne, the War Secretary, was accused of negligence, incompetence and infirmity of purpose, and there were calls in the press for his impeachment.

But the accession to power of a Liberal ministry in the winter of 1905–6 awakened anxieties of a more deep-seated kind. For the Liberal Party contained within it 'pacifist' elements, eager to reduce 'bloated arms expenditure' and convinced that international conflicts could be resolved by the application of reason and goodwill – foolish sentiments at the best of times, thought most Conservatives, but suicidal folly when considered against the background of growing Anglo-German tension. It was not seriously argued that the Foreign Secretary, Edward Grey, or the Service Ministers were blind to the danger from Germany; but it could plausibly be claimed that the Liberal Government was inhibited in its diplomatic activities and in its defence planning by the need to propitiate its own 'pacifist' left wing. It was thus in a mood of despairing rage that many Conservatives watched their beloved country sliding to disaster (or so they believed), while the Opposition proved itself powerless to persuade the electorate of the dangerous situation in which it had been placed by an irresponsible Radical ministry.

Simultaneously there was mounting apprehension in Conservative quarters at the spread of 'socialism'. This phrase, though often on the lips of Conservatives, lacked a precise meaning. It might on some occasions be a reference to the increasing self-assertion of organised labour, the growth of trade unionism or the activities of avowed socialists. More often, however, the invocation of socialism denoted bitter hostility to the social-welfare legislation of a Liberal Government that was allegedly stirring up class animosities by promising the poorer electors material advantages to be secured by the despoilation of the rich. Whether or not Conservatives were being entirely serious when they called radical ministers such as Lloyd George and Winston Churchill 'the Reds' is a question which lies outside the scope of this essay, as does the further question of whether or not the Government's policies did indeed have the 'revolutionary' implications which their critics claimed to see in them. Suffice it to say that, in sponsoring old-age pensions, health and unemployment insurance and the like, the Liberals were undoubtedly rewriting the ground rules of British politics in a way that threatened both the electoral and the economic interests of their opponents.

Between 1909 and 1911 all these anxieties coalesced to bring the 'crisis of Conservatism' to a climax. Lloyd George's 'People's Budget' of 1909 precipitated a constitutional crisis, in which the Liberals took active steps to curtail the powers of the House of Lords by removing its absolute veto on legislation. In pursuit of this goal, the Government appealed to the country and was twice confirmed in power, though now reduced to dependence on its Labour and Irish Nationalist allies. Moreover, the constitutional crisis proper coincided with a naval panic ('we want eight and we won't wait!') occasioned by an acceleration in the German shipbuilding programme, and the Navy issue made a prominent appearance in both of the two 1910 general elections. But the failure of the Opposition to shake the electorate out of its preoccupation with domestic political issues raised some worrying questions about the 'state of the nation' and about the Conservative Party's relationship with the masses whose support it needed to mobilise.

However, as is well known, the turbulent events of 1909–11 did not simply polarise British society into left and right, Liberalism and Conservatism. They also triggered off a bitter dispute within the Opposition ranks, which culminated in Balfour's resignation in November 1911 and the election of Andrew Bonar Law as his successor. The issue directly responsible for the disruption was the issue of what tactics to adopt once the Government's hated Parliament Bill had entered the Upper House. But this particular controversy would not have been so acrimonious had there not also existed a more fundamental 'crisis of Conservatism', as outlined above. Under the weight of this crisis, the forces of the right, which were every bit as fissiparous as the forces of the left, splintered into a variety of factions, each with its own programme and strategy. The stratification of the right was complex, and made the more so by individuals who shifted their stance or moved from one group to another; but, at the risk of some oversimplification, it makes sense to distinguish between three differing responses to the crisis and between three corresponding groups within the Conservative Party.

First, there were the traditional party members, Balfour at their head, who saw the function of Conservatism as being that of preserving 'national' institutions and putting a brake on reckless and ill considered change. The constitutional crisis, it is true, caused even the most soft-spoken of the Opposition leaders to voice strong criticism of what they saw as the 'revolutionary' and 'unconstitutional' behaviour of the Government. But, basically, traditional Conservatives believed that there was no viable alternative to abiding by the rules of the party game, taking each issue as it arose, and waiting until such time as their opponents destroyed themselves by their own cupidity and folly and an electoral reaction set in in the Conservatives' favour. In the interim all that could be done was to guard jealously the party's interests and traditions, since the Conservative Party was seen by this group as an institution worth preserving for its own sake, as well as being an instrument for furthering the national good. These cautious and traditional attitudes, however, aroused impatience in certain quarters of the party, especially among many of the younger members, who protested that this fossilised Conservatism, while it might satisfy the average member of the Carlton Club, was too negative to have an appeal to the modern electorate.

But these critics have in turn to be broken down into two groups. The first of these groups was composed of those who, from the time of the Boer War onwards, had identified themselves with the fashionable catch-cry of 'national efficiency'. Acutely aware of Britain's declining influence in the world, they tended to take the view that the historic feud between the two major parties was now, at best, an irrelevance; at worst, a danger to the state. Ideally, responsibility should be handed over to a highly trained managerial élite – perhaps to 'men of business', perhaps to 'scientific experts'. In the interests of 'national efficiency', they also hankered after some 'national government' that would combine the talents of all the 'first-rate men' and shelve traditional party issues, such as the denominational dispute over education, Ireland and the drink question, so that national energies could be directed into preparations for a possible war with Germany and for adapting British society for economic survival in an increasingly competitive international world. Two of the heroes of the imperialistic wing of the party were to some extent identified with this approach: Joseph Chamberlain, on whom party loyalties always sat lightly, and Lord Milner, the former High Commissioner in South Africa, who, on his return to England, had come out as an open critic of the 'rotten system' of party politics.[2]

Interestingly enough, events seemed to be playing into the hands of this group in the course of 1910. After all, the Constitutional Conference, which sat intermittently from June to November of that year, represented a more or less serious attempt by the two party leaderships to reach an agreed settlement on the vexed issue of the powers and composition of the House of Lords. But party 'collusion' did not stop there. For in October 1910 Lloyd George approached Balfour with a project for setting up a 'national government' of the kind of which 'national efficiency' advocates had long dreamed. For obvious reasons the delicate discussions to which Lloyd George's initiative gave rise took place in circumstances of secrecy. But politicians and political journalists were alerted to what was afoot by a series of letters in *The Times* – advocating a 'federal' solution of the Irish problem – written by Milner's disciple, F. S. Oliver; and also by the propaganda being put out in the influential Conservative paper the *Observer*, the editor of which, J. L. Garvin, had been entrusted by Lloyd George with the task of creating an atmosphere conducive to national unity.[3] Thus, when the secret coalition talks broke down in November and the Constitutional Conference also ended in failure, many Milnerite and Chamberlainite MPs harboured the suspicion that Balfour, with characteristic over-caution, had allowed a great historic opportunity to pass him by.

But the second group of Balfour's critics took a quite different view of the crisis, and this is the group that forms the nucleus of what I shall call the 'Radical Right'. These Conservatives did, it is true, subscribe to many of the causes promulgated by the disciples of Chamberlain and Milner: tariff reform, Army reform, a big Navy, 'constructive' social reform and so on. But they had diametrically opposed views about what was the correct political strategy. Thus, the Radical

Right, far from welcoming the suspension of the party struggle in the summer of 1910, had greeted the convening of the conference with a shudder of apprehension. While conceding that their leaders could hardly have refused the invitation to confer, they suspected that the sole purpose of the exercise was to get the Asquith Government 'off the hook', and they feared that the Conservative leadership, in its simplicity, was only too likely to fall into the trap.[*] Subsequent rumours that some sort of compromise over Ireland was in the air caused further unease. In the first week of October 1910 many of these right-wing critics had come together to form the 'Reveille' movement, which aimed at committing the Unionist Party to 'a more vigorous constructive programme' but which was also clearly intended to keep a watchful eye on the leadership.[5] Thus, far from criticising Balfour for his unwillingness to grasp the 'historic compromise' that Lloyd George was offering him, the Radical Right was rather disposed to pick a quarrel with Balfour over his apparent disinclination to fight the Liberal enemy with the necessary ruthlessness and determination. Smouldering suspicions of this kind gave way to open hostility when in the following year Balfour advised his supporters to beat a tactical retreat over the Parliament Bill. The diehard peers (several of whose leaders had signed the original Reveille manifesto) came out in rebellion against the defeatism of the party leadership, and many Unionist MPs and party workers associated themselves with this stand; even Milner and his friends, now that a 'national settlement' had been rejected, joined in the fight.

But the paradox of the situation was that, although purporting to act as the custodians of Conservative principles, diehard leaders, such as Willoughby de Broke, in fact had a highly ambivalent attitude to the Conservative Party, and were already engaged in an analysis of the political system that was to put them some way outside the pale of Conservatism, as that creed is usually understood. This much will become apparent when we examine their creed in greater detail. But the point must be established at an early stage because it helps to explain why these ultra-Tories so often found themselves collaborating with patriotic zealots who had never in their lives been true Conservatives at all. In fact, the Radical Right embraced many former Liberals who had subsequently broken with Liberalism in protest against its alleged 'pacifism' and 'anti-imperialism'. A prominent example of this political type would be the scaremongering journalist Arnold White, who had stood as a Gladstonian Liberal in the 1886 general election, but whose notoriety in the Edwardian period derived from his work for the Navy League, the National Service League, the Eugenics Education Society and the anti-aliens movement. [6] One can perhaps also include in the Radical Right a few 'rogue socialists', such as Robert Blatchford, whose hatred of Germany had overcome their hatred of capitalism; and other variegated adventurers, who calculated that demagogic imperialism might bring them financial rewards and personal prominence.

The Radical Right was not, of course, a 'party'; it did not have a proper organisation of its own. The Radical Right can perhaps best be described as a collection of super-patriots unable for one reason or another to identify with their 'natural' party, or as a movement of rootless nationalists who felt alienated to a lesser or greater extent from *all* the major political organisations of the day. But, though diverse in social origin and liable to quarrel on specific issues of policy (for example, they were divided in the bitter controversy between Admiral Fisher and Admiral Charles Beresford), these people owned allegiance to a common set of attitudes and viewed politics in a way which gave them a distinct identity. This made the Radical Right a force to be reckoned with in Edwardian politics.

The distinguishing feature of the group was its unbounded confidence that 'the people' could be won over to the support of imperialistic objectives if a direct appeal were made to their patriotic instincts. The Radical Right was a 'populist' movement in the sense that it believed that ties could be forged between the masses and the Government by means which circumvented the party machines and the party leaders. [7] The underlying assumption was that there existed vast numbers of 'silent voters' and 'little people' who were exasperated with the conventional system of politics, which ignored their interests and point of view, but who would eagerly respond to the patriotic call of duty.

The populism and demagoguery of the Radical Right can be seen in the attitude that its members adopted towards the working class. Essentially, they believed that the good sense of the British people would triumph over the errors and follies of the Radicals and socialists who claimed to speak in their name. Leopold Maxse, the editor and proprietor of the monthly *National Review*, lamented 'the total ignorance of the working classes who are rarely given a chance of understanding the problem of national security' and who had 'simply been cruelly exploited by self-seeking Demagogues'. [8] The bitterness of the Radical Right against Balfour and the 'party mandarins' derived in large part from their conviction that the 'man in the street' was being needlessly alienated from the Unionist cause by Balfour's pose of aristocratic detachment. But, if the gospel were preached to the working classes in language they could understand, the Radical Right believed that all 'decent' workmen would enthusiastically respond. The present alliance between the manual workers and the Liberal Party was, they said, merely a transient phenomenon. Approached in the right way, working men were as patriotic as anybody else, as had been shown by the labour movements in Australia and New Zealand, which had come out in support of compulsory military service. The diehard peer Willoughby de Broke was absolutely certain that 'we can get the best working men on our side, and divide them against the agitators'; it was an indictment of the flabby leadership of the Unionist Party that it had failed to elicit the instinct of patriotism which existed amongst the working-class electorate.[9]

In general, the Radical Right was not easily frightened by democracy. Indeed, from 1910 onwards this group strongly pressed for the referendum as a device for ascertaining the popular will – and not simply because this gave a tactical advantage to the opponents of home rule and other legislative measures likely to be introduced in the near future by the Liberal Government. 'The one thing most dreaded by Demagogues is a direct reference to the people', declared the *National Review* in December 1910.

Nor, surprisingly perhaps, did all members of the Radical Right give way to feelings of dismay during that period of industrial turbulence between 1910 and 1914 known as the 'great labour unrest'. It is true that Arnold White, who was a frequent contributor to the journals run by the Anti-Socialist Union,[10] was reduced to a state of near hysteria by the miners' strike of 1912: he predicted that a protracted stoppage would mean the wiping out, by pestilence, starvation and civil commotion, of a considerable portion of the 17 million people inhabiting the industrial north; and he therefore called for the establishment of a committee of public safety armed with draconian powers, while himself joining one of several volunteer police forces.[11]

But this was not how Maxse's *National Review* reacted to these events. Maxse himself seems to have experienced a positive sense of exhilaration in contemplating the wave of industrial disturbance, because, as a tariff-reformer, he took this as proof of the collapse of the free-trade system. He seems, in fact, to have perceived organised labour's new mood of self-assertion less as a threat to the whole social order than as providing useful ammunition that could be fired off against the number-one enemy: the despicable Liberal administration.[12]

Naturally, all members of the Radical Right disliked socialism, but socialist agitators, in Maxse's phrase, were 'known to the police', and neither as dangerous nor as troublesome as middle-class Radicals. Thus, the *National Review* did not treat the Labour MPs as a serious force to be reckoned with and usually referred to them simply as one of the constituent elements in 'the Coalition'. In the 1910–14 period there was a plausible case to be made out for the view that the Labour Party's boasted independence was a mere pretence and that the only valid political distinction was that between groups which opposed and groups which supported the Asquith Government. Maxse and his friends could also claim, again with some justification, that the Labour Party in no way represented the average working man. The Labour politicians, they alleged, had been bought off with public posts and in other ways merged into the governing coalition, greatly to the indignation of thousands of manual workers, who were now in open revolt against their leaders. In this situation the Radical Right thought it quite possible – and eminently desirable – to organise the return of 'patriotic' working-class candidates in complete independence of the Liberals. Without going into much detail, they also adumbrated a 'constructive' social and economic programme, of which the central plank was tariff reform, but which also included Poor Law reform and smallholdings legislation; an appeal along these lines, they confidently proclaimed, could hardly fail to elicit a sympathetic response from the masses.

Yet if, as was here claimed, the working classes were potential allies of the imperialists, why had the union between the two forces not in fact taken place? To this the Radical Right had three main answers. Firstly, they laid great blame on the flaccid leadership supplied by Balfour and his cronies. Secondly, they believed that the whole political process was being distorted by a variety of corrupt practices. Thirdly, they feared the activities and influence of 'alien' groups within British society which, they alleged, were working for the destruction of the Empire. Each of these three lines of argument will now be examined.

We have already seen the collision between the Radical Right and the party leadership during the constitutional crisis. The outcome of this crisis made many diehards increasingly ambivalent about the Conservative Party itself. Thus, in August 1911 several of the leaders in the revolt were seriously discussing the possibility of forming a new, breakaway organisation.[13] This did not happen, in part because confidence in the official party revived with the election of Bonar Law as leader – the 'Reveille' promptly disbanded to mark its support of him.[14] But a rooted dislike of all parties as such continued to be a characteristic of this group. Patriotic idealism, it was felt, tended to wither once it had become institutionalised; enthusiasts then found themselves repeatedly being outmanoeuvred by 'mandarins' and wirepullers, whose instinct it was to settle political disputes by compromise arrangements. This offended members of the Radical Right, who, like the ideologues of the extreme left, could not live with political complexity but demanded inflexible adherence to principle and prophesied disaster if their own favoured solution to a difficulty was not implemented *in toto*. In short, the Radical Right approached political conflict with the mentality of the combatant, not the negotiator. And this readily explains why they should so ardently have supported the Ulster loyalists after 1912, since here was a congenial cause to join – a cause in which courage and determination were the cardinal virtues and where victory seemed likely to go to the side which showed the more inflexible will-power.

A particular bugbear of the Radical Right was the political lawyer who hired out his intellect to the party machine that employed him. Devoid of political convictions of their own, such lawyers were eminently suited to the 'game' of party politics, where silver-tongued advocacy was valued rather than administrative capacity. Moreover, not knowing to what constructive purposes they should put power when they had won it, political lawyers, it was said, invariably degenerated into time-servers, obsessed with their ministerial salaries and the lucrative opportunities opened up by a successful parliamentary career. The Radical Right also perceived that the camaraderie of the Bar fostered friendly relations between politicians of different parties, so providing yet another example of the tendency for party controversy to decline into a frivolous and insincere game.[15] Maxse was especially perturbed at the social ties between the two front benches which existed when Balfour was leader and feared that weekend parties and encounters on the golf links were having a deleterious effect on important national interests. Like Hilaire Belloc and the Chesterton brothers, and for similar reasons, many diehards had come round by 1911 to the view that the two front benches were in 'collusion' to damp down the enthusiasm of their innocent supporters[16] – a line elaborated in greater detail in Hilaire Belloc's and Cecil Chesterton's *The Party System* (1910). Even after the replacement of Balfour by the intransigent Bonar Law, these suspicions lingered on. 'I am afraid that both Front Benches will be found on the side of the "Hush-Ups"', wrote Willoughby de Broke in August 1913; 'they do love one another so.'[17] The Radical Right could envisage the nightmarish prospect of the Unionist leaders reaching an agreement with the Asquith Cabinet over some compromise formula which would settle the Irish question at the expense of the loyalist population of Ireland. Ulstermen were publicly advised to keep a firm grip on their rifles and not repose too much trust in their self-proclaimed 'friends' on the Opposition front bench. For the Ulstermen, at least, political conflict was deadly earnest; but could the same thing be said of the professional politicians?

This attack on the party system was sometimes extended into an indictment of the corruption which was allegedly poisoning British political life, and this was the second reason given for the failure of the Government to enlist and organise the patriotic enthusiasm of the masses. At the centre of the web of corruption, as the Radical Right saw it, stood the Liberal ministers and their backers – frequently identified as 'Cobden millionaires' and 'Radical plutocrats'. Maxse, in particular, was animated by an almost pathological hatred of rich Liberals who indulged in 'class politics' while continuing to lead lives of unbridled self-indulgence and luxury.[18] But their charges were not confined to charges of vulgarity and hypocrisy. By 1912, if not earlier, the Radical Right had convinced itself that the failure of the imperialistic ideal, could be ascribed to powerful financial and business interests, of which the Asquith ministry was the 'willing tool'. 'The money bags', so ran the complaint, had been mobilised to thwart their schemes of national regeneration.

The press, too, was alleged to be biased against the imperial idea, partly because of the formal control over newspapers exercised by 'Cobden millionaires' such as George Cadbury, the proprietor of the *Daily News* (an organ of the so-called 'Cocoa Press'), but also because the owners of the big newspaper syndicates had been corrupted by honours and the offer of peerages: this was said to have happened to the Harmsworth brothers.[19] It was even suspected that editorial policy was being secretly censored by business interests who could bring pressure by threatening an advertising boycott[20] – the same explanation that Mosley was later to use to explain his poor press coverage in the 1930s. This belief that they were operating from a situation of acute disadvantage against a powerful and wealthy establishment gave Radical Right propaganda its distinctive note of underdog insolence.

The desire to expose the creeping corruption in high places led journalists such as Arnold White into a succession of campaigns against individual politicians whose integrity had been called into question – usually, but not always, Liberal politicians. But, by the end of the pre-war period, there was less interest in the peccadillos of individuals than in the alleged corruption of the whole political process. Increasingly, the Liberal ministry was portrayed as a gang of adventurers on the make. In Maxse's words, men such as Asquith 'are little better than pirates – they are out for loot'.[21] In particular, the Liberals' willingness to keep the allegiance of their Irish allies by introducing a third home-rule bill in 1912 was seen as a corrupt bargain whereby the Radicals sacrificed their real convictions in order to retain their ministerial salaries. This was the main theme in a public speech of intense bitterness delivered in May 1914 by Rudyard Kipling, who, on this as on other occasions, clothed in memorable language political opinions that were commonplace in Radical Right circles.[22]

The Government as a whole was also repeatedly arraigned for perpetrating 'jobs' – a charge echoed by the Opposition leader, Bonar Law, who claimed in January 1912 that the Liberals had created a vast spoils system on the American model. Here the Liberal ministry was certainly open to attack, since the extension of the social services taking place under their auspices involved the creation of thousands of public posts which were filled by appointment or after interview, without recourse to open competitive examinations. A blue book published in 1913 revealed that over 7000 officials had been appointed in this way to posts worth £100 a year or more.[23]

The Radical Right was on even stronger ground when it joined up with Belloc and the Chestertons and raised a hue and cry about the Liberals' trafficking in honours and peerages. Of course, this method of raising funds and enlisting support goes back some way before 1906: the honours list of the outgoing Balfour administration, for example, had been widely criticised.[24] But it was difficult for even the apologists of the Campbell-Bannerman and Asquith governments to deny that under Liberal rule these dubious practices had become more prevalent. By May 1908 the Government had already created twenty-three temporal peers, which, as one Radical backbencher pointed out, was more than had ever been created in the past in such a short period of time.[25] Many of these peerages had obviously been bestowed on rich men who had contributed to party funds in the clear expectation that they would soon be rewarded in this way.

The 'scandals' attending the honours system came in for sporadic parliamentary debate in the period 1908–14. In 1913 Belloc and the Chestertons pressed home the attack by setting up the 'National League for Clean Government', which intervened in by-elections and asked embarrassed candidates on whose money they were standing.[26] Understandably, the Opposition front bench held aloof from this campaign, but the Radical Right felt no such inhibitions, since it enabled them to dramatise their theory that the Asquith administration was the most corrupt in British history – at least since the days of Robert Walpole.

All these accusations were being broadcast *before* the so-called Marconi scandal broke in 1912.[27] (Two prominent ministers, Lloyd George and Rufus Isaacs, and a former Liberal Chief Whip, the Master of Elibank, were accused of speculating in Marconi shares at a time when the Government was negotiating a contract with the English Marconi Company for the construction of a chain of wireless stations.) This is not the place to analyse the complex story of the Marconi affair, nor to discuss how far the criticisms of the Liberal ministers were justified and how far they were merely an expression of party spite. But it is worth emphasising an often forgotten point: that the Radical Right press had previously been regaling its readers for many months with tales of ministerial corruption and impropriety. In these circles the Marconi affair simply provided hard evidence of speculation, deception and dishonesty which had long been suspected but were now demonstrated for all the world to see. The scandal could also be used to point an anti-semitic moral, another reason why the Radical Right took it up. Finally, a lasting effect of Marconi was to encourage muck-raking journalists to look for other cases of political corruption.[28] This process of exposure, it was hoped, would make the mass of ordinary working people see the machinations of the ruling élite, which had so unscrupulously abused its power to deceive and manipulate a gullible populace.

This attack on corruption in high places was closely linked to a vendetta against 'traitors' in British society, the 'enemy within'. Here was a third reason offered by the Radical Right to explain why the patriotism of the masses was not being tapped. Aliens, indifferent to or contemptuous of, national interests had, they said, infiltrated into positions of influence where they could thwart or distort the national will. Preoccupied as they were with the threat of war, it is not altogether surprising that the Radical Right should have exhibited these xenophobic tendencies. Moreover, the authoritarian cast of mind characteristic of this group allowed no place for legitimate political differences of opinion which rational debate could resolve: either one acknowledged one's obligations to the Empire or one stood a fair risk of being denounced as a 'traitor', a word used by the Radical Right on the smallest provocation.

Especially vulnerable to such attacks were Radicals who wanted an accommodation with Germany: if not exactly agents of the German Government, these 'cosmopolitan cranks' were thought to be playing the Kaiser's game; as such they had to be destroyed before they succeeded in destroying the British Empire. 'Domestic Germanophiles' were doubly at risk if they were of German origins or sported German-sounding names – as did the Radical MP Sir John Brunner, of the chemical firm of Brunner, Mond and Co., who was actually of Swiss extraction, though this did not prevent him from being singled out for a viciously unfair attack in the pages of the *National Review*.[29]

Strictures against the 'undesirable alien' were equally often a prelude to thinly veiled attacks against the Jews, or sections of the Jewish community, particularly successful financiers and self-made businessmen, whose vast wealth and social ostentatiousness were portrayed as a threat to the old-fashioned British virtues. For example, the entry of rich Jews into 'Society' and their prominence in King Edward VII's entourage aroused considerable unease in Radical Right circles. It was also argued that such Jews, because they were 'aliens' or 'cosmopolitans', had no interest in Britain except for the opportunities it offered for making money. In the *National Review* of July 1913 Maxse took these strictures one step further when he speculated about the unexplained reasons which made 'cosmopolitan Jews . . . almost always prepared to do Germany's dirty work'. That the material existed for a full-blooded anti-semitic agitation of a Continental kind seems highly likely judging from the post-bags of Maxse and White.[30] But in fact the final step – of denouncing Jews simply because they were Jews – was a step that was rarely taken. It may also be significant that nearly all members of the Radical Right had *supported* Dreyfus in the 1890s.

But the mixture of prudence and moral scruple which held back the Radical Right from attacking the Jews in unmeasured language was not there to moderate its comments about the Irish nationalists. From the start, resistance to home rule was obviously an essential part of this movement, and in the search for traitors in high places the home rule MPs provided obvious targets. The Radical Right did not take seriously the claim of Redmond and other Irish leaders that they wanted nothing more than a modest measure of self-government within the British Empire. The Irish were seen as rebels who had placed themselves outside the bounds of civilised society through their association with the perpetrators of agrarian outrage in the 1880s, the dynamiters, and the Clan na Gael in America, which continued to supply them with much of their money. More than anything else, this link with the anglophobic Irish Americans, who openly exulted in all Britain's misfortunes, enraged the Radical Right, as indeed it did all Unionists; and the return from a fund-raising tour of America in September 1910 of Redmond, the 'Dollar Dictator', determined to exact home rule from the Liberal Government as the price of his support for its continuation in office, was seen in Radical Right circles as an enormity which justified any kind of opposition protest. The Irish were traitors, but so too were Liberal ministers who parleyed with them and agreed to 'toe the line'. The Radical Right threw itself with fanatical enthusiasm into supporting the Ulster resistance movement from 1912 onwards.[31]

In short, the Radical Right was xenophobic, demagogic, and attracted to 'conspiracy theories' which seemed to explain the strength of the 'enemy' and its own relative powerlessness. Also, although its spokesmen were often intelligent and well educated men, Radical Right propaganda took on an increasingly anti-intellectual hue. There was even a strain of nihilism, a tendency to engage in iconoclastic attacks on all authority. White, for example, persistently questioned every established institution – except the existence of the Empire itself. Even towards the monarchy his attitude was ambivalent. (The same can be said of the diehards, who felt that they had been outmanoeuvred during the constitutional crisis by 'Court and Cabal'.[32]) White felt positive hatred for the bureaucracy, especially for the aristocratic personnel of the Foreign Office and other 'mandarins' of the upper Civil Service, whom he castigated as an inefficient little clique mainly concerned with protecting their privileged position. 'Old fogeys' in the War Office and retired generals in their bath chairs who obstructed the work of defence reorganisation were also obvious targets. Moreover, 'High Society' was decadent and effete; the public schools and universities were failing to supply a practical training for the country's governing class. And scathing attacks were made on parliamentary institutions as such, while party politicians were ridiculed as mere 'talkers' and compared unfavourably with 'men of action'.[33]

This anti-parliamentary rhetoric easily shaded off into a cult of violence. Whether calling for a preventive war against Germany or rushing forward to enlist in para-military bodies that could fight in Ireland, should civil war break out there, the Radical Right seemed to be positively eager for a bout of blood-letting that would put an end to sentimentality and humanitarian humbug and restore the British nation to its former manhood.[34] Using the fashionable rhetoric of 'Social Darwinism', the Radical Right preached the necessity of struggle between nations, races and social types for the evolutionary progress of mankind. Moreover, these people lived in a state of perpetual tension, ever conscious of the fragility of the social order and the dangers that threatened it from within and without. Street fighting in London, bloody insurrection in India, the yellow peril, civil war in Ireland, a German army rampaging through the eastern counties looting and destroying: these were the fears that haunted the Radical Right and gave urgency to its writing and oratory.

Because they believed the country to be virtually in a war situation, these groups called for the immediate adoption of universal military training, as advocated by their hero, Lord Roberts. They also contributed powerfully to the 'spy mania' which swept over the country after 1908, regaling their audience with stories of sinister personages 'plotting the map of Essex and photographing the country – not in the interests of art', and keeping a watchful eye on German waiters, publicans and musicians, who were thought to constitute a potential fifth column.[35] It can readily be imagined, therefore, with what relief and delight the Radical Right reacted to the actual advent of war in 1914.

This brief description of Radical Right attitudes indicates the existence of a body of opinion in Edwardian Britain which seems to foreshadow the fascism of a later generation, though it is unwise to transport this term out of the historical period where it properly belongs. More pertinent are the many resemblances between the Radical Right in Edwardian Britain and analogous groups in Wilhelmine Germany, such as the Pan-German League. These Anglo-German analogies are highly instructive, not least because they raise the question of why radical nationalism did not have the same influence and importance in Britain as it clearly possessed on the other side of the North Sea.

An explanation of this is to be found within the preceding analysis. For a start, the Radical Right carried its distrust of organisation to the point where it failed to organise its *own* members and potential supporters for effective action. True, the leading figures who have been discussed in this essay can be found taking part in specialised pressure groups, such as the National Service League and the extremist Imperial Maritime League. But they never formed themselves into an organisation of their own.

More relevant to the Anglo-German comparison is the fact that (leaving Ireland to one side) Britain lacked a *Mittelstand* in the German sense, that is to say, a pre-industrial grouping of peasants, self-employed craftsmen and small businessmen detached from the institutions of both labour and capital; yet these were the groups which, one supposes, would have responded most readily to Radical Right rhetoric.[36] In consequence, though the Radical Right was well represented in the press,[37] its journalistic spokesmen were not articulating the interests and prejudices of any readily definable or identifiable social constituency. Moreover, the aristocratic faction within the movement, including, for instance, Willoughby de Broke, could never quite bring itself to make a clean break with the Conservative Party, since, however much it might criticise the party and the whole 'system' of which it formed a part, the countervailing tug of history and tradition was too strong.

Finally, the political culture of Edwardian Britain remained permeated with liberal values that offered a barrier to the spread of Radical Right ideas. Respect for parliamentary institutions, the party system of government, free trade, a volunteer army, freedom of speech and association, religious and racial toleration and so on were important elements in British – if not in Prussian – political tradition. Even the Radical Right could not entirely escape the influence of these prevailing ideas, try as it did to discredit many of them. For example, though much of its propaganda was anti-semitic by implication, the Radical Right always hotly denied the charge of being anti-semites. Even Arnold White was in the habit of pretending that he was only warning Jews for their own good of what might befall them if they obstinately clung to an 'anti-national' line.[38] This may be judged hypocritical. But, as the adage has it, hypocrisy is the tribute which vice pays to virtue, and such disclaimers are interesting as an indicator of the constraints within which the Radical Right operated in these pre-war years.

For, in the last analysis, the Radical Right failed. When the war broke out, a Liberal administration was still in existence and the Opposition had not been 'reconstructed' in any particularly radical way. Almost by definition, perhaps, the members of the Radical

Right stood somewhat on the fringes of the world where important political decisions were reached. On the other hand, the activities of these men cannot be ignored in any serious study of Edwardian Britain. Periodically, they burst in upon the political scene with dramatic effect: for example, playing a prominent part in driving Balfour from the Unionist leadership in 1911 and making the running in the Marconi affair. More generally, they can be seen as part cause and part symptom of the hysteria which enveloped British domestic politics on the eve of the First World War. Finally, and most important of all, there was the contribution made by the Radical Right in drawing attention to the German danger and in whipping up anti-German feeling in the country at large, thereby heightening the Anglo-German antagonism and creating the atmosphere in which the advent of war could be so widely welcomed in August 1914. It was only during the First World War itself, perhaps, that the Radical Right really came into its own.[39] But that is another story and it would take us beyond the chronological confines of this volume.

5. The Character of the Early Labour Party, 1900-14

DENNIS DEAN

In the closing days of February 1900 a conference of trade unionists and principal socialist societies took place at the Memorial Hall in Farringdon Street. Its purpose was to discuss the formation of an independent working-class party. The occasion was hardly an auspicious one, since the attention of the nation was directed to events in South Africa. While delegates heatedly debated issues of independence and socialism, London was celebrating the relief of Ladysmith. No time for consolidation was allowed, for by October 1900 a general election had to be faced. Only two Labour Representation Committee candidates were elected, both heavily dependent on Liberal support. In other areas, where Liberal voters were less sympathetic, candidates were heavily defeated.

As I hope to show, the rapid rise of Labour to power after 1918 has meant that historians of the Edwardian era have made much of the event. Biographies of the more important Edwardian politicians have often hinted that particular courses of action were taken because the new formation was recognised as a potential danger to older parties. Peter Fraser made the point that Treasury officials thought that Chamberlain's tariff-reform campaign was intended to woo trade unionists, who were suspected to be moving to protectionism.[1] By contrast, Winston Churchill's bitter disagreements with his own party arose from a conviction that Chamberlain's proposed course of action would strengthen the socialists in the new party, who would claim that industrialists were behind tariffs, and that workers would suffer through higher prices for food. So deeply did Churchill feel about this danger that he was prepared to change his party. The Edwardian political scene was pervaded by speculation about new political alignments to replace the major parties. Whether the talk was of liberal imperialism, Milnerite efficiency groups or social radicals, a continuous theme was the need to win over working-class support. Although it was soon evident that the Labour leadership was far from revolutionary, there was anxiety in political circles about the party's following. Strikes, particularly in the railways and the mines, erupted into violence and counter-displays of military and police power. Thus George Dangerfield's classic study of pre-war Britain presented a liberal society on the verge of destruction.[2] Historians with varied Marxist inclinations, constantly looking for the revolutionary crisis in industrial Britain, have been in turn excited and dismayed by the years after 1910. Dramatic outbursts of political and industrial protest by an ever-increasing number of workers, driven to despair by declining living standards, were allowed to peter out by 1914, because of inadequate political direction from the parliamentary and trade-union leaders or from their rivals, the Marxist socialist groups. Certainly few recent historians have ignored the intense Labour and working-class activity in the Edwardian period.

The most significant pioneers, Hardie, Henderson and MacDonald, never found time to set down their recollections, and some who did, notably J. H. Thomas and J. Clynes, left only brief sketches.[3] Only Snowden produced a lengthy assessment of his life, and in 1934, when his memoirs appeared, despair and bitterness dominated much of his attitude to the other Labour leaders. Thus at the top, among the major figures, was continuous petty jealousy, contrasting with, in the early days, heroic self-sacrifice among the following, which impelled him to write, 'they were really poor and what they gave to the movement involved real sacrifice on their part'.[4] Circumstances surrounding the fall of the Labour Government in 1931, and particularly MacDonald's behaviour, blurred assessment of the early years from within the party. Thus MacDonald was seen as an ambitious political opportunist from the start, while Keir Hardie, increasingly rejected from his death in 1915, became the figure of absolute integrity and loyalty to the people. *The Common People*, an influential study published in 1938, hailed Hardie's arrival at Westminster in 1892 as a triumph of the ordinary man against the people. 'He was escorted to Parliament in a charabanc in which was playing a small brass band. He himself wore a cloth cap. The clothing was natural to him and so to his supporters were the charas and the musicians.'[5] Only with Kenneth Morgan's recent biography has a truer picture emerged of a man often distrusted by other Labour leaders, and frequently remote from the ordinary working people.

George Dangerfield's interpretations of the Edwardian age, in which he saw a Labour Party preaching on class lines as one of the major factors undermining liberal England, has profoundly influenced much thinking by other historians. According to this view political liberalism was dying before the Asquith–Lloyd George rift in 1916 sealed its fate, and Labour is seen as a destructive political force. Perhaps the most thoroughly researched inter-war work on this phase in British history is contained in the closing volumes of Élie Halévy's massive account of Britain since 1815 – one of which was entitled *Imperialism and the Rise of Labour*. As a staunch, old-fashioned radical, Halévy did not welcome the birth of the Labour Party, which he regarded as one of the symptoms of Britain's decline from Victorian prosperity. Increasingly middle-class individualism and the dissenting outlook were being undermined by the collectivist attitude, which was influencing even Conservative and Liberal thinkers. Halévy was not entirely carried away by his outlook, and recognised that the British Labour Party was a very different species from its more doctrinaire socialist counterpart on the Continent. It was left to Sir Robert Ensor, a Labour sympathiser of the early days, in the influential Oxford History of England volume *England, 1870–1914*, to see the party's creation as one more aspect of the transformation of 'English government into a democracy',[6] a process that was marked by good sense among both the governing class and labouring men.

Following the Labour Party's massive success after 1945, studies of its origins have proliferated. General histories have continued to appear at steady intervals, but the growth has been among monographs covering all aspects of the early years, including the motivation of different components, the kind of socialist commitment taken up and the spread of Labour ideas in the regions. A major landmark was the appearance, in 1954, of Henry Pelling's *Origin of the British Labour Party*. Dr Pelling's theme was that the energy of certain socialists converted reluctant trade unionists to political action. Clegg, Fox and Thompson, in their *History of British Trade Unions since 1889*, explain the need for caution, and this theme was taken up in studies of individual unions.[7] Much emphasis here has been put on the miners' union, perhaps because of its size in the 1890s, or as a result of the particular position which it achieved in later Labour history between the wars.

Since the Labour Party itself has often been bitterly divided on the issue, it is not surprising that Labour historians have found it difficult to explain the meaning of socialism for the new party. Most of the early leaders spoke of socialism but never very fully explained its meaning. Several studies of the party's attitude to unemployment, education and Empire have failed to discover a distinctively socialist outlook.[8] This has enabled writers such as Rodney Barker, Kenneth Morgan and the contributors to A. J. A. Morris's collection on Edwardian Radicalism to argue that the divide between progressives and Labour around 1900 was a very narrow one, with Labour, even after the successes of 1906, a pressure group never going much beyond narrow electoral considerations and demands for the redress of trade-union grievances. Rodney Barker has contended that a distinctive Labour Party came into being with the war, and, following that, a new constitution and programme, 'Labour and the New Social Order'.[9] For Ben Pimlott and David Howell the events of 1931 marked the divide, and the present party with its emphasis on public ownership, priorities and planning emerged in this period of revaluation.[10] Even Dangerfield's persuasive view of a dying liberalism cast aside by new political forces has forced sharp criticism. Liberalism has been seen as a reviving force, strengthened by the reforming ideas of 'new liberalism'. These ideas were sifted and transmitted to the Asquith Government by astute politicians such as Lloyd George and Churchill. Marxist historians have explored the growth of working-class political consciousness and the various socialist groups. Walter Kendall has condemned the Social Democratic Federation for its sectarianism and isolation from the trade-union ranks.[11] Professor Hobsbawm has attributed lack of success for the Marxist groups to the manipulative skill of the entrenched ruling class, who used the wealth of the colonial Empire to buy off sections of the working population with social-reform programmes. R. D. Challinor has regretted that the Socialist Labour Party, an offshoot of the Social Democratic Federation, lacked an intellectual cadre to give the group a sound political education.[12] The stress on working-class political activity has probably encouraged social historians to examine the distinctive texture of Edwardian working life, embracing not only conditions of work but also family life, living conditions and recreations.

Without doubt, trade unionists formed the backbone of the new party, a fact that was reflected in the occupations of the bulk of Labour MPs in 1906. An extensive election campaign would not have been possible without trade-union affiliation fees. Before 1906, the occasional independent Labour member, such as Burns and Hardie in 1892, was elected, but the career of Burns was to show that a long stay in Parliament meant making peace with the Liberals. Even in 1903, Richard Bell, supposedly an advocate of separate Labour representation, left the small group of Labour MPs to work with the Liberals. On the Labour Representation Committee itself, the socialist societies, although they had secured a substantial presence, were heavily outnumbered by trade unionists, especially after 1901, when the Social Democratic Federation and the Fabians ceased to attend. Nevertheless, the impression has often been given that the trade-union majority was outmanoeuvred by the socialists. Summing up the 1900 conference, Roger Moore, a recent writer, comments, 'But in the end Hardie managed to get most of what he wanted and gained for the ILP [Independent Labour Party] the most influential position in the new group.'[13]

Part of the explanation for this passivity was their apparent obsession in the late Victorian period with caution, a desire to be acceptable and an overbearing urge to appear respectable. Most of the union officials who did sit as Liberal MPs from 1885, Burtt, Fenwick and Broadhurst, afterwards appeared as subservient tools of Gladstone. In an influential article, R. V. Clements defended them from the charge of accepting the theories of political economy almost slavishly.[14] Again, the drive to make the trade unions appear as an improving force has only just begun to appear as a method of defence rather than as a form of subservience. In a world in which human labour was not widely valued, respectability, in T. R. Tholfsen's view, was the means to impress on society the dignity of labour.[15] It was true that union leaders often talked about harmony and conciliation, but often only to extract concessions from suspicious governments. Those that adopted this softer line, and association with the Liberal Party, often pointed to the degree of recognition for trade unionism secured by the legislation of the 1870 period. Younger elements were often more doubtful about tactics and argued that the position of the worker had not markedly improved by 1900. Ammunition for this view was provided by employers, who still found it difficult to accept the presence of trade unions within their industries. Railway companies fought bitterly against negotiations with the Association of Railway Servants until 1907. Significantly, the motion calling on the TUC Parliamentary Committee to bring together Labour and socialist bodies to discuss the formation of a Labour alliance was proposed by the union's moderate General Secretary, Richard Bell, who was doubtlessly influenced by the strength of the railway directors in Parliament.

Criticism of trade-union 'moderation' was expressed by the Social Democratic Federation. Its leader, H. H. Hyndman, saw the stolid union membership, together with the network of chapels, temperance societies and mutual-aid organisations, as instruments to accommodate workers to existing society. Even the weapons of the highly skilled unions, notably the limitation of entry to a craft by stringent apprenticeship laws, disturbed him, for it often created barriers between the skilled and the unskilled. Craft unions often did regard the unskilled with as much suspicion as they viewed employers, and widely believed that trade unionism could flourish only among the skilled. Yet Hyndman was slow to detect a changed attitude from the middle 1880s, when skilled workers began to believe that their own survival depended on extending union activity to a wider section of the working population. Younger trade unionists such as Mann or Thorne either assisted in the creation of the new unions in the later 1880s, or campaigned to open up their own craft unions to the less skilled. In 1892 Mann succeeded in widening membership of the engineers' union.

The differing attitude of the craft unions and the general unions to the use of the strike weapon or independent political activity has often been raised, but by the 1890s the struggling general unions were prepared to adopt a less aggressive stance. At city and town levels, the formation of trade councils, often influenced by socialist elements, ensured that the various unions began to pool their ideas. Industrial unionism spread throughout mining, building and the railways, and many of the smaller craft societies were absorbed into larger bodies, though on the railways, for instance, drivers, foremen and clerks strenuously resisted amalgamation with the National Union of Railwaymen.

Historians such as Paul Thompson and Standish Meacham have insisted that by 1914 the working-class community was almost self-enclosed.[16] Urban historians in their studies have indicated that outer suburbs of cities were reserved for the employing and professional classes, who sped to their work in the new forms of transport through an inner ring of housing reserved for the working class. Places such as nonconformist chapels, once the meeting place of employers and skilled workers, were no longer frequented by the wealthier industrialists, who had formed their own congregations in the new suburbs. A working-class subculture of music halls, clubs and popular songs was spreading, and attachments to football clubs were being instilled. In the latter part of the Victorian period, further advances in technology increased the size and the scale of industry, after crushing the smaller workshop and its skilled workforce. Advances in retailing, transport and distribution created a new labour force and increased the army of managers, supervisors and salesmen, who formed, with shopkeepers, smaller manufacturers and clerks, a lower middle class. In spite of difficulties in defining its scope and size, Geoffrey Crossick has endowed this lower middle class with characteristics that separated it from the rest of the workforce.[17] Their position in society concerned them intensely, and generally within an industry their sympathies were with employers rather than unions. Often their children had access to some form of secondary education, which further divided them from the worker, whose children found their ambitions crushed by the restricted nature of the 1870 Education Act. Some form of academic ability, rather than the industrial skill of engineers and mechanics, became the means of social mobility and 'improvement'. Many traditional skills were being broken down by the employers, who were thus able to weaken the bargaining power of the skilled operative. Tension and suspicion between skilled and unskilled did not disappear entirely and remaining skills were often jealously guarded against newcomers, but insecurity of employment did promote solidarity among labouring men and often confirmed the predictions of socialist agitators about future prospects.

Improved consumption of meat, fruit and vegetables appears to indicate that the living standards of the working class were rising. Yet trade-union leaders in the 1890s were clearly anxious about the economy and the employers' ever-tightening scrutiny of wages and restrictive practices. Trade-union demands for the eight-hour day received a hostile reception from many employers. Industrialists, who had often been unable to consult each other in past decades, because of commercial rivalry and intense individualism, began to form associations. The lesson of the 1889 dock strike, in which the various employers were in disarray, was not lost. In 1896 the Employers Federation of Engineers Association was formed, and within a year, they had defeated the demands of the engineers for an eight-hour day. This defeat certainly influenced the powerful engineering union to undertake a slow reappraisal of its attitude to independent political action.

Proof of an employer's counter-offensive has also been ascribed to the formation of the National Free Labour Association. John Saville, while admitting that the importation of non-union labour in industrial conflicts was far from new, has concentrated on the degree of organisation and the existence of a central body.[18] Its chief agent,

William Collinson, was an ex-trade unionist who believed that the unions no longer preached class harmony and self-improvement. On the whole, his activities were restricted to the docks and places of work using unskilled labour. Bitter clashes between union and non-union labour at these places put doubts in the minds of the educated professional classes, who in the previous decade had seen trade unionism as an instrument to improve the outlook of working men.

Decisions in the courts on such sensitive issues as picketing, protection of union funds and liability for damage during the course of a strike provoked uncertainty among the union leadership, who had believed themselves protected by the legislation passed in the 1870s. Working men were uneasy in the legal system and disliked, often with good reason, judges, magistrates and lawyers. Events in the United States, especially the use of injunctions to curb labour-union activity, were carefully watched. Hardie and MacDonald were quick to hammer home the need for the Labour Representation Committee after the Taff Vale decision. Courts generally were severe where property was damaged, whether by individuals or by organisations, although it must be said that it is unlikely that the Taff Vale decision was taken specifically with a view to crushing trade unions. Concern about the decision did not lead to a total rush towards a separate party, and Bell, the leader of the union involved, was prepared to use the decision to restore his authority over local militants. Other means of influence were at the disposal of the trade-union movement. In the 1890s the machinery of the Parliamentary Committee was improved by the use of a permanent legal adviser and insistence on regular attendance by its members. Liaison with the Liberal Party through Sir Charles Dilke, and the decided coolness of the Salisbury Government after 1895, encouraged many influential leaders to press for closer links with the official Opposition. By 1903, however, it was clear that the Liberal Party and the TUC Parliamentary Committee were unable to work out an agreed policy on Taff Vale. There was a sharp rise in the number of unions affiliating to the Labour Representation Committee, and an agreement to strengthen central finances.

Campaigns to rid the nation of bad legislation were a feature of Victorian political life. The most successful example had been the repeal of the Corn Laws. What made many unions hesitate to affiliate in 1900 was the declaration of permanent independence proposed by the Labour Representation Committee. Throughout the nation union membership was very patchy, and in London, for instance, largely lacking in numbers. Industrial unions encouraged a spurt in the later

1880s but the following decade saw little growth and the total throughout the nation did not exceed one and a half million. Occupations such as agriculture were hardly touched by the unions, and the strength was concentrated largely in heavy industry and textiles. Coal and cotton dominated trade unionism, and neither industry contained unions pressing for independent political action. Miners were already represented at Westminster because there were some constituencies almost totally dominated by the industry, and even the most reluctant Liberal association was compelled to accept union officials as their candidates. They formed the nucleus of the Liberal–Labour group, and, until death or retirement at the beginning of the century, exerted a strong influence against separation from the Liberals. Even after the miners had voted, in 1908, to affiliate to the Labour Party, their representatives in the Commons were reluctant to accept the decision. Textile workers were more scattered, but in Lancashire large sections of them followed the county's popular Toryism. A recent study of the electorate after 1885 has indicated the uphill task of any party trying to establish itself from a trade-union base.[19] The cost of elections, harshness of residential qualifications and the difficulties of registration ensured, until 1918, that large numbers of the male population remained without the vote. In the circumstances, cautious union executives were disinclined to plunge their resources into foolhardy political enterprises.

One further factor producing hesitation was the prospect of a new independent party splitting a trade-union movement that already was characterised by sharp internal differences on a wide number of issues, ranging from the necessity for an eight-hour working day to the promotion of state welfare, which Dr Pelling has shown to have been unpopular among many of the workers.[20] Debates at the annual Congress in the 1890s alarmed the leadership, because younger elements seemed determined to create a separate party to advance the cause of socialism. Arguments put forward by Tom Mann, in particular, tried to prove that a socialist party would, in contrast to the Liberals, who tended to give prominence to Church disestablishment, local option or home rule, accord to the working man the highest priority for his demands. In 1893 and 1894, these socialists pushed through Congress motions calling for public ownership of the main industries. One year later the leadership struck back, excluding the socialist-dominated trade councils from voting at Congress. The major figures resisted the continuous undermining of their authority, and disliked advocates of socialism, who often spent much time arguing about incomprehensible ideas. In any case, the trade-union leadership, mostly non-conformist in religion, were not prepared to dismiss questions of religious liberty and local option as lightly as some of the socialists were.

In these circumstances much of MacDonald's time in the early years of the Labour Representation Committee was spent reassuring cautious trade unionists that independence did not mean dangerous innovation. Even at its foundation meeting the Committee did not rule out co-operation with the Liberals. No attempt was made to impose outside candidates on constituencies and socialism was kept in the background. MacDonald did recognise that these tactics might eventually lead them back into the Liberal fold, and he worked hard to produce an evolutionary political philosophy that would set the party apart, and at the same time act as a bridge for Radicals to cross. Lack of interest from the Fabians, the withdrawal of the Social Democrats, and the weight of trade-union representation meant that the Committee lacked intellectual theorists to assist MacDonald. By-election successes in 1902–3 brought Shackleton, Henderson and Crookes into Parliament and these men looked very similar to their Liberal–Labour colleagues, differing only in their determination to stand up against local Liberal oligarchies.

It was not always easy to keep contact with the Parliamentary Committee of the TUC, still inclined to the Liberal–Labour position, but in 1905, the uneasy toleration paid off. By the terms of the Caxton Hall agreement, electoral contest between rival Labour candidates was avoided. MacDonald's presence as secretary and Hardie's sporadic interventions gave the impression that the socialists were firmly entrenched, and trade unionists did change more frequently than the politicians. This reflected not disinterest, but the fact that the Edwardian period did see an expansion of trade unionism, which took up most of their time. Certainly this expansion was of vital importance in breaking down regional and religious loyalties which the other political parties could exploit. Union militancy in one region often produced a revival elsewhere. The agitation of South Wales miners after 1908 encouraged the flagging energies of the Cardiff and Swansea dockers. Ultimately the development of the new party owed much to trade-union growth, and trade unionists' casting their votes for Labour as a mark of loyalty. As the party grew in size it took on many of the practices of the trade-union movement in its organisation.

In his description of socialist societies, Dr Pelling has distinguished between those that integrated Labour and trade-union opinion and those of a disruptive influence. Hyndman's Social Democrats, in spite of early success, were too inclined to preach violence and atheism, both of which horrified working people. Although the Championites were enthusiastic for an independent party based on trade-union strength, Champion marred his initiative by the violence of his dislike for Liberals, which made him willing to explore electoral pacts with Conservatives. Generally, the Fabian Society's parliamentary commitments and refusal to accept Marxism without question have earned praise, but there were traits that made the society less valuable. In spite of the spread of provincial Fabians, the outlook remained predominantly metropolitan, and its leaders had little contact with the unions. During the early years of the Labour Party the Webbs were totally immersed in plans to use the existing parties for their schemes for social reconstruction, and had great hopes of Rosebery, Churchill and even Balfour. Only Beatrice Webb's disappointment with the Poor Law Commission, Liberal and Conservative suspicion, and later wartime experiences convinced them that the Labour Party was the instrument of change.

Much importance has been attributed to the work of Hardie's Independent Labour Party. Keir Hardie's skill has earned the praise of gradualists, moderates and outright socialists, and, in turn, his refusal to collaborate with the Liberals and his determination to work with trade unionists and Radicals has met with approval. Many of his own attitudes, even after two excellent biographies, still remain a mystery, including even the circumstances of his conversion to socialism.[21] What is clear is that in the early 1880s Hardie was a self-improving working man, respecting but by no means deferential to the local middle class. Memories of early life underground never left him and he made no secret of his humble origins. At the same time, even when he had rejected Liberalism, he continued to believe that most educated and professional men were anxious to improve the lot of the workers. Throughout his political life he resisted calls to exclude non-trade unionists and professional people from a Labour Party. The longer, too, that he remained in politics, the greater grew the distance between himself and the impoverished sections of the population. Slums, squalor and city life generally appalled him, and this sensitivity made him work for speedy change rather than awaiting distant socialist utopias. Just as William Booth linked his message with the relief of destitution, Hardie held that the advance of socialism and a new socially responsible attitude among the masses depended on the diminution of poverty. His own struggles for improvement, together with those of others, convinced him that it was wrong to exclude working men from political life. Therefore his own position was scarcely that of a revolutionary, but rather one of insistence that the worker should have a larger share in the existing social and political order which he had helped to create.

Hardie's own rebellion from his radical roots was repeated throughout the country, notably among the northern towns, in which independent Labour groups came into being in the early 1890s. Radical noncomformity, hostility to the privileges of the Anglican church, and an older Chartist tradition created conditions for independent political activity. Disillusion with the slow progress towards democracy in the Liberal Party, even after massive Whig defection in 1886, added to the feeling of alienation. Scattered associations eventually came together in 1893 to form a national Independent Labour Party (ILP). Unity was not easily created, because each branch continued to believe that it was a sovereign body, free to express its own views. Unity of a kind was achieved by the constant journeys of lecturers such as Hardie and Snowden. More important was the fact that most northern cities were honeycombed with ethical societies, Labour churches and Clarion clubs inspired by Blatchford's journalism, all of which created an environment for independent-minded working men to enjoy. Often in the forefront were middle-class sympathisers such as the Glasiers, whose horror of the degradation of industrial society was roused by the writings of Ruskin and Morris. Social Democrats, as a result, found Hardie's following confused, and even hypocritical, as they appeared to mix talk of revolution with images of class harmony. An early supporter, Blatchford, soon grew to dislike the puritan atmosphere of ILP meetings. The outlook, however, made it easier for trade unionists to move from association with Liberalism to Labour.

It was the socialism of the ILP and the early Labour Party that aroused the Edwardian wealthy to form anti-socialist unions and talk of bloodshed. Recent historians such as David Marquand and Kenneth Morgan have argued that socialism was only one ingredient in early Labour thinking. Most of the pioneers had some glimmerings of Marxism, and like Hardie were excited by the vision of a future classless society, but were more likely to have been impressed by Ruskin or Morris or some mystical religious experience of their own.

In fact the early leadership was steeped in a version of history that gloried not only in the distinctiveness of the British political system and its liberties, but stressed the participation of working people in the more important constitutional events. In this kind of society there was no need for a Marxist upheaval. Hardie did participate in the continental socialist congresses, at which bitter debates took place between orthodox Marxists and the revisionists, but he probably believed that many of the arguments were inappropriate for Britain, which could be transformed gradually into a socialist state. On the other hand, it has been argued that the creation of the ILP was part of the socialist revival of the 1880s and that it clearly pushed Hardie towards a class-conscious party aiming to destroy industrial monopolies. Later, the obsession with access to Parliament and the manoeuvrings for seats shifted the perspective away from socialism. In the process, Hardie's influence diminished and politicians such as MacDonald took over. This view clearly presumes that the differences between the two men were more ideological than personal. A survey of the major debates within the party, ranging from the absence of a socialist commitment, which so clearly angered Hyndman, to the demand that the parliamentary party accept total direction from the annual conference, found the two men in agreement. In 1903 Hardie supported MacDonald's pact with the Liberals, and in 1908 he condemned Victor Grayson's parliamentary behaviour and refused to join in his demands for a more socialist programme.

In the Edwardian period the fortunes of the Liberals were closely interwoven with the rise of Labour. Gladstone's strength as leader after 1867 had been his ability to prevent the spread of class politics by his intuitive exploitation of important moral issues, such as the conduct of foreign policy or Irish Church disestablishment, which aroused the passions of the entire community. With his retirement in 1894 this crusading spirit tended to wither away. The Liberal Party was unable to disentangle itself from the Gladstonian legacy and found it difficult to adopt a programme that was in line with its increasingly important working-class support. Local Liberal associations added to the problem by rejecting the leadership's advice to accept trade unionists for office. Even the extent of the 1906 victory caused difficulties, for, although the party gained widespread support from the industrial population, the defence of free trade also brought back a sizeable number of the wealthy financiers and industrialists. Thus, the dilemma after 1906 was to try to hold on to both sections of support. Only Lloyd George, who used issues such as social welfare, constitutional reform and a land campaign, all of which were presented as means of preserving the existing social order, attempted to satisfy these conflicting interests. By 1914, however, Conservatism was clearly identified as the party of property, while Labour was seen as the workers' party. There was no room, as 1924 and 1929 were to show, for a Liberal Party trying to hold the balance.

This influential view has underestimated the ability of the Liberal Party periodically to renew itself. At election times, a whole array of societies and sects, part of a wider liberalism, was brought into action. Other elements were more in evidence by the 1890s, as Welsh home rulers, social radicals and Liberal–Labour worthies linked up with the Gladstonian rump. Liberal agents were convinced that the working-class vote was on their side, if only apathy and, in some regions, a popular nativist Toryism could be overcome. Even a display of independence, providing that the Liberal leadership was able to handle labour carefully, was not necessarily dangerous. Issues continued to exist to bring them together. Keir Hardie was so deeply distressed by the Boer War and fears of the growth of militarism that he shared platforms with anti-war Liberals and proposed a Liberal–Labour coalition under John Burns.

Co-operation too, was secured at the time of the 1902 Education Act, and the emergence of Chamberlain's tariff-reform campaign provided further opportunities to work together. Liberals were genuinely afraid that men such as Chamberlain and Milner intended to use the campaign as a stepping stone to a new political structure that would weaken the authority of Parliament. Strident anti-foreign propaganda and elements of social insurance alarmed trade-union leaders, who feared that a Bismarckian coercive state might be in the offing. Herbert Gladstone's task, of securing the most formidable anti-Conservative vote at the next election, was made easier. In areas such as Lancashire, where the Tory machine had been shaken by tariff reform, it was possible that Labour candidates would be more likely to capture seats. As regards other areas, he was anxious that Liberal candidates would be spared a contest with the well-entrenched Conservative organisations, while coping simultaneously with Labour or socialist contenders.

For his part, MacDonald did not want the new party to appear too openly anti-Liberal, and he also wanted the scarce resources available to it to be used in constituencies where it was most likely to succeed. He, himself a candidate for the two-member constituency of Leicester, was aware of the advantage of running nominees together from both parties. The practice of Whigs and Radicals' dividing up a two-member constituency was an important precedent. In September 1903 the Gladstone–MacDonald pact, intended for one election only, was agreed, although a hasty, less amicable understanding was secured for the 1910 elections.[22] At local level, not all Liberal associations or socialist groups accepted the national agreement. In the north-west, where the Liberals were most anxious for allies, the agreement was enthusiastically observed, and thirteen of the 1906 Labour contingent came from this area. The signatories were well pleased. Herbert Gladstone had secured a maximum anti-Conservative front, and MacDonald saw a parliamentary party, often the mark of permanence, emerging. Trade unionists were pleased at Liberal success, and gained the nagging power of a body of independent-minded working-class MPs.

Labour's independence was far from assured by the 1906 election. Where the party had involved itself in three-cornered contests, little success was achieved. Only five Labour MPs had fought off Conservative and Liberal opponents. The programme had contained little novelty, and most emphasis was put on the defence of free trade. Moreover, Liberal politicians, enjoying the fruits of office after a long period of opposition, no longer showed signs of factionalism. Indeed, Lloyd George's social-welfare programme continuously kept an inexperienced leadership on the defensive. Militant socialists resented amelioration, and some trade unionists were angered by the principle of compulsory insurance. Labour, too, suffered as a result of the 1909 budget and the subsequent House of Lords controversy, for in a crisis of this nature all the constitutional traditions of the Liberals made them the superior partner. Radicals talked of a broad progressive alliance, a mirror of the Progressive Party on the London County Council, but essentially dominated by Liberal politicians. Two elections in one year further strained resources, and encouraged Liberal managers to take a tougher line on electoral deals. Labour was warned to restrict itself to the seats captured in 1906, and that further flurries of independence would invite Liberal retaliation. Only the accession of miners' MPs, many of whom remained Liberals at heart, increased the party's strength. Until 1913, when the Liberals pushed through the Trade Union Act, which allowed unions to introduce a political levy, a near-bankrupt party was not in a position to dictate to the Liberals. By-elections after 1911 seemed to confirm that the progress of Labour had been checked.

The Liberal Government's ability to keep Labour as a junior ally had flaws. Much of the ability to out-manoeuvre its leaders depended on energetic ministers such as Lloyd George and Churchill. By 1911 the latter had become immersed in the Admiralty, and Lloyd

George's devotion to social welfare began to lag. Large sections of the parliamentary party remained staunchly Gladstonian, and Asquith himself had little sympathy for new and progressive Liberalism. Even the Radical section of the party was scarcely able to form the bridge with Labour. Its members were intensely individualistic and represented a wide variety of opinion. Although many·of them were anxious to make Edwardian industrial society more humane, they feared much of Labour's talk about dismantling private industry. Strikes and industrial conflict caused difficulties for Radicals, who often abhorred the use of the weapon to win a dispute. Apart from Hardie and MacDonald, Labour spokesmen were woefully ignorant of foreign and imperial affairs, which were often the most abiding interest of Radical societies. At local level, often in the industrial boroughs, the election of Labour councillors pushed Liberals into fusion with Conservatives.[23]

In addition, by 1914 there were growing signs too that the Labour Party was maturing. A group of leaders, who continued to exercise direction until 1931, had established themselves. MacDonald's authority grew, through his speeches, writings and parliamentary skill, and Henderson was beginning to use his talents to organise the party. J. H. Thomas and J. Clynes formed the links with trade unionism, and in Snowden a formidable, if orthodox, financial spokesman had been found. At first, the annual conferences were not easily controlled, as delegates asserted their right to act as the parliament of the party. By 1914 MacDonald and Henderson, skilfully playing on emotions of loyalty and the need for discipline, comfortably controlled the wilder conference elements, aided by the use of the trade-union block vote. In the large industrial regions the presence of the party was increasingly felt, as a web of city and town Labour parties, often trade councils by another name, were set up. Thus, the latter stages of the period under study saw the coming together of a whole variety of working-class endeavours into a wider Labour movement. A disciplined, stable organisation was prepared to take advantage of the leap into mass democracy which came with the end of the 1914–18 war and the 1918 Reform Bill. This, rather than the syndicalist fury, was the true legacy of the pre-1914 period.

6. Irish Home Rule and Liberalism

ALAN O'DAY

'WHETHER it begins with Ireland and ends with Wales, or begins
with Wales and ends with Ireland' home rule is objectionable, said
Arthur Balfour in 1898 in the House of Commons debate on the resolution for 'Home Rule all-round'.[1] In 1898 there was a Tory ministry
and the discussion was still largely academic, but by 1910 the home-
rule dispute was again coming to the fore. Then Balfour stated his
own and the Tory Party's concern that the United Kingdom constituted one nation and that home rule would lead to its disintegration. He argued that, 'while I admit differences of degree, I will never
admit that the Irishman is one race of inhabitants and England or
Scotland or Wales is another race'.[2] The debate on home rule neither
began nor ended during the Edwardian age, but during that time it
developed special characteristics. Moreover, the debates revealed
much about the potential and adaptability of British institutions. But
perhaps the most surprising element of all is that the home-rule
disputes occurred – much less that they reached such dangerous
intensity. The Edwardians displayed remarkable energy in attacking national ills, yet seemingly by 1914 they had allowed the
country to hover on the brink of civil war over Ireland, while feelings about the disestablishment of the Church in Wales were
scarcely more tempered. Why did this remarkably resourceful
generation prove so resourceless when facing the question of domestic arrangements in the Celtic parts of Britain?

Historians and others looking back on the Edwardian years have
usually seen in them a misspent Indian summer, at least in so far
as Ireland is concerned. George Dangerfield's influential, if much
criticised, *The Strange Death of Liberal England, 1910–14*, from the
vantage point of the 1930s, saw the Irish question after 1910 as one
of the central elements in the erosion of those values and attitudes
which had made Victorian liberal England possible. His emphasis
was particularly on those resorts to militancy and violence as a
substitute for the discussion and compromise which were so vital to

the efficient functioning of liberal institutions. From this perspective the villains of the piece appeared to be the House of Lords (prepared to abuse its power in order to thwart the legislation proposed by democratically elected MPs), the Conservative Party (members of which actually encouraged armed resistance to Irish home rule), Ulster Unionists (who by their unconstitutional actions brought about a permanent division of Ireland) and members of the British Army (those who identified with and encouraged open mutiny to a legally constituted government). Recently, Mr Dangerfield's *The Damnable Question* has taken up the thread again after a forty-year interval and suggested that the logical conclusion to the 1910–14 Irish crisis was the 1916 rising in Dublin.

Though Dangerfield's details have been modified by a number of historians and the battle for home rule and Ulster resistance to it can now be seen with considerably greater clarity, most agree with Dangerfield's basic analysis. Even Lord Blake, a semi-official Conservative Party historian, has treated the party's involvement in Ireland during the Edwardian years as a regrettable aberration from the path of successful adaptation of Toryism to mass democracy. A number of assumptions are made in the specialised and general accounts of the period: that home rule for Ireland was a long-overdue reform; that the issue was largely a replay of the late-Victorian dispute; and that British resistance was a peculiar and unfortunate exception to an otherwise remarkable record of peaceful adjustment to the forces of democracy, industrialisation, nationalism and modernisation. While Marxist and other social historians have vigorously demonstrated that such adjustments were by no means smooth, for even these writers Ireland has remained a unique case. Two recent books of considerable interest, Paul Thompson's *The Edwardians: The Remaking of British Society* and H. V. Emy's *Liberals, Radicals and Social Politics, 1892–1914*, make the point indirectly by virtually ignoring both Ireland and the Irish question. Where Dangerfield assigned Ireland a central role in the demise of liberal England, the social history now in vogue sees in it at best an impediment to the tackling of the real issues before the Edwardians or at worst as something irrelevant.

But, while it is possible to regret the way in which the Irish issue turned out, it can be demonstrated that it was by no means irrelevant to the wider problems facing Edwardian Britain. Neither was it a unique case. Both Wales and Scotland shared many of the same attributes and sought at least some of the same goals. Asquith, in introducing the Government of Ireland Bill in 1912, called it 'only the first

step in a larger and more comprehensive policy',[3] thus confirming the
fears of those many opponents of home rule who had always insisted
that Ireland was just the thin end of the wedge. During these years
Winston Churchill, then a Liberal minister, went further and even
proposed a scheme which gave parliaments not only to Ireland, Scotland and Wales but also to regions of England, something unknown in
England since Stuart times, and even then in not so extreme a form.[4]
More surprisingly, a number of Conservatives associated with the
Round Table proposed and debated various schemes of domestic and
imperial federalism in which Ireland, for example, would bear
towards England a similar relationship to that which Ontario bears
towards Canada (surely an inappropriate analogy, for Quebec would
have been more accurate). However, main-line Conservatism continued to be doubtful of the worth of home rule. Yet we should not
allow hindsight to obscure our vision. After the war, this remarkable
and open debate on home rule and federalism was largely forgotten:
the Irish issue remained to be solved. Yet, at the time, the Irish issue
was seen to have implications of great importance for the whole of the
United Kingdom.

There were some who said that the Celtic 'revolt' would affect
Britain's status as a world power. It is often noted that domestic tensions over Ireland ran so high that some doubted Britain's capacity to
unite against Germany. In the Reich itself this belief was widespread
if, in the event, mistaken. Less frequently, Britain's nationality problem and proffered solutions are equated with those of Austria–Hun-
gary, Germany, France and the United States. And to some extent the
ability of each of these powers to deal with problems of nationality
would define their role in world affairs in the twentieth century. So it
seems evident that the question of Ireland was neither a unique domestic problem nor an issue of a variety specific to Britain.

Though the Irish question forms the main subject matter of this
essay, these wider issues must be kept firmly in mind. In contrast to
the case of Scotland and Wales, the subject of Edwardian Ireland has
produced a vast literature, a testimony to its prominence and importance. Irish nationalism is said to have a more ancient lineage and to
have had more fervent native backing than did the corresponding
movements in Scotland and Wales. Even Dr Kenneth Morgan's
illuminating study of Wales tends to support this view, although Professor H. J. Hanham's treatment of Scottish nationalism is a little less
prepared to concede the primacy of Irish feeling.[5] Ireland, however,
was at the centre of the stage for two other major reasons. First, she

had far greater representation in the House of Commons than had either Wales or Scotland – indeed, more than both combined. This representation gave her unusual strength, which was rather increased than otherwise as a consequence of the Reform and Redistribution Acts of 1884–5, which gave all three Celtic countries somewhat greater representation than their respective populations warranted. This imbalance, already evident then, was further accentuated by the Edwardian years, since in the interim the population of England had grown and that of the Celtic fringe decreased. In the years after 1900 Ireland had at least forty more seats than her population justified. Secondly, within Ireland the provisions of redistribution overcompensated the predominantly Catholic areas at the expense of the Protestant districts of the north-east. In total, Irish nationalism enjoyed an enormous advantage in the House of Commons and this was defended with great vigour. Nationalists were always prepared to resist any enfranchisement or redistribution (such as that proposed by Conservatives in 1905) that threatened their vital strategical advantage. Catholic Ireland supported its case with a relatively efficient political organisation.

Yet Ireland's advantages were also potentially her defects. For quite obvious and good reasons, nationalists tended to concentrate their energies on the House of Commons, where they could play such an influential role. This meant a neglect of alternative approaches and, in practice, an almost ruthless suppression of dissent from strict parliamentary strategy. It is not hard to see why Irish politicians such as John Redmond and John Dillon chose to become supreme parliamentarians, for, aside from personal inclination, it seemed that ultimately this course had much to offer. But the weakness of the position was that everyone knew that the House of Commons was in a sense 'unrepresentative'. This awareness turned opponents towards other means of expression and particularly to challenge the concept of parliamentary supremacy. The irony was that those who sought fundamentally to change the constitution relied primarily on so-called constitutional tactics, while those intent upon what they saw as the preservation of the Constitution (the Unionists) were forced to turn to an extra-parliamentary strategy. The struggle for the Constitution, then, is central to the Irish question. Ireland is, thereby, at the heart of a wider issue in British history – the question of what should a legitimate government be constituted. How should change be brought about in the Constitution?

It is true that on the surface, always excepting the emergence of the problem of Ulster, the Irish question in the Edwardian period closely resembled that which preoccupied the Victorians. It is usually claimed that Ireland had a long sense and tradition of separateness and had always sought autonomy. Tactics and specific goals differed over time – whereas Wolf Tone and Patrick Pearse resorted to armed rebellion, Daniel O'Connell, Parnell and John Redmond followed a constitutional path – but a self-governing Ireland was always the intention. Popular representatives might quarrel among themselves and differ on the precise shape of a future Irish regime but the basic demand for self-determination remained unscathed. F. S. L. Lyons, in *The Irish Parliamentary Party, 1890–1910*, has taken note of this spirit in observing that over the long years of intrigue and bitterness between 1890 and 1914 the Irish electorate never wavered in support of some species of home rule. Against this background, the formal arguments for and against Irish home rule from 1910 do seem to be very much a repetition of those heard in the 1880s and 1890s. With Gladstone's Government of Ireland Bill in 1886, Ireland's minimum demands were apparently settled, and from an Irish perspective it seems that only details – admittedly some of them crucial – remained to be fixed. Generally historians accept that Liberals, with some considerable faintness of heart, stayed broadly true to their Gladstonian home-rule traditions. To achieve home rule, it seemed that a sufficient Liberal majority, dependent on nationalist support and a curtailment of the veto of the House of Lords, was essential. Historians see this classic juxtaposition as emerging after 1910, opening the way to the long-expected home-rule solution. Home rule, if overdue, was a popular, just and optimistic resolution of the ages-old issue of Anglo-Irish relations.

In accord with this view is the accepted opinion that the Conservatives, who had little interest in or sympathy for Ireland, were confronted with the prospect of Irish home rule and forced to respond with an alternative policy: that of 'killing Home Rule with kindness'. The Tory view, it is said, was governed by blatant and naïve economic materialism, which wrongly believed that Irish souls could be bought with English pounds. During the long period of Conservative rule, governments applied this economic recipe to Ireland, but in the end the Irish, although better off in a material sense, were true to their ideals as expressed in the demand for home rule. Conservatives, short on ideas when faced with the loss of the Lords' veto, had at last to face the prospect of an Irish parliament. Out of desperation they encouraged the Ulster revolt, in a last stand against the democratic decision for home rule. Those aspects of the Edwardian Irish question which were new were no less regrettable because they too undermined the essentials of liberal democracy. Like most facile explanations, this overview has many grains of truth, but in fact the reality was far more complex than this suggests.

The Victorian period produced two major ideological approaches to the issue of the Celtic fringe. These were the 'pluralist' and the 'organic' conceptions of the British state. Pluralists, gradually and over time, came to argue that Britain was made up of distinctive communities with separate and valuable traditions. It seemed wrong, therefore, to impose completely 'English and essentially Anglican' ideas and institutions on these communities. By doing so in the past, great damage had been done: loyalty could be regained only by permitting, indeed even encouraging, these distinctive societies to exist by removing the shackles of 'alien' institutions (where this was demanded by a clear majority of the people of the affected community). When sufficient appropriate concessions were made, the whole of the British Isles would be fused into a new and stronger nation based on the principles of merit, self-respect and humanity. John Morley argued that Irish government must be reshaped 'so as to leave room for an independent and spontaneous growth of Irish civilisation along its own lines'.[6] The pluralist approach was essentially the ideology which Gladstone developed, based in part on his observations of mid nineteenth-century colonial relations and in part on the practical lessons taught by his mission 'to pacify Ireland'. Gladstone's ideology was never systematised but evolved over three decades. The home-rule debate in 1886 marks the fullest flowering of the pluralist position and the point at which it came to be identified with the Liberal Party. From this time at least, Gladstone became increasingly receptive to the idea of Irish and Welsh distinctiveness. In the case of Wales he displayed substantial sympathy with demands for disestablishment of the Church and for some other nationalist goals. And, as Sir William Harcourt, briefly Liberal leader, saw it in the late 1890s, Ireland was held by force, a wholly inadequate basis for an effective national relationship.

Because Gladstone and Liberalism have become almost synonymous in the minds of historians, we should not be misled into thinking that Gladstone's pluralism represented the mainstream of Liberal thought on the nationality issue. In point of fact Gladstone's conversion to pluralism drew him away from the ethos of the party. At heart, Liberalism, as J. R. Vincent demonstrates in his *The Formation of the*

British Liberal Party, 1857–1868, was a doctrine for outsiders and, by emphasising governmental and administrative efficiency and the granting of privileges based on merit, stressed the *integration* of pluralist communities. British subjects who were neither Anglican landowners nor English found acceptance and status based on the Liberal concept of a meritocracy. At its best Liberalism provided a means by which members of religious, national and social minorities could be integrated into the wider community on terms of ostensible equality. Logically, therefore, the doctrine of the Liberal Party had always been inclusive, while Gladstonian pluralism was exclusive. Hence, when many late-Victorian Liberals accused Gladstone of abandoning true Liberalism, they had this in mind. For contemporaries, however, the issues were not always very clearly defined. Nevertheless, the tensions engendered by this ideological split were important within the post-1886 Liberal Party. Many Liberals, notably the Rosebery and imperialist wings, never wholly accepted home rule, on political, emotional or ideological grounds.

An alternative ideology, that of organic unity within the British state, was associated with Conservatism and was fully championed by the Tory Party after 1886. Balfour's plea in 1912 that, 'while I admit differences of degree, I will never admit that Irishman is one race of inhabitants and England or Scotland or Wales is another race' is a clear exposition of this doctrine. Conservatives believed that open recognition of states within a state would cause the weakening and ultimately the disintegration of Britain both at home and abroad. They believed that the communities were interdependent, and that only harm could result from breaking the bonds of interdependence and challenging accepted power and social structures. The case for organic unity could be put by a Scottish Liberal such as Lyon Playfair, who worried in 1885 about an education proposal which might 'accentuate the differences between England and Scotland for the future, and ... tend to convert Scotland into a Province with the narrower peculiarities of Provincial existence'.[7] A Conservative in the Edwardian era could say that 'Wales has never been a nation.'[8] In less pleasing language another characterised Welsh nationality as something of interest only to students of folklore and archaeology. There was a marked tendency for proponents of organic views to denigrate the distinctiveness of native Celtic traditions, to speak in harsh radical terms, and to offend in general the sensibilities of Celtic peoples. L. P. Curtis's *Apes and Angels* affords an all-too-graphic glimpse of contemporary pictorial representations of Irishmen. But behind such words and pictures there was a good deal less of the racial overtones than we of the present day are wont to see. Rather more, they represent a fundamental belief in the preservation of the ideal of a unified British community. British organic ideology can be viewed profitably against a European backcloth. Eugen Weber has demonstrated the development of similar theories in France in his *Peasants into Frenchmen: The Modernisation of Rural France, 1870–1914*. These developments had their parallels in Germany and also in the United States (as shown in Robert Wiebe's *The Search for Order*).

But, as in the case of pluralist thinking, the rival doctrine of organic unity was often muddled and half articulated, and only became firmly associated with a party as a consequence of Gladstone's home-rule proposal of 1886. Yet it had two powerful advantages over its adversary: it had the legitimacy of tradition and it was an excellent attacking doctrine. Whereas pluralists sought fundamental constitutional change, organicists sought none. Whereas home-rulers were divided even in their own ranks as to the appropriateness of their solution, Unionists were united. Where the Liberals argued that a stronger Britain would emerge from the acceptance of pluralism, Conservatives were clear, consistent and persuasive in their insistence that home rule could only result in the collapse of Britain. It is hardly surprising that in the years down to 1914 organic ideology held the field.

Furthermore, the Conservatives held another decisive advantage over the Liberals in the late Victorian years: an alternative policy of 'killing Home Rule by kindness' and 'twenty years of resolute rule'. It could safely be confessed that Ireland had been less than well treated in the past, but Tory arguments that the drastic measure of home rule with all its attendant danger should be deferred until remedies had been applied and the healing process had taken place held considerable attractions. In fact, in the 1880s and 1890s a section of the Conservative leadership, headed by Arthur and Gerald Balfour as Chief Secretaries for Ireland, and followed by George Wyndham at the beginning of the new century, showed how constructive an organic approach could be. From 1898 much local government fell into nationalist hands in those parts of Ireland where the nationalists formed a clear majority. Redmond spoke of it as a great achievement for Ireland and later called the Land Act of 1903 'the most substantial victory gained for centuries by the Irish race for the reconquest of the soil of Ireland by the people'.[9]

The Tory approach was castigated by opponents at about this time precisely because of its coherence and apparent success. Lloyd George put the case:

> the Tory policy towards Ireland was the policy of giving them millions of pounds to buy land, make harbours, build railways and even to supply them with potatoes. They would give them everything except freedom. . . . The Liberal policy was no more subsidies, no more grants, but that of power to work out their own salvation.[10]

Whether Conservative reforms could indeed have killed home rule is a moot point, necessarily, but the principle enshrined in the various pieces of legislation proposed during these years was that great concessions, even those acknowledging Celtic distinctiveness, could be made to Ireland, and by implication Scotland and Wales, so long as parliamentary sovereignty over the British Isles was maintained intact. Less helpful to the cause of peace was the tendency of Conservatives, in the midst of talk of reform, to speak offensively of the very peoples who had to be reconciled.

Towards the end of the 1890s the polarity of pluralism and organicism was beginning to break down. Pluralism had never entirely won the hearts of Liberals and now suffered from a number of body blows. The removal of Gladstone from politics and the succession of Lord Rosebery followed by that of William Harcourt (neither of whom was particularly enamoured of home rule) signalled a moving away from the extreme party position of 1886 and 1893. During these years the feeling was widespread in the Liberal ranks that home-rule policies would condemn their party to perpetual exclusion from office. H. McCready has shown that even Gladstone's son, Herbert, when Liberal Chief Whip, came to adopt a restrained position on the desirability of home rule.[11] By the twentieth century, the struggle between pluralists and organicists had become less of a fight between Liberals and Conservatives and, moreover, had been won clearly by the organicists, as both Liberal and Conservative parties moved towards a more moderate position.

Attitudes to the nationality problem were further complicated by yet other currents of thought and by some unexpected permutations of older ideas. This had the effect of de-escalating the Irish controversy. The most important of the new forces was the emergence of the labour movement. For the present, Labour supported home rule, but principally on the grounds that this unresolved conflict only served to get in the way of the restructuring of society which the movement desired. In June 1914 the *Irish Worker* observed 'with the rise of Home Rule comes the inevitable fall of the Home Ruler'.[12] Socialist thought had more in common with the Tory concept of a unified kingdom than with the pluralist ideology. Although party alignments tended to obscure this fact, the redirection by Labour of conflict into a contest between capitalists and proletariat was significant.

A second complicating current of thought arose from the Celtic cultural revival in Ireland. The movement is often associated with the literary genius of W. B. Yeats and J. M. Synge and with the Gaelic language and ideals emphasised by Douglas Hyde. While cultural nationalism was by no means unified, it did tend to draw attention away from the goal of political home rule and to emphasise the importance of the regeneration of Ireland by Irish minds and hands. Similar movements were making an impact in Wales and Scotland. Joseph Lee, in *The Modernization of Irish Society, 1848–1918*, has argued persuasively that Hyde's Gaelic League was essentially a backward-looking movement attempting to resist the advance of the urban, industrial world. Its intellectual origins lay in a confused mixture of pluralist and organic doctrine: the effect was to erode still further the old polarity and, in fact, to challenge the whole basis of the Irish parliamentary movement. But the impact of the cultural revival was restricted in the main to a group of Dublin intellectuals. In isolation it would have been insignificant; what gives it importance is its confluence with other cross-currents undermining the authority of traditional parliamentary nationalism.

But the most potent challenge to appear on the Irish side was that mounted by William O'Brien, a home-ruler. He was becoming, in practice, more concerned with the need for social reform in Ireland, particularly of land-ownership, and was beginning to see home rule *per se* as a dangerous *cul de sac*. He was impressed by Conservative attempts at constructive Irish legislation and increasingly impatient with the obstruction of Unionist attempts to improve Irish conditions by some nationalists. O'Brien came to believe that full home-rule government could come only in conjunction with other measures and only when all classes of Irishmen were prepared to co-operate. His attitude was encouraged by a number of influential Irish Unionists, especially the Earl of Dunraven and Sir Horace Plunkett. O'Brien's importance lies in the fact that he was a nationally known politician with a considerable following among the agrarian population who had a distinctive alternative policy to that of the official party and yet did not need to resort to the extremes of the cultural revivalists. The years 1900–4, and particularly 1902–4, were the peak period of O'Brien's influence both within and outside traditional parliamentary nationalism. After this he became increasingly estranged from the party leadership and its policies. At the beginning of the Edwardian period, however, O'Brien's outlook seemed in harmony with other developments in Irish and British politics and to herald the dawn of a new era in the nature of the Irish question.

The Edwardian period, then, opened with the emergence of significant and fresh attitudes to the impasse over Ireland. On all sides there were men unimpressed by the avenues travelled by the late Victorians and willing to consider new pathways. Even important nationalists had become disillusioned by the solution offered by pluralism and were prepared to welcome fresh attempts to solve the old Irish grievances. Co-operation rather than confrontation seemed the hall-mark of the new reign. Developments in Wales seemed to confirm that the high tide of pluralistic nationalism had passed in the 1890s and that Welsh politics would become reintegrated into those of the United Kingdom as a whole.

This expectation was not to be realised. The devolution crisis of 1904 marked the beginnings of the reassertion of conventional party alignments on the nationality issue. Partly, this was a consequence of traditional suspicion of Unionism on the part of hard-core Irish party members, epitomised by John Dillon, but, more especially, it was because the Balfour ministry was under fire from many quarters. For the first time in a decade the Liberal Party seemed to have a real chance of returning to power and nationalists expected to gain more from their traditional allies than from their traditional opponents, the Conservatives. During 1905 the alliance between nationalism and the Liberals was considerably consolidated.

This alliance between Irish parliamentarians and Liberals, however, was based on a clear understanding that, although the projected Liberal ministry would not renounce home rule as its long-term objective, home rule would be explicitly ruled out of the legislation programme of the next government. James Bryce in early 1905 summed up the Liberal position: 'as to Home Rule, no one thinks it possible to bring into the next Parliament a bill like that of 1893. But probably there may be some further steps towards granting local powers and removing topics from the British Parliament, while retaining its ultimate control.'[13] Liberals adopted this view partly because home rule was regarded as an electoral liability. Asquith argued that, 'if we are to get a real majority in the next House of Commons, it can only be by making it perfectly clear to the electorate that . . . it will be no part of the policy of the Liberal Government to introduce a Home Rule bill in the next Parliament'.[14] In addition, Liberal interest in home rule flagged: some believed that 'probably there are fewer British Home Rulers than there were in 1886 and 1893'; to many it seemed that 'when they have got the land much of the steam will have gone out of the boiler'.[15] Several members of the Cabinet formed by Campbell-Bannerman stipulated that there be no home-rule bill. Although the new Liberal Government would continue to express sympathy with Irish demands and pledge to carry on affairs in Ireland, 'so far as existing circumstances permit, in a spirit regardful of the wishes and sentiments of the Irish people',[16] this was not because of the party's strong pluralist instincts but rather the contrary. Step-by-step, governmental, economic and social reform was proposed but little support for Gladstonian home rule was expressed. Even Campbell-Bannerman, more of a pluralist than his followers, publicly urged Irishmen to accept instalments of 'representative control . . . provided it was consistent with and led up to the larger policy'.[17] And John Morley, hitherto Gladstone's home-rule policy lieutenant and biographer, was now at pains to de-emphasise the home-rule issue in the total Liberal programme.

Had the nationalists in Parliament really been committed solely to home rule at this juncture, as they always insisted they were, this Liberal proposal would have been totally unacceptable. However, even the resolve of the Irish party wavered at this point. Some Irishmen outside the party were eagerly exploring alternative approaches which placed less stress on the priority of home rule. Party leaders sought more immediate reforms, partly because of the demands from Irish constituents and influential pressure groups, and partly to gain credit for themselves while forestalling their critics and opponents at home. For, as long as the party concentrated only on the achievement of home rule, its appeal in Ireland itself was narrow and it was fast appearing irrelevant to the pressing needs of Irish life. For this reason, John Redmond and Dillon were happy to walk this path with the Liberals in 1905, provided that all appeared faithful to home-rule principles. In February 1905 Herbert Gladstone noted that Redmond 'has to maintain Home Rule as a minimum . . . but fully realises the difficulties of the Liberal position. Thinks Home Rule will come by degrees, and not unreasonable.'[18] Campbell-Bannerman had an interview with T.P. O'Connor and Redmond in

November 1905 in which the Irishmen revealed themselves as congenial and accommodating on the issue of home rule.[19]

On balance, the Liberal ministry was begun at a propitious moment for the Irish. Co-operation was the underlying spirit of the hour; home rule was played down; and the Unionist Party was prepared to minimise its opposition to certain proposed Irish reforms. A bill for the construction of labourers' cottages had been proposed first by Wyndham and this reached the statute books as a Liberal–Irish measure in 1906. Similarly, the Land Bill of 1909 was allowed to pass with the tacit approval of the Unionist leadership.

But in other ways the years from 1906 to 1908 brought rather mixed blessings to the Irish. The question of the financing of denominational schools again bedevilled the Liberal–Irish alliance, although the nationalist leaders never allowed the gulf to grow too wide. Some opponents of the Irish party used the occasion to attack the parliamentary leadership. The Archbishop of Westminster, however, did much to bolster the position of Redmond and Dillon and to minimise criticism of the nationalist–Liberal alliance. But the schools controversy revealed one strain of nationalist thought which has not attracted much comment. At the height of the controversy in autumn 1906 Dillon warned the Government that they were drifting into 'a conflict with the House of Lords in which the House of Lords are in the right and they are in the wrong'.[20] Dillon's curious statement seemed to presuppose not merely the legitimacy of the upper house in the modern Constitution but also a vigorous denial of Commons supremacy if the Commons sought to modify the Constitution or act unjustly. No nationalist leader made any similar assertion when the issue of Irish home rule re-emerged, yet Dillon's opinion did provide some justification for the Lords' resistance to home rule when it was again proposed – a situation charged with some irony. Moreover, it was apparent that nationalists objected more to the specific application of the British Constitution than to its principles – even the role of the House of Lords was grudgingly acknowledge when it suited Irish Catholic needs.

More unsettling yet for nationalist–Liberal relations was the tenor of James Bryce's Chief Secretaryship in 1906 and the fate of the abortive Irish Councils Bill in 1906 and 1907. Traditionally nationalists complained that Ireland's elected representatives, namely themselves, were not consulted on Irish policy and administration. A Liberal government was expected to take a more regular account of popular feeling. In practice Bryce was as aloof and disdainful of nationalist MPs as his Conservative predecessors. Bryce was much influenced by Sir Anthony MacDowell, Under Secretary, who hoped to strengthen a moderate middle party in Irish politics and was hostile to traditional parliamentary nationalism. Though Bryce was succeeded by Augustine Birrell in 1907, who did take more account of Irish-party wishes, considerable goodwill and common ground had been eroded during Bryce's term of office. Increasingly, the Irish party found that it needed to establish a more independent position relative to the programme of the ministry or else lose credibility at home. For this state of affairs, Bryce and MacDowell must carry a generous measure of blame.

The tangled story of the Irish Councils Bill is at the heart of the disintegration of the 1905–6 alliance between non-home-rule Liberalism and nationalism. The bill underwent several metamorphoses. Its essential feature at all stages, however, was to provide increased local participation in and some degree of local responsibility for certain parochial Irish administrative affairs. For a number of Liberals, the bill was intended as a substitution for home rule, but for many others it represented but a further step along the path to full home rule. The bill was conceived and drafted under Bryce without consultation with the leaders of the Irish party. This, of course, was a deliberate tactical decision. Redmond worried that the new body 'created irrespective of the existing Irish members would totally reduce the importance of the latter and practically deprive them of the power of criticising most branches of the Irish administration', which was,[21] not surprisingly, the intention of the bill. Bryce, then, by ignoring the official opinion of the Irish nation, broke one of the mainstays of the alliance – co-operation. Birrell energetically attempted to repair the damage but suspicion lingered, as Sir Anthony MacDowell remained Under Secretary until 1908.

During the early months of 1907 the Councils Bill was the object of intensive Government attention. Birrell and his colleagues were under the impression that the nationalist party would give the bill guarded support. Many were simply deeply shocked when Redmond, at the national convention called to consider the bill, rejected the proposed legislation wholesale. Thereafter, the Government dropped the proposal and Birrell lamented ever touching it. Many Liberals continued to believe that Redmond privately favoured the bill but had been forced to oppose it because of clerical pressure and fears of native Irish opposition. Nationalist unity thus had been preserved. Bryce, by this time ambassador to the United States, summed up this prevalent feeling:

> The Irish leaders, if they honestly meant to pass the bill – and very likely they did – made two great mistakes. The first was in letting their people expect a large measure. The bill ought from the first to have been represented as neither home rule nor a substitute for it. The other mistake was to let judgment go by default against it. They ought to have gone to Ireland and explained the bill and shown how, though it wasn't home rule, it might be worked so as to do much good.[22]

The muddle over the Councils Bill revealed a great deal about the tenuous nature of Irish–Liberal co-operation. The views of the Irish were sought only in the bill's later stages, and, indeed, for a long time Irish leaders were actually ignorant of the precise nature of the proposal. During the long period of speculation, false expectations were given a chance to develop in Ireland and the final product was, therefore, a disappointment to almost everyone. The bill, even Birrell's version, was not a proposal likely to generate enthusiasm among the Irish and hence not one on which Redmond would be willing to stake his reputation. Domestic Irish opposition to the bill was allowed to emerge, and the Irish party, split internally over the bill in any case, was in a dangerously vulnerable position if it elected to support the Government's measure. The Church, the extremists, the Healy and O'Brien factions, and even an influential segment of the nationalist press were hostile. Irish America, source of the party's finance, would neither understand nor endorse such a bill. A. C. Hepburn rightly lays considerable stress upon nationalist fear of O'Brien's and the Irish American opposition.[23] The incident demonstrates the real restraints on Redmond's freedom of action, especially when he was confronted with a proposal for which he did not feel personal enthusiasm. Equally, it revealed to many Liberals the fundamental weakness of Redmond's position and the tremendous difficulties, not to say waste of time, involved in trying to negotiate 'step by step' Irish government reform.

The lessons drawn from the Councils Bill affair were, therefore, to affect the whole course of the home-rule question fundamentally. For Redmond, it implied that, while piecemeal social and economic reforms might well be negotiated on their merits, it was far too dangerous to co-operate with the Liberals on any governmental reform short of home rule. The Irish leadership now pursued a policy of home rule or nothing. It sought to reaffirm the supposed Liberal commitment to eventual home rule by making the issue central in the next general election and introducing a bill in the next Parliament. There was no expectation that full home rule would be achieved – that was not the point – but it was essential for the party's survival as leader of nationalist opinion in Ireland that the commitment be reaffirmed and strengthened. The leadership had detected that 'step by step' legislation was directed more against the paramount authority of the party than against Irish grievances: as a policy it was a commodity which the party could scarcely welcome.

Birrell, more sensitive to the predicament of the Irish than most of his colleagues, captured the essence of the new situation when he wrote to Campbell-Bannerman,

Redmond's position is a tricky one. I think he has saved himself for the present, but only by the skin of his teeth. . . . This next session will be watched with scrutinizing eyes by the whole country. He can't rest on his oars for a single moment. . . . The impression is general in Ireland that the parliamentary party have allowed *home rule* to be *shoved under* and that it can't emerge for at least a decade. Were the impression to become a belief, Redmond and his whole party would be *kicked into space*. Their maintenance fund would disappear and the *sinn fein* . . . would reign in their stead. . . . If he can't gain our support then he must fight us *tooth and nail* and at least half his supporters would be just as well pleased if *he decided to fight us*.[24]

Redmond himself put the case simply: there could, from an Irish point of view, be 'no half-way house between despotism and home rule'.[25]

For Liberals the experience was even more chastening. Some would continue to hanker for the formula proposed in the Councils Bill but most rather agreed with Birrell that the idea should never have been touched. In retrospect, the affair seemed only to have served to expose the weak points of the Government's Irish policy without achieving anything positive. At this juncture the Liberal Party faced an acute crisis. The bulk of the party and its leadership had explicitly turned its back on Gladstonian home-rule policy for the foreseeable future. 'Step by step' reform had proved attractive to them because it made possible a number of constructive proposals consistent with an organic concept of the British state. From 1907, however, the Liberals were again without a coherent and politically defensible Irish policy. The pluralist position was a minority view even within the party and step-by-step reform had been ruled out of court by events. In the absence of a party view, minorities within the party had the field to themselves. In 1905 and 1906 a return to the Gladstonian policy had been almost inconceivable: in 1907 and after, the pluralists held the policy initiative by default. It was a remarkable reversal of party policy, the origins of which rest evidently in the Councils Bill affair. The Liberal Party was now reconciled to pluralist policies not out of conviction or argument but out of a poverty of alternative solutions. To formalise this state of affairs, all that were needed were a general election and the need to win Irish votes.

Historians have not taken a great deal of notice of the Councils Bill episode nor given it appropriate weight, yet it seems to have been one of the most critical incidents shaping Edwardian attitudes to Celtic questions. It was the beginning of the decisive stage of the constitutional crisis: now the confrontation between pluralists and organicists re-emerged. The question of the authority of House of Commons majorities (especially tactical majorities rooted in an absence of policy) was imminent. Had it not been for the cohesion of the Liberals on other than Celtic issues, a further party split would not have been improbable. And suggestions for a coalition arrangement in 1910 should be seen against this background of the growing desperation of many Liberals that they were being pushed into a dangerously undesirable position on a wide range of topics.

Awareness of the importance of the Councils Bill incident also helps us to realise that the two general elections were not so decisive in terms of home-rule policy as it is usually assumed. While it is true that the Liberals became more dependent on Redmond at this time and that at election time he probably reached the peak of his apparent influence on British politics, the inability of the majority of Liberals to evolve a viable alternative policy to Gladstonian home rule meant that the field had already been abdicated to the pluralists. Indeed, to Liberals Redmond's insistence on the primacy of home rule alone was something of a godsend, because it enabled them to apportion blame to him for what was bound to be a contentious and unpopular bill. Furthermore, it provided certain Liberals, notably Lloyd George, with an effective scapegoat should the policy prove unsuccessful; it opened up the possibility of a realignment in

politics; and it justified special concessions to Ulster as that problem began to edge to the forefront of people's minds.

Home rule was not brought before Parliament until 1912. Its
introduction as a bill marked the continuation of a longstanding
crisis which was to recede only with the outbreak of European war.
Attention focused on the proposal itself and, most particularly, on the
demand for special provision for the Protestant portions of Ulster.
Subsequently, historians have emphasised the critical nature of the
Irish question in these years, but, on closer analysis, this may seem
unwise. In a sense, the lines of dispute then marked were the natural
consequence of the introduction without conviction, by a Government
majority without a policy, of a highly unpopular piece of legislation.
For opponents the only path open was one of open resistance, especially when a large majority of the population in north-east Ireland
made it amply clear that it would not accept what it saw as disenfranchisement from Britain. Such an appeal was difficult to resist. The
many conferences and proposals for a resolution, particularly in 1914,
took place in an atmosphere of unreality. The real issue was much
larger than Ireland: it concerned the nature of governmental authority and legitimacy. Liberals and many subsequent historians have
seen it as an argument over the ability of House of Commons majorities to legislate, but the fight over Irish home rule symbolised an even
more fundamental crisis. Could ephemeral political majorities, perhaps elected to Parliament for entirely different reasons, impose an
apparently objectionable minority policy on the whole country without resistance? Conservatives were reasonably united in answering
'No' and even Liberals were not answering unanimously in the affirm-
ative. The question was complicated by the fact that the position of
the House of Commons had changed considerably in the past
hundred years: no longer was its claim to legitimacy, even supremacy, in the Constitution unassailable. The unpopularity of home
rule made this a suitable test case for Commons authority. If a conclusion can be reached, it should be that the home-rule crisis in 1914
demonstrated the limits of parliamentary government in the Edwardian age and not that it was in itself novel. The essence of the crisis,
as we have seen, was to be found in the years 1907 and 1908. Asquith
was to discover, as Edward Heath did over labour legislation in the
1970s, that mere majorities, however arrived at, are insufficient to
carry very unpopular measures in the country.

The Irish crisis displays other less auspicious aspects of Edwardian politics. The failure of Liberal policy after 1907 suggests that

the critics of Liberalism have a good case. The most important suggestions for a resolution to the Irish problem were those for 'Home Rule all-round', for which there was no established popular demand. Redmond and Dillon always saw it as a potential diversion from real home-rule policies: it is difficult not to accept their view. 'Home Rule all-round' was evidence not of the vigour of Liberal political thinking but of its poverty. Nevertheless, what emerges is not a picture of imminent Liberal disaster, as Dangerfield would have us believe, but a panorama of the rigidity of conventional party structures and loyalties, which perhaps, following Max Weber's analysis, could be broken only by some major crisis, such as that provided by the Great War. The strength of party probably inhibited political realignment, despite increasing support for a non-pluralist approach to Celtic problems. In addition, it is worth speculating on the intensity of the Celtic crisis had Britain's economic performance between 1870 and 1914 not been so very lame. Many of the Irish arguments, those of men such as Patrick Pearse, were to centre on how poorly Ireland had fared under the Union. Frequent attempts were made to justify self-government in terms of the essential economic regeneration which was expected to follow as an almost automatic consequence of home rule. Britain, then, may be seen to have been both unlucky and inept in confronting centrifugal tendencies at a time when she was also proving incapable of building the just, meritocratic society promised by the Liberals for so long.

A closer examination of the Irish question during the Edwardian era suggests that Dangerfield's emphasis on the erosion of what may be called liberal ideals is to some extent confirmed but in other ways modified. Dangerfield was right to stress a decline in these values but less than accurate in ascribing a date for the 'death' of liberal England and substantially incorrect as to its causes. It would be an exaggeration to say that liberal Britain collapsed at Irish hands, but the dispute over Ireland deserves a central place in any analysis of 'The Strange Death of Liberal England' and can be seen to highlight the political and constitutional ailments of the age. That the crisis emerged at all is the strangest feature of all. Between 1900 and 1907 only a minority of thinking Englishmen were convinced pluralists and a Gladstonian solution did not appear likely to appear on any government's programme of legislation. The circumstances which led the Liberal Government to propose a pluralist solution demand our attention more urgently than the Irish grievances themselves. For they are symptomatic of a fundamental political, societal and constitutional turmoil. There can be little doubt, that if the Irish question presented a golden opportunity to the Edwardian generation to demonstrate its healing powers, it was an opportunity which was very much missed.

7. The Family and the Role of Women

SUZANN BUCKLEY

I do not see why the only way in which women can advance should be along the road to female suffrage. The existing social fabric rests upon the assumption that the family is the unit, and not the individual. It is impossible to deny that an attack upon the existing social fabric must imply an attack upon the family.

Mrs Creighton, in *The Nineteenth Century*, xxxvi (1889) 347

The women's movement has now in a word a more universally human, a less onesidedly feminine character. It emphasises more and more the fact that the right of woman is a necessity in order that she may fulfil her duties in the small, individual family, and, exercise her powers in the great, universal human family for the general good. The new woman does not wish to displace man nor to abolish society. She wishes to be able to exercise *everywhere* her most beautiful prerogative to help, to support, to comfort. But she cannot do so, long as she is not free as a citizen and has not fully developed as a human personality.

Ellen Key, *The Woman Movement*, trans. M. B. Borthwick (1912)

These observations by an opponent and proponent of the enfranchisement of women capture the crux of the Edwardian female-suffrage debate. Central to any discussion of votes for women was the question, how will such a change affect the family? Despite the contemporary emphasis on the relationship between votes for women and possible changes in the family, most historians have not developed this point. They have tended to focus either upon the functions of members of Edwardian families of various classes or upon the political conflicts over female suffrage. Indeed, most of the historiography on Edwardian women falls into the latter category. Ray Strachey's *The Cause* (1928), Constance Rover's *Women's Suffrage and Party Politics in Britain* (1967), and David Morgan's *Suffragists and Liberals* (1974) discuss the political aspects of the women's movement from the 1860s through to the 1900s. George Dangerfield's *The Strange Death of Liberal England, 1910–14* (1936) treats the suffrage campaign as a manifestation of middle-class female rebellion against the prevailing Edwardian norms of security, respectability and political compromise, and Andrew Rosen's *Rise Up, Women!* (1974) analyses the militant campaign of the Women's Social and Political Union. More recent work does at last link women's familial and political concerns. *One Hand Tied Behind Us* (1978) by Jill Liddington and Jill Norris examines suffrage activities by working-class women in local areas in order to determine how these women managed to combine political campaigning with family and work commitments. They thereby develop the important theme set forth by Hannah Mitchell in her autobiography, *The Hard Way Up* (1968). She vividly recalls the difficulties of some married activists:

> No cause could be won between dinner and tea, and most of us who were married had to work with one hand tied behind us, so to speak. Public disapproval could be faced and borne, but domestic unhappiness, the price many of us paid for our opinions and activities, was a very bitter thing. But neither deterred us, and we carried on.[1]

Clearly, any comprehensive perspective of the suffrage movement must relate familial concerns to political activity. This consideration is essential before one can determine the validity of Mrs Creighton's fear that votes for women entailed an attack upon the patriarchal family structure. Before this can be done, however, it is necessary to consider ways of analysing the modern family, usually defined as members of the same kin who live together under one roof, and the role of women.

Social scientists and historians of the family and the role of women have tended to examine these elements in relation to such aspects of modernisation as rapid industrialisation, urbanisation, bureaucratisation, increased social mobility and political participation and decreased authority of moral and social institutions. Some have employed psychological and sociological methodologies or analysed patterns of employment, social-policy legislation and domestic and work conditions in order to connect aspects of modernisation with disruptive changes in the family. Others, particularly Michael Anderson in his classic study *Family Structure in Nineteenth Century Lancashire* (1971), incorporate these approaches into examinations of how such

factors as family size, patterns of intimacy, economic needs, delega-
tion of authority, codes of conduct and nature of ideals both shape and
reflect events and forces outside the family. This more inclusive
method can be very helpful in determining the role of women within a
family. However, as pointed out by Gerda Lerner in her seminal study
'Placing Women in History', women cannot be examined solely as
members of families.[2] Studies of women in history thus must not only
substitute new periodisation for the traditional politically determined
historical divisions, but also consider women as more than members
of families. They should examine women with respect to such pertinent categories as class, production, reproduction, socialisation, sexuality and female bonding. New directions in family history thus must
be combined with the new methodologies in women's history in order
to explain why the patriarchal structure of the Edwardian family
remained intact when it was seemingly threatened by changes or demands for changes in the subordinate position of women.

One of the most obvious characteristics distinguishing Edwardian
families from those of previous decades was that they contained fewer
children. Edwardians thus continued the birth-control trend of the
late Victorian period. Between 1900 and 1909 the birthrate was 27·50
per 1000, as opposed to 30·02 per 1000 in 1890–9.[3] In addition, the Victorian pattern of more women than men continued. This contributed
to an uninterrupted increase in the number of unmarried females who
were over nineteen years of age (all figures are per 1000):

	1891	1901	1911
Unmarried	281	298	302
Married	585	576	579
Widowed	134	126	119

At the same time, as the following figures indicate, the decline in the
percentage of employed women who were ten years of age or older was
slightly reversed:

	1891	1901	1911
Percentage	31·14	29·1	29·7
Total working population in millions	4.016	4.171	4.830

The percentage change came essentially from unmarried females.
From 1901 to 1911 the proportion of unmarried females increased from

523 per 1000 to 545 per 1000. The increase for married women was considerably less dramatic: 132 per 1000 in 1901: 136 per 1000 in 1911. Widows also exhibited little change. Furthermore, many of the recently employed females were finding posts in the new middle-class occupations that continued to develop as a result of economic, political, scientific and technological changes. Expanded overseas trade, increased government services and health and education facilities provided work in commerce, the Civil Service, medicine and education. Unmarried educated middle-class women who had taken advantage of the expansion in education opportunities for females could readily compete with males for posts in these areas. Extensive use of typewriters and greater demand for ready-made clothing and packaged foodstuffs increased substantially the number of jobs for upper working-class women in clerical work and retail sales.[4] These factors of fewer children and greater employment opportunities suggest changes in the traditional domestic role of many Edwardian women. However, at least two very important questions about these factors remain: how specifically did they affect the position of women, and how did they relate to women's demand for enfranchisement?

Those less directly affected by greater employment possibilities for females were married women. Only about one in four married women worked outside the home. The census of 1911 thereby could conclude: 'There remain the married women, the great bulk of whom are fortunately in this country free at all ages to devote their attention to the care of their households.'[5] A primary task in this domestic sphere was the care of children. As Anna Davin illustrates in 'Imperialism and Motherhood', during the Edwardian years public discussion of infant life and child health took on new importance as various discussants stressed the importance of children as a national resource. Children, it was argued, were crucial to the maintenance of the Empire. Without them, Britain and the Empire would be unable to withstand economic and political competition from the expanding powers, Germany and the United States. Yet, as exponents of the imperial view lamented, the birth rate declined while the infant mortality rate rose. Imperialists tried to counter these trends by promoting an ideology of motherhood. Women of all classes were urged to see their duty and reward in bearing healthy members of the imperial race. They were strongly encouraged to seek professional guidance in mothering skills. The authorities emphasised that a mother neglected her duty if she failed to devote her time to the care of her children. As part of the motherhood ideology, mothers were expected to supervise their daughters' upbringing in order to instil in them the virtues of the imperial domesticity.[6] Consequently, a decline in the number of children did not necessarily mean much freer time for married women. Also, the number of domestic servants declined during this period, from 1009 per 10,000 in 1901 to 915 per 10,000 in 1911. Hence, some women, especially from middle-class homes with modest budgets, probably spent more time on household tasks as well as on child care.

The decline in the birth rate and increased concern with the well-being of future generations of the Empire was accompanied by the growth of new parental attitudes towards children. Increasingly, parents viewed children as individuals to be trained to become ladies and gentlemen. Some middle-class parents, beset by mounting financial burdens, were determined that their children would, if nothing else, be able to maintain their class status by being versed in respectable ways. Socialisation by mothers, particularly in the lower middle classes, thus became quite important in inculcating the tenets of respectability in children. For example, as Sidney Ford, a member of the lower middle class recounts, Mrs Ford was

the dominating personality. . . . She insisted on the observation of manners at the table and towards other adults; prevented him from playing in the streets, and was appropriately horrified by any sign of influence from such sources, like swearwords [and] all the time she was looking for me to improve my mind.[7]

To some extent the situation was similar in working-class families. However, for some within this group, fewer children could produce stresses for married women. In the upper and middle classes, family planning stemmed to some extent from a husband's desire to maintain his family's standard of living, and the decision to limit the number of children was usually based on consent between husband and wife. This was less frequently the case in working-class families, where fewer children threatened many male workers' concept of manhood. At a time when unstable working conditions were disturbing his self-image of a strong male, fatherhood could give the male worker some status in a predominantly male culture. Rejection of this compensation could be unsettling and too high a price to pay in order to alleviate the financial burden of many children. Often, then, a working-class woman could not obtain her husband's co-operation in birth control, and if she did not want another child her chief recourse was to the dangerous practice of abortion.[8]

A decline in the birth rate and a decline in child mortality among working-class families also had ambiguous implications for mothers. It encouraged them to make a greater emotional investment in each child. Yet this occurred when child mortality was still sufficiently high, especially among the working class, to result in most instances in the death of at least one youngster per family. But the death of a child could no longer be accepted with fatalistic resignation, especially as medical reformers espousing the cult of motherhood linked child mortality with working mothers and inadequate working-class diets (the usual fare for poorer working-class children comprised small quantities of tea, butter and unwholesome packaged white bread). Thus, even though on the one hand a mother could feel justified in not working, on the other she might be guilt-ridden about not bringing in some extra income with which to buy better food for her children.

In addition to these tensions, a working-class mother, either working or non-working, had to deal with the influence of voluntary societies and schools upon her children. Boys and girls increasingly spent their little free time participating in activities sponsored by middle-class reformers, who intended that such organisations as the Girls' Friendly Society and the Boys' Brigades should uplift the working-class children to their norms. Schoolteachers were equally anxious to inculcate middle-class standards, particularly of hygiene. The conflicts that resulted from this sort of public interference of one class with the heretofore private concerns of another class is graphically described as follows:

> A young girl was called to account for a dirty wrist which was disfigured by a birthmark. The child came home, boiled water, and scrubbed at the offending spot in hope of giving satisfaction. Her mother worked herself into an understandable righteous fury: 'I'll pull her blooming hair off'. And her daughter was certain she would at least have hit the teacher had she not herself intervened to prevent the confrontation.[9]

Despite these problems, married working-class women were generally content. As a result, many married women felt no need to question the subordinate role of women in work and politics. Their sphere was the home and in that environment they felt equal or superior to their husbands. 'They enjoyed a certainty about the rightness of their role',[10] and this was sufficient for them at a time when economic, social and political conditions afforded no alluring alternative to the security of traditional familial structure and customs. Besides the fact of no readily visible alternatives, the prevailing familial situation among working-class families was reinforced by the mores of large numbers of Irish and Jewish immigrants, who tended to settle in working-class neighbourhoods. For these groups, tradition and religion emphasised patriarchal structures and few Irish or Jewish women questioned their position within this hierarchy.

No doubt many middle- and upper-class married women also enjoyed a certainty about their roles. Those who did not could retreat into respectable middle-class bouts of melancholia or into tolerated upper-class affairs. As long as an affair neither provoked scandal nor led to divorce it was accepted as a reasonable means of dealing with those marriages that were based on little more than a desire to preserve the financial and social position of the upper class. But, as Vita Sackville-West describes in her novel *The Edwardians* (1930), an affair that might cause a scandal had to end. Scandal could not be tolerated, because it would entail a loss of respect *vis-à-vis* other classes. Divorce could not be accepted, because it would not only upset many of the arranged marriages between members of the upper class, but also threaten the whole social order. Families in all classes might adopt this procedure, and the ensuing break-ups in the structured family would eventually take their toll on a hierarchical society already beleaguered by challenges to the existing social and political structure. Despite the appointment in 1909 of a Royal Commission on Divorce and Matrimonial Clauses, the question of divorce was kept basically where the King wanted it to remain: in the category of subjects 'which cannot be discussed openly and in all its aspects with any delicacy or even decency before ladies'.[11] Sickness and affairs were accepted safety valves for an unpleasant marriage; divorce was an unacceptable form of dangerous radicalism. Indeed, for all his dalliances, Edward VII tried to serve as a model patriarch to all his subjects by taking a strong public stand on the importance of the family.

Of course, not all married women were content with the conventional home life or the accepted alternatives to it. Some married women, together with single women, did not conform to prevailing norms. Working-class women such as Hannah Mitchell combined family life with participation in political and trade-union activities. Others, such as the middle-class type depicted by H. G. Wells in *Ann Veronica* (1909), rebelled against the social and moral conventions imposed upon them. Rejecting the double standard that allowed men social and sexual freedom while denying it to women, young wives whose husbands spent long periods away from home because of duties in the outposts of the Empire took to dining out with male friends. Others experimented with trial marriages or claimed the right of unmarried women to bear and raise children out of wedlock. A few may have become lesbians. Most women, however, accepted conventional social and moral standards. They deplored the double standard not because it suppressed female sexuality, but because it encouraged male incontinence. For example, some women denounced the divorce laws, which allowed a woman to be divorced for adultery, but required a man to be guilty of adultery plus cruelty, desertion, sodomy, bestiality or rape. These laws, the women argued, condoned male adultery by suggesting that adultery was a less serious offence for a man than for a woman. Christabel Pankhurst also attacked the double standard, for its harm to her ideal of a chaste society. In her book *The Great Scourge and How to End It* (1913), she contended that a sex war whereby wives refused sexual contact with husbands might be necessary, unless promiscuous men who consorted with prostitutes stopped spreading venereal disease to innocent wives.

Thus, for the majority of discontented middle-class women, social purity rather than sexual freedom was the predominant aspect of any sexuality issue. Certainly, despite Dangerfield's curious interpretation of the suffragettes' solidarity as a non-sexual form of lesbianism, there is no evidence to suggest that many of the suffragettes had homosexual tendencies.[12] Dangerfield, on this point, clearly reveals ignorance of female bonding. In this respect he does not differ substantially from many of the suffragettes' male opponents, who equated the suffragettes' unorthodox political acts with deviant social or moral behaviour. But this equation of sisterhood with homosexuality is merely a convenient, albeit inaccurate, way for anti-feminists to dismiss the significance of an episode when thousands of women from various classes banded together for enfranchisement and proceeded to harass a male-dominated political and social structure by peaceful and violent means.

A desire to have the political power to legislate for social purity was definitely one reason why women wanted the vote. Specifically, they wanted to enact social-purity laws, in order to strengthen the family by protecting women and children from the effects of vice. Laws for temperance and control of sexual vice might spare women from abuse by drunken husbands or from the ills of prostitution. For example, some argued that, if the age of consent were raised, young girls would be less likely to fall into the clutches of white slavers. Also, stricter laws against brothels might reduce the incidence of prostitution as well as the rate of venereal disease. Working together with moral and just men, many women hoped to be able, as Ellen Key argued, to exercise their 'powers in the general universal family for the general good'.

Besides wanting to transform 'the Angel in the Home' into the angel in the House of Commons, many women sought the vote because of economic issues. Distressed by financial problems, working-class female activists hoped that the vote would help to bring about measures designed to improve the lot of both employed and un-employed working-class women. In this respect, Andrew Rosen's explanation that Hannah Mitchell's political activity resulted from a deep dissatisfaction with married life needs qualification. Her bitterness was directed not against the family *per se*, but against an economic structure that made things so difficult for working-class women to maintain the well-being of their families.

Protest stemming from economic issues was by no means limited to working-class women. Although middle-class female proponents of enfranchisement did not, unlike working-class women, usually see the vote as a means of changing the economic structure, they did envision that votes for women would help them to secure their place in the workforce. Despite the gains made by unmarried women in the new occupations, their position was vulnerable. The new occupations were rapidly becoming overcrowded, and in the competitive market employers tended to favour hiring men instead of women. Even if women were able to find employment, their salaries and chances for advancement were less than those enjoyed by their male counterparts. For example, the White Paper in 1911 on secondary-school teachers' salaries and superannuation showed that the average salaries in grant-earning secondary schools were £438 for headmasters, and £332 for headmistresses; £168 for male assistants and £123 for female assistants. Edwardian women protested against this situation by demanding equal opportunities and equal pay with men. Their protests did not receive a sympathetic hearing from those who clung to the traditional assumptions that women should be subordinate to men, and that men, as heads of families, needed and deserved better pay and prospects than women. Frustrated by this unresponsive reaction, these women joined with other women to press for the vote.[13]

Proponents of female enfranchisement sometimes met with well-meaning rebuffs that pointed out that the status of women, especially among the upper and middle classes, was improving. It was argued that the Married Women's Property Act of 1882 and legislation that allowed some women to vote in municipal elections and to sit on school boards and boards of guardians indicated a willingness to make women's status co-ordinate rather than subordinate.

This type of paternalism, expressed by both female and male opponents of female suffrage, merely reinforced the feeling of dependency felt by discontented women. They reacted by becoming more determined to secure the vote. But, although they made some progress, victory eluded them in part because they failed to stir up widespread interest in the subject. (In 1903 the main suffrage society, the National Union of Women's Suffrage Societies, had only sixteen constituted branches.) It remained for the Women's Social and Political Union (WSPU) to vitalise the issue by serving as an umbrella organisation and by attracting publicity by means of militancy.

Initially purporting to be an organisation for championing the interests of working-class women, by 1906 the WSPU had abandoned this pretence. Women of all political sympathies and classes were encouraged to join the WSPU. The battle of votes for women was thus no longer associated either with a movement of élite ladies or with the parochial policies of the Independent Labour Party. Equally important, the battle was no longer necessarily peaceful. Determined to draw attention to the issue of women's suffrage, Christabel Pankhurst and other members of the WSPU embarked on a militant policy of disruption of public meetings and destruction of property. The publicity given to these tactics and the imprisonment of the militants pushed the franchise struggle out of the wings into the centre stage. The WSPU and the older suffrage societies, which disapproved of militancy, greatly increased the number of members and the financial support.[14]

Ultimately, however, neither violent nor peaceful acts alone secured women the vote. Suspension of militancy during the war made it easier for politicians to endorse enfranchisement, but the number of changes brought about by the war and the desire of politicians to enlist women's support for post-war reconstruction measures made it prudent to enfranchise most women over thirty years of age. Some women had to be included in the political process, because, as Asquith, who had bitterly opposed such a measure during his tenure as Prime Minister, stated, it was expedient. Among other things, if women were to support government plans to place returning soldiers in jobs held by women, they had to be co-opted. Limited enfranchisement was the logical means of gulling women into believing that they would at last have 'the power and the right of making their voice directly heard'.[15]

To the Edwardian suffragettes the Representation of the People Act of 1918 appeared to be the long-awaited triumph of virtue and justice. After generations of struggle some women supposedly could begin to 'exercise *everywhere* [their] most beautiful prerogative to help, to support, to comfort'. It would require the rude experiences of subsequent years to demonstrate that the vote had been given rather than won, and therefore that women's prerogative would be exercised in a subordinate rather than co-ordinate role. Enfranchisement of women may have slightly modified the patriarchal political system, but it did not alter the patriarchal ideals. This type of change would have required radical rather than reform measures. Foremost among these would have been an attack upon the patriarchal family structure, which either shaped or reinforced the ideals. But, contrary to Mrs Creighton's fear, few perceived the existing family structure as an obstacle to equality. It would in fact have been difficult to do so, in view of the strong institutional and ideological bulwarks for the family. Furthermore, few wanted to perceive the family in such a light. Whatever the class, most women saw the family as a symbol of order and comfort in a world apparently marked by disorder and discomfort.

8. Edwardian England and the Coming of the First World War

COLIN NICOLSON

I

THE outbreak of the First World War marked the end of the Edwardian age in a tragic and dramatic fashion, and, while many institutions survived the war remarkably unscathed, its impact upon the social structure and psychology of the nation was colossal. Edwardian England, that chronologically vague but none the less very recognisable epoch, may have survived Edward the Peacemaker, but it unquestionably ended in the mud of Passchendaele and on the banks of the Somme, and, less heroically, but with no less finality, in the factories and shipyards of a nation mobilised for total war.

With the publication by the early 1970s of all official documents, the diplomatic origins of the war have been studied in such detail that it is unlikely that they will reveal further secrets. On one level, the diplomatic documents provide an adequate explanation of the events of July and August 1914. The war came about because of the alliance systems, the miscalculations of statesmen, and the relentless operation of military machinery, war plans and timetables which 'carried the nations to war by their own weight'. This explanation is superficially satisfactory when applied to events on the Continent, but in the case of Great Britain most of it is irrelevant. Britain had no formal alliances, and she did not possess a large army which made statesmen the prisoners of complex mobilisation and war plans. Indeed, only two days before the declaration of war, the majority of the Cabinet were disputing Britain's legal and moral obligation to fight; and, even after war had been declared, arguments were still raging about whether Britain's 'contemptible little Army' should be sent to Europe at all.

A purely diplomatic explanation of Britain's involvement in the war, which gives pride of place to *Primat der Aussenpolitik*, the pre-eminence of external factors in the making of foreign policy, is clearly inadequate: it leaves too many questions, even diplomatic questions, unanswered. How was it, for instance, that in 1914 Britain had incurred a commitment to fight that was at the same time so ill defined that senior Cabinet ministers did not understand it, and yet sufficiently binding to involve the country in a war for which she was militarily and strategically unprepared? Why was there such a gap between Britain's diplomatic commitments and her ability to fulfil them effectively? Why was it that Britain's armed forces, upon which she had lavished the highest per capita expenditure in Europe, were insufficient either to deter an enemy or to enable the nation to remain securely neutral? Would a less ambiguous statement of Britain's position have had the effect of restraining and deterring Germany?

Many of the questions raised by Britain's situation in August 1914 lie in the realm of social and political history. Was there any connection, whether indirect and informal or sinister, between the decision to go to war and the fact that Britain was facing unprecedented industrial strife and incipient civil war in Ireland? Why was there such a contrast between the ambiguous and tentative attitude of the British Government and the massive popular enthusiasm that greeted the war and sustained it for four years? Why did the apparently powerful forces of pacifism and internationalism that had done so much to shape Britain's stance in the years before the war collapse so ignominiously? Had the politicians, hypnotised by the persistence of the Gladstonian tradition and deafened by the articulate clamour of the Radicals, misread the popular mood?

Perhaps the answer to these questions lies not so much in the interplay between nation and nation, but in the peculiar structures of the foreign-policy-making process in Edwardian England. Various turbulent currents of opinion and attitude were fighting for predominance within Edwardian society: traditional idealism and a new realism, pacifism and militarism, isolationism and commitment were all striving to express themselves, beating often in vain upon the walls that sheltered the foreign-policy-making élite. Much of the explanation for the ambiguities and paradoxes that manifested themselves in August 1914 lies in the dichotomy between the popular will and the official interpretation of that will.

II

Once the European states had emerged from their struggles for national existence in the last quarter of the nineteenth century, and once the natural forces of economic development had begun to redress the anomaly of Britain's early industrialisation, it was inevitable that Britain would have to seek her security through co-operation with other powers. The humiliations of the Boer War merely served as a catalyst to a wide belief which already existed that the decline of Britain must be reversed.

Most attempts at reform foundered upon deep-seated traditions, institutions and structures that had grown up in Britain over many centuries, unshaken by internal war and revolution. It was only in the field of foreign policy that change could easily be effected, for, as A. J. P. Taylor shrewdly remarks, foreign policy is a matter of talk not action,[1] and, merely by 'talking', it was possible to bring about in the period between the Boer War and the First World War a fundamental change in Britain's diplomatic stance. The creation of an armed force that would make diplomatic pledges credible, required 'action', however, and here politicians were brought face to face with the same problems that were retarding and obstructing change in other areas.

In retrospect, the most striking feature of Britain's diplomacy in the years before 1914 is the lack of real options open to the decision-makers. British statesmen were propelled by the relentless dynamics of international politics into a position over which they had very little control. The country whose pre-eminence had given her the luxury of choice in foreign policy for generations was faced with remarkably little choice once she had been forced to emerge from isolation.

Once Joseph Chamberlain's brave but impractical scheme for retreating into an imperial fortress had proved a chimaera, there were only two courses open to Britain: friendship with France and Russia, or friendship with the Triple Alliance powers of Germany, Austria and Italy. In fact, events conspired to rob Britain even of this option, and propelled her helplessly towards France.

It was generally agreed by contemporaries that Sir Edward Grey's speech to the Commons on 3 August 1914,[2] when he convinced the House of the need to go to war, was one of his greatest political triumphs. The emotional appeal of that speech was based on support of Belgian neutrality, but its rational appeal lay in its advocacy of the need to support France against German aggression, although 'as regards our freedom to decide in a crisis what out line should be . . . the Government remained perfectly free'. In other words, support for France was vital to Britain's national interest, but Britain would not express that support through any explicit commitment. Britain was prepared to go to war on behalf of France, but she was not prepared to tell her so.

Only three days before this speech, Grey had told the outraged French ambassador, Jules Cambon, that Britain was 'free from engagements', and that she would have to 'decide what British interests required us to do'.[3] Cambon's disgust at this rejection of any British obligation was understandable, for almost everything Grey had done since entering office could legitimately be interpreted by the French as an avowal of support. 'The Entente', wrote Eyre Crowe in an attempt to stiffen his chief's resolve, 'has been made, strengthened and put to the test and celebrated in a manner justifying the belief that a moral bond was being forged'.[4]

Cambon's bitterness over Britain's legalistic detachment while his country was 'sliding over the precipice into the boiling cauldron of war' is understandable. Scarcely a month had passed during the past eight years without the Foreign Secretary's affirming his faith in the Entente. Had Grey been merely affirming his faith in a ten-year-old colonial agreement, the significance of which presumably ended with the disputes it settled? The French might well have concluded that Grey saw the Entente as having some deeper significance than that.

The logic of Britain's national interest argued clearly that she could not allow France to be defeated by Germany. Britain's military preparations, however puny, and her covert strategic dispositions pointed to a commitment to fight in northern France; she had given the key of her Empire into the keeping of the French Mediterranean fleet and laid the western coasts of France wide open to German attack. When the crisis came there was never any real chance of her deserting France; and yet she refused to make her commitment explicit. As Winston Churchill said in 1912, 'everyone must feel who knows the facts that we have all the obligations of an alliance without its advantages, and above all without its precise definitions'.[5]

III

Three things must strike any observer of Britain's helpless position in

1914; the ambiguity of her diplomatic stance; her lack of ability to influence events, because of military weakness; and the divorce that seemed to have taken place between diplomacy and strategy.

Grey had two foreign policies: one, an explicit position which denied any formal obligations to any other power; the other, an implicit position that derived from ten years of tacit military co-operation with France. When the crisis came, Grey found that neither his explicit nor his implicit positions could be sustained, because they were not supported by military capacity. The 'free hand' was significant only if it carried a big stick, and the balance of power could be maintained only by the exercise of power: that is, by action or the threat of action, not merely by talk. Implicit support for France was meaningless, not only because it was unclear, but also because Britain lacked the armed might to deter Germany.

Many people after the war believed that 'a perfectly explicit statement as to Britain's conduct in certain eventualities' would have deterred Germany. If this view constitutes 'the greatest myth of pre-war diplomacy',[6] it is because Britain had no power to influence events at this late stage. The French hoped that a clear British diplomatic commitment might deter Germany, and they needed the moral support that even one British soldier on French soil would give them, but they knew that any war against Germany would be settled within the first few weeks in a massive collision of conscript armies in the plains of Flanders and Picardy. If the vast unleashing of men and materials envisaged in the Schlieffen Plan was to be countered, it would be by the equally massive armies of France. In such a contest, Britain's tiny standing army of 100,000 effective men was too small and too far away to influence the result, and if the Schlieffen Plan succeeded, the support of the Royal Navy in the Channel and the North Sea would be superfluous.

It is not surprising that the confusion and ambiguities of Britain's diplomacy were reflected, and to some extent explained, by confusion within the armed services themselves over their shape and role. This confusion was most clearly manifested in the acrimonious meeting of the Committee of Imperial Defence which took place in August 1911 and in which many of the problems of Britain's changed diplomatic and military position were discussed.

The crux of the meeting was a bitter argument – which reflected many of the dilemmas of Britain's ambivalent international position – between the Admiralty and the War Office over the role of the British Expeditionary Force (BEF). The Admiralty argued, in Fisherite terms, that the BEF should be used as an adjunct to a naval war, as a flexible force which could be landed at any point on the coast of Europe under the massive protection of the Royal Navy. The Generals had a totally different conception of the BEF's function: it should be clearly committed, they argued, to a predetermined position alongside the French and Belgian armies to fulfil a specific strategic role.

The Navy's preference conformed closely to Britain's explicit diplomatic position. If the nation was primarily concerned with monitoring the European balance, it was logical to command a response which could operate against or in conjunction with any European power. If the main threat of Britain's war effort was to be expressed through the Army, why was the Army so small, and why had so much money been lavished on the Navy? Any plan to deploy the BEF in a predetermined position on the Continent must surely imply the very commitment to France that Grey was so anxious to deny.

The Navy's arguments may appear a more logical strategic expression of Britain's diplomatic position as it was constantly and publicly reiterated in the years before the war, but it was not just because the First Sea Lord expressed these arguments so badly that they were defeated in August 1911. It was Grey's implicit policy that had carried the day. A continental commitment had been incurred in all but name, and it was left to the Army Chiefs of Staff to translate that commitment into action with the totally inadequate force that Parliament had allowed them.

General Henry Wilson, the Director of Military Operations, despite his madcap politics, had a very clear idea of the military implications of Grey's diplomacy, and strove, within the limitations imposed upon him by the size of the BEF, to give some substance to Grey's implicit promises. It is not surprising that Wilson allowed the BEF to become too much of an adjunct of the French army, nor is it surprising that Wilson was a vocal advocate of conscription. Although he believed the British could make a contribution to stopping a German advance, he knew that the BEF was too small to play a really independent role. He suspected that the only effective way to deter German aggression was by making a clear diplomatic commitment to support France and translating this support into action by rapidly deploying a large conscript army within a clearly defined Anglo-French defensive plan.

It is typical of the muddled thinking about defence matters before the war that the Admiralty's defeat in 1911, and the move towards a continental commitment, had no effect on the Government's vast expenditure on warships, nor upon naval strategy. The Cawdor Programme of 1904 was sufficient to give Britain an unassailable lead in capital ships. 'No matter how fast Germany built', writes Jonathan Steinberg, 'as long as Britain remained resolute, the gap between the powers remained the same. . . . By implication, the German fleet could never meet the threat for which it was designed, nor grow rapidly enough to make that threat less ominous.'[7] Britain won the naval race in 1914, but the victory was irrelevant: the war at sea turned out to be an affair of submarines, blockades and technical superiority. Even if a 'new Trafalgar' had been fought, it would have been irrelevant to the security of France and the outcome of the Schlieffen Plan.

As a result of diplomatic ambiguity and military weakness, Britain found herself in August 1914 in a position where she was unable to influence events or to deter Germany. How did this situation come about? Sir Edward Grey was a man of great intelligence, experience and power; the Army Chiefs of Staff were far from being the blimps and idiots that it was fashionable, until recently, to portray them as being. The answer to many of the problems posed by Britain's equivocal position in 1914 stems from the ideological framework within which Edwardian foreign policy was made.

IV

From the early nineteenth century onwards, two conflicting traditions have contended for prominence in the making of British foreign policy: traditions that are usefully summed up by the descriptions 'idealist' and 'realist'.[8]

The 'realist' tradition, expressed in some measure by such diverse exponents as Palmerston and Churchill, saw Britain's pre-eminence as the result of war and conquest. Britain's military might was the shield that had saved her from Napoleon and protected her while she grew rich and developed her unique institutions, and the sword that had enabled her to conquer half the world. Conflict and war, they believed, were an inevitable part of man's condition, and the pursuit of the national interest was a legitimate concern of governments. It was, therefore, the duty of governments to provide sufficient armed force to secure that interest.

The 'idealist' tradition developed by nineteenth-century radicals such as Cobden and Bright, and put into occasional practice by Gladstone, also grew out of the immense wealth and security of mid nineteenth-century Britain. Secure behind their fortuitous thirty miles of protective water, and grown rich through the equally fortuitous combination of circumstances that had made their country the first industrial nation, many Britons felt able to view the problems of the world with a proprietorial and critical gaze, and to draw from contemplation of advanced institutions of their own country an extremely optimistic philosophy of international politics.

Man, the idealists believed, had reached a stage, epitomised by their own country, where his natural condition was peace. If some nations, such as Belgium, Turkey and above all Russia, showed, by Congo atrocities, Bulgarian horrors or Persian persecutions, that they still had some way to go in the march to civilisation, it was the duty of those who had already reached that state to encourage these laggards, if not with gunboats, then at least with the full weight of their moral broadsides. As for disputes between nations, these could be settled by reason and conciliation: wars, therefore, were obsolete, as well as expensive, diversionary and a sport for the aristocracy, and foreign entanglements and armed forces were unnecessary and unacceptable.

The Edwardian 'Establishment' seems to have been deeply imbued with the realist tradition. The speeches, correspondence and writings of the Royal Family and its advisers, the chiefs of the armed forces and most Army and naval officers, the Civil Service, including the officials surrounding Grey at the Foreign Office, the owners and editors of virtually the whole of the popular press, the masters of public schools and many university professors and churchmen were deeply permeated by its influence.

The idealist tradition, upheld by a small but talented and articulate group of editors, politicians and writers, was much less pervasive, and carried little weight in the Establishment; its strength lay in the massive prestige of its Gladstonian heritage, and above all in the fact that its main vehicle, the Liberal Party, held power during these crucial years. At the time of the Agadir crisis in 1911, no fewer than fifteen out of nineteen members of the Cabinet had some sympathy with neutralist and pacifist ideas.

Certainly until 1912, most of Grey's policies were abhorrent to the Radicals. They feared that he had made secret agreements with the French, and that he was dragging his feet over attempts to mend fences with the Germans. They regarded the Russian entente with particular distaste, claiming that Grey had sold out to the Russians in Persia; and, having 'been taught to writhe at the merest mention of cruelty and oppression',[9] they duly squirmed when Grey seemed to be condoning Tsarist oppression in that country. Above all, the Radicals resented a constantly growing expenditure on arms: this ran directly counter to the Gladstonian tradition and seemed to confirm the dire prognostications of their more pessimistic prophets.

The Radical revolt against the Government's foreign policy culminated in a major confrontation following the Agadir crisis of 1911. Shocked by the realisation that Britain and Germany had nearly gone to war, Radical members of the Cabinet began to ask embarrassing questions about the precise nature of Britain's commitments to France. The Prime Minister deemed it wise to appoint a Cabinet Committee on Foreign Affairs, in which he and Grey for the first time revealed the existence of the military conversations with France. On 27 November Radical discontent exploded in a bitter Commons debate on foreign affairs in which Grey's alleged secretiveness, the weakness of parliamentary control, and the direction of Britain's affairs were attacked with unprecedented ferocity.

Throughout 1911 and early 1912, Grey and the Foreign Office faced their greatest challenge from the Radical wing of the party. Most members of the Cabinet and a large section of the Commons put Grey and his policies under enormous pressure, and there is some evidence that this pressure resulted in a change of course in Grey's policy which had a significant bearing on Britain's position at the time of the crisis of 1914.

From 1912 onwards, Grey became far more critical of Russia's activities in Persia and allowed the movement towards Anglo-Russian military co-operation to languish. Towards Germany, accepting Lewis Harcourt's suggestion that Germany's restlessness could be calmed by the acquisition of territory at the expense of Portugal, he adopted a policy that twenty years later would be called 'appeasement'. During the Balkan Wars he played a role of arbiter and honest broker that struck a responsive chord in the Radical breast; it seemed to the idealists that Grey had at last discovered the truth of man's innate reasonableness, and to the Germans that Britain had resumed that same detachment that had allowed her to view indulgently the crushing of France in 1870. It was in his schizophrenic attitude to the Entente that Grey's change of course was perhaps most damaging: on the one hand he encouraged naval co-operation, which in its strategic implications went further than any previous commitment; on the other hand his disavowals of any diplomatic obligation to France grew in frequency and vehemence. Cambon's efforts to obtain clarification of Britain's position met with obstinate prevarication. In the Cabinet and the Commons the Foreign Secretary and the Prime Minister lost no opportunity to declare Britain's freedom from engagements, a sentiment that was no doubt as welcome in the Willhelmstrasse as it was in the offices of the *Manchester Guardian*. It was not surprising that Bethmann Hollweg was tempted to gamble on British neutrality, that the French Assembly passed new conscription laws which increased their armed forces by many times the size of the BEF, or that General Wilson should dream of the end of 'Squiff and his filthy cabinet'.

Whether it was Radical pressure or personal inclination that caused Grey's diplomacy to move even further in the direction of ambiguity after 1912, it is true that many of the constraints that bound him stemmed not just from the political power of Radical pressure groups, but also from the far more intimidating 'unspoken assumptions' of the mid-Victorian idealist tradition.

It had become accepted that Britain as a democracy could not, in Grey's words, 'enter into permanent engagements with another power', although she had done so many times in the past and would do so again in the future. It was an unchallenged assumption amongst politicians that compulsory military service in peacetime was unthinkable; Britain was forced to rely, as a reflection of her diplomatic will, on the six divisions of the BEF, which, as 'the best possible Army that time and circumstances allowed', had only been obtained by Haldane 'in the face of hostile critics both within and outside his party, in the Cabinet, the Commons and the Press'.[10] It is symptomatic of the stranglehold that the idealist tradition held on British policy that Haldane was able to achieve this limited goal because of constant and pious disavowals of the need for conscription, and the support of that eminent Gladstonian Sir Henry Campbell-Bannerman.

The real power of the idealist tradition in Edwardian politics lay not so much in the political manoeuvring of its acolytes in the Cabinet and the Commons, but in the lingering beliefs and assumptions about the limits of political action that restricted the options of the decision-makers who lived in the long shadow of its dead heroes.

The idealists were far more influential than their numbers warranted, because they rode on the back of a great tradition, and because they commanded a majority in the Cabinet. Perhaps their greatest weapon, however, lay in the fact that Sir Edward Grey 'instinctively shared many of the principles which drove Radicals to protest against his policy',[11] and in many ways was 'much nearer to the Radicals than he was to Eyre Crowe or Arthur Nicolson of the Foreign Office'.[12]

At first sight, Grey, the Liberal imperialist and member of the Liberal League, seems to belong clearly within the realist tradition. He was a strong advocate of Empire, and supported Milner for most of the Boer War. He believed in the inevitability of competition and conflict between nations, and regularly sided in Cabinet discussions with the group demanding higher military spending. Since the 1890s he had made no secret of his suspicion of German intentions and his determination to thwart them. In all these ways Grey's views were very close to those of his officials, but there was another side to Grey's philosophy and that made him surprisingly amenable to the idealist critique.

Grey believed strongly that Britain's interests lay in maintaining the balance of power, that rather simplistic conception that John Bright had dismissed as a 'foul idol', but which was none the less part of the 'enlightened' tradition of equipoise and rationality from which Bright himself derived. Grey's belief in the balance of power was coupled with a conviction that Britain had a special mission to act as the fulcrum of that balance, throwing her weight, preferably through reason and concilation rather than war, between contending continental power blocks. Underlying this was an assumption that disputes were essentially soluble, and that the protagonists were motivated by, and amenable to, reason. This conviction not only made it difficult for Grey, like Neville Chamberlain after him, to comprehend or deal with irrational forces, but also made him very sympathetic to many of the optimistic assumptions of the idealists.

Grey's attitude to the use of armed force was not as clear-cut as may appear from his sympathy with the Navy League; indeed, his enthusiasm for the Navy pointed to the existence of a characteristic equivocation. Despite the fact that the logic of Grey's diplomacy pointed to the conclusion that a future war would be fought on land in Europe, his advocacy of a 'blue water' fleet presupposed that any future war would be a naval contest, one that would be defensive, detached, balancing and comparatively bloodless – a reflection of Grey's character, perhaps, but not of his diplomacy. Grey had in fact a deep aversion to war, as was manifested in his helplessness and incompetence once war broke out.[13] While reason might convince him of its likelihood, he tended to avert his gaze and close his mind to the prospect of what would happen if reason and statemanship broke down. 'If we are engaged in a war,' he told Parliament with extraordinary naïveté in

August 1914, 'we shall suffer but little more than we shall suffer if we stand aside.'

V

If the Radical idealist wing of the party was strong enough to distort Government policy, why was it not strong enough to keep Britain out of the war? Right up to the last minute it seemed that Arthur Nicolson's fear that 'supposing a collision did occur between France and Germany we should waver as to what course to pursue until it was too late'[14] came very close to fulfilment. On 30 July, four days before the declaration of war, John Burns recorded that the Cabinet had 'decided not to decide',[15] and next day Lewis Harcourt was convinced that 'this Cabinet will not go into the war'.[16]

The nature of Britain's military commitment was in doubt even longer. On the very day that the Cabinet belatedly accepted Britain's obligation to fight in certain circumstances, the Prime Minister, in a letter that must to some extent justify Amery's contention that Asquith held 'a season ticket on the line of least resistance', proclaimed that 'the despatch of the Expeditionary Force to help France at this moment is out of the question and would serve no object'.[17] Indeed, it was not until 6 August, two days after the declaration of war, that the decision was made to dispatch the BEF.

Despite this extraordinary procrastination, and despite Ponsonby's claim that nine-tenths of the Liberal Party in the Commons was neutralist, and the belief of Asquith and Churchill that three-quarters of the Cabinet would not countenance it, Britain did go to war. How can the complete eclipse of pacifism and idealism be explained?

Part of the answer lies in the fact that, despite their brave showing in the Cabinet and Commons battles of 1911 and 1912, the strength and confidence of the Radicals seems to have declined greatly by 1914. Ironically, at the very time that it seemed that the idealist tradition had reasserted its influence over the foreign policy of the Liberal Party, many of its assumptions were beginning to crumble.

Norman Angell's rational but naïve contention that war was obsolete, because of its economic implications, was particularly damaging to the pacifist and idealist cause. Angell expressed the perennial dream of eternal peace in modern and scientific terms, and at the same time undermined the Radical attack upon 'Liberal imperialist' foreign policy by challenging Hobson's theory of the inevitability of imperialist conflict. If war was unreasonable and unlikely, the need to control the actions of their own government was less pressing. Angell's arguments seemed to be borne out by the obvious lack of belligerence on the part of British business interests, which had the effect of 'hypnotising' the anti-war movement during these years.[18] The inference was that, if war was not the inevitable culmination of the economic and imperialist process, and was indeed inimical to that process, it could come about only as a result of the irrational militarism of Britain's enemies. It was clear that, if another crisis occurred, it would not be easy for Radicals to withhold their support from a Liberal government that resisted irrational militarism.

Lloyd George's 'betrayal' in his Mansion House speech of July 1911 not only deprived the Radicals of their most forceful leader, but also brought them face to face with certain contradictions, within their critique of international politics, that undermined the very basis of their philosophy. In 1911 Britain stood on the brink of war with Germany, and many of the abstractions of Victorian idealism melted in the fires of an imminent cataclysm.

These unpalatable but inescapable realities raised questions that undermined most of the tenets of the pacifist and neutralist case. Was it logical to decry attempts to maintain the balance of power, now that Britain's safety so obviously depended on the equilibrium of Europe? If maintenance of the equilibrium meant supporting France against Germany, was it rational to object so strongly to the Entente? Was it consistent, in the existing European situation, to advocate both disarmament and isolation? Above all, was it reasonable or ethical for the Radicals to refuse to support their own Liberal Government if it resisted aggression by a power whose system and philosophy they so much feared and hated? Even in 1911, one wonders if the logic of realities was already so strong that 'a "Belgium" was really necessary to bring them into line, should the Government opt for involvement in a continental struggle to preserve the balance of power'.[19]

Indeed, the attitude of the Radical Left towards pacifism had always been equivocal. Rivalling their belief in the inherent rationality of mens' actions was a powerful tradition of moral militancy, which found the use of force in a just cause acceptable and even desirable. Since the middle of the nineteenth century, the cult of the 'Christian warrior', the growth of military imagery and organisation in evangelical religion, and the acceptance of imperialism as a prelude to missionary conquest had become important components of the ideology of the idealist left.[20] In Edwardian England, militancy, whether it was expressed over Ireland, in industrial disputes, or in the struggle for women's suffrage, was perhaps the most characteristic feature of the age, and it was as much a part of the emotional baggage of the left as it was of any other section of society. When it was combined with the peculiarly British form of moralistic patriotism, which claimed a special role for Britain as the arbiter of world affairs and the upholder of Christian civilisation, these ideas made it comparatively easy to accept that the decision by a British government to go to war was tantamount to the proclamation of a moral crusade.

VI

By about 27 July 1914, Grey had become convinced that the militarists were controlling policy in Berlin and that Germany was exacerbating the European crisis rather than helping to solve it. He was enough of a realist to understand the implication of this development, and all his energies from 27 July to 3 August were bent on the task of convincing the Cabinet and then the Commons that Britain might have to go to war.[21]

On the whole, the Cabinet was extraordinarily ignorant about foreign affairs, partly because of the concern of many members with domestic matters, and partly because of a secretiveness on the part of Grey that most of them were happy to condone. In July the Cabinet's time was taken up almost exclusively with Irish affairs, which were entering a critical phase at the very moment the Sarajevo assassination took place. Ministers had not discussed foreign affairs for a month when Grey brought up the Serbian crisis on 24 July, and for many ministers it took time to adjust their minds to an apparently trivial Balkan dispute. As Winston Churchill recalled in prose that matched the momentousness of the occasion, 'the parishes of Fermanagh and Tyrone faded back into the mists and squalls of Ireland and a strange light began immediately but with perceptible gradation to fall and glow upon the map of Europe'.[22] The perceptible gradations that Churchill detected were at first clear only to the more informed and acute members of the Cabinet: 'Why four great powers should fight over Serbia no fellow can understand' complained John Burns.[23] Over the next few weeks it was the task of Grey to make the Cabinet aware of the significance of these developments.

It soon became clear during the endless Cabinet meetings and private conclaves of the next few days that Grey's task was not as daunting as it might have appeared some months before. As we now

understand much more clearly, the apparently overwhelming neutralist group of some fifteen ministers was neither as coherent nor as
fixed in its position as sometimes appeared before the war. The group
lacked leadership: the only real candidate, Lloyd George, probably
had the gifts to mobilise men to avoid wars as well as to win them, but
he had shown in 1911 that he was no pacifist, and in late July he was
being briefed about military realities by one of General Wilson's
aides. To some extent, realism grows with nearness to the realities of
power, and, when these experienced politicians were faced with an
actual crisis, without the leisure to adopt theoretical positions, they
eventually responded to its exigencies. Few of them were opposed to
war in any circumstances; it is quite correct to describe them as
'waverers' rather than pacifists or neutralists, and certainly not correct to describe them as idealists.[24] The problem faced by Asquith and
Grey over the next few days was to discover the particular gradation of
circumstances which would allow various members of the Cabinet, in
good conscience, to jettison their opposition to war.

One circumstance that certainly would not satisfy the Cabinet
would be a war in support of Russia over Serbia. Many members of
the Cabinet, and almost all the Liberal press, remained fixated on the
Balkan aspects of the crisis and seemed unwilling or incapable of
exploring its western European dimension. 'We care as little for Belgrade as Belgrade for Manchester', proclaimed the *Manchester Guardian* on 30 July, and went on to ask, 'Why should the Slav be so much
dearer to us than the Teuton?' The next day the *Guardian* woke up to
the fact that Britain 'by some hidden contract had been technically
committed, behind her back, to the ruinous madness of a share in the
wicked gamble of a war between two militarist leagues on the Continent'.

In the Cabinet meeting of 2 August, Grey, with belated candour,
spelled out the extent of Britain's commitments to France: 'We have
led France to rely on us', he explained, 'and unless we support her in
her agony I cannot continue at the Foreign Office.'[25] It was at this
meeting that the Cabinet accepted the probability of war by author-
ising Grey to tell the French ambassador that the Royal Navy would
protect the coast of France from any German aggression. Whether or
not the resistance of Radical ministers had been softened by the
suggestion that Britain would be involved solely in a naval war, their
decision was the death blow for British neutrality and a capitulation
for the idealists.

A Cabinet that was apparently overwhelmingly neutralist had at last accepted the reality of Britain's vital interests. Britain could not afford to see France defeated. Her ports would become German naval bases and her dockyards would turn out German battleships; France's colonies would provide raw material for German factories, and her enslaved economy would make Germany an overwhelmingly industrial giant. All this had been clear for at least ten years, but it was only accepted when Britain stood on the brink of war. It is significant that it was accepted before the question of Belgian independence became an issue.

It is difficult to avoid the conclusion that the crucial *volte-face* in the Cabinet on 2 August 1914 was the result of consideration of *Realpolitik* rather than moral obligation. The numerous Cabinet meetings and conclaves which took place during the stifling days of late July and early August, with their Byzantine disputes about the exact nature of Britain's obligations and the frenetic searching for formulae that would enable them to be fulfilled, were little more than a prolonged placation of the Liberal conscience. To make the decision palatable to the Cabinet, the Liberal Party, and even to Grey himself, what was needed was, in the cryptic phrase of the supreme realist, Churchill, 'a casus belli wh[ich] everyone here w[oul]d understand'.[26] The ghost of idealism required that the decision for war should be expressed in terms of moral crusade.

A convenient focus for that crusade was the issue of Belgian independence. Britain had shown herself willing in 1870 to ignore the Treaty of 1839, and there were several ways she could have plausibly avoided supporting Belgium without outraging international law. Asquith told the King on 29 July that supporting Belgium was matter of 'policy rather than of legal obligation'.[27] On 30 July Grey rejected a German pledge to respect Belgian neutrality and concealed another German approach, on 1 August, from his colleagues. For some ministers the Belgian issue was a 'heaven sent excuse for supporting a war';[28] for Grey it provided a rich theme for his muddled but highly effective speech of 3 August.

VII

The declaration of war on 4 August can be seen as a victory of the forces of realism over the forces of idealism in Britain's foreign relations. It was clear that the strength of the idealist traditions which had done so much to shape Britain's policy in the pre-war years had been greatly overestimated. It is possible to explain the processes by which the idealists were able to influence policy in terms of their influence within the ruling Liberal Party, and the particular susceptibility of the Foreign Secretary to their point of view, but where did the strength of the realists lie?

It is difficult to discover any formal ways in which the right influenced diplomatic decision-making, although it has long been argued by determinist historians, who see the First World War as the inevitable culmination of late nineteenth-century imperialism and capitalism, that the agents of these forces, businessmen, armaments manufacturers, generals and admirals, unrepresentative governments and the aristocratic and bourgeois agents of their foreign policy, had a powerful influence upon the making of foreign policy. Professor Fischer has shown that, in the case of Germany, such arguments are difficult to refute;[29] but, much as one might suspect similar tendencies to exist in England, most historical inquiry has tended to deny the existence of such pressure.

It has been suggested, for instance, that many people in Britain welcomed war as a diversion from the threat of industrial strife and civil war over Ireland. Certainly Asquith realised that the war crisis would 'have the effect of throwing into the background the lurid pictures of civil war in Ulster',[30] and later wrote about the 'luck' that had saved him from painful decisions over Ireland in July 1914, but there is little evidence to support an argument that any persons or groups were actively seeking a diversionary war in 1914.

The armed forces certainly strove mightily to influence governments to support the strategic option which favoured their own interests, but pressure from the Army and Navy through the Committee on Imperial Defence (CID) was singularly ineffective in influencing diplomacy. Victory or defeat in CID meetings, as shown in 1911, had little bearing on the shape of subsequent military planning. The failure of the generals, with their strong inclinations towards conscription and their belief that, to have any impact upon British policy, the ententes should be transformed into alliances, was a major reason for Britain's helplessness in 1914.

Despite the fact that sources of strategic commodities such as oil were becoming the concern of the Foreign Office, the contention that business interests had any significant direct influence on foreign policy is also difficult to substantiate. Those business pressure groups that existed at this time, such as the Anglo-German Friendship League, were working for peace, not advocating an imperialist war, while the Radical belief that 'merchants of death', and 'armour plate' had an evil influence upon British foreign policy has recently been exposed as yet another rickety plank in the collapsing edifice of Radical mythology.[31]

Perhaps the greatest barrier to external influence on the making of foreign policy was the nature of the Foreign Office itself. For various reasons the permanent officials who shaped policy were particularly impervious to outside pressures. They were educated in the classic Victorian tradition, which ensured that they were not only ignorant of business and commerce but also contemptuous of what they regarded as its base and contemptible motivations. Moreover, their conduct was governed by a proud tradition of incorruptibility, and by strict rules of conduct such as the Bryce Memorandum of 1886. Their formulation of policy was based implicitly on a belief in *Primat der Aussenpolitik*, which allowed no place for the distortion of policy by trivial and short-term domestic interests. They believed in a dispassionate formulation of policy which derived a classical and largely static analysis of the balance of international forces, and the place that history had given England within that system.[32]

The Foreign Office officials were comparatively impervious to external pressures, but they were themselves formidably placed to wield influence. There is no doubt that almost all the officials had Unionist sympathies. Many of them had personal links with the Court, with conscriptionists and hard-liners such as Henry Wilson, and with various right-wing journalists. Their inclination was strongly in favour of a 'realist' foreign policy, and almost all of them accepted Crowe's belief that the Kaiser was seeking 'the establishment of a German hegemony at first in Europe and eventually in the world'.[33] The Radicals were convinced that Grey was the 'prisoner of his officials', but recent research suggests that 'the influence of the Foreign Office did not match the skill and elegance with which its advice was often proffered'.[34] Officials had a well defined conception of their advisory role, which they rarely overstepped, and from 1906 onwards they were confronted with a veritable keep of defensive detachment in the shape of Sir Edward Grey.

Domestic pressures were a crucial factor in Britain's decision to go to war in 1914, but they did not conform to the patterns of *Primat der Innenpolitik* that Fischer has detected in imperial Germany, nor did they stem from any desire for a diversionary war. In Britain, pro-war sentiment manifested itself more subtly, through the operation of party political machinery reacting to the tremendous weight of public opinion, which showed itself willing, and even anxious, to accept the challenge of war.

It is difficult, in the light of the appalling events that followed the decision to go to war, to accept that anything as trivial as party political considerations played a part in that decision. Politicians had little understanding of the kind of war that would follow their decision, however, and there existed a bitterness, one could almost say hatred, between the parties that made the prospect of coalition or a transfer of power abhorrent. Those leaders in both parties who were prepared to go to war were certainly aware of the susceptibility of Cabinet ministers to the prospect of loss of power. Asquith and Grey constantly made it clear that they would resign if the Cabinet voted for neutrality, and the Conservatives made it clear that they supported Grey and would continue his policy if the Government fell.

The reluctant majority in the Cabinet were aware, therefore, that they could not prevent the implementation of Grey's policy, which would continue under a coalition or Tory administration. The balance of political power in Britain was tilted in favour of fulfilling the tacit commitments that Grey had undertaken, and those commitments would be fulfilled despite Grey's refusal to admit them and even if Grey retired to the back benches.

Even before war had been declared there was evidence that the tentative attitude of the Government, both in preparing for and in taking the decision to go to war, was out of step with the national mood. Lloyd George, whose intuitive rapport with public opinion was one of his most valuable political assets, was impressed by, and may well have been influenced by, the cheering crowds who lined the streets through which he drove to attend the agonised conclaves of the decision-makers. Indeed, it is doubtful whether any Cabinet minister or member of Parliament was unaware of the public mood and unmoved by it in making his decision. Labour politicians soon realised the dangers of going against public opinion by 'attaching themselves to . . . a potentially ruinous foreign policy based on radicalism', and 'the perils of attempting to stand against the government and against public opinion'.[35]

The Belgian issue was not only a moral escape route for the idealists, but also 'proved to be a catalyst which unleashed the many emotions, rationalisations and glorifications of war which had long been part of the British climate of opinion'.[36] In August 1914 politicians, their sensitive antennae tuned to the nuances of the public mood, recognised that war was more acceptable to the British people than a dishonourable peace, and acted accordingly.

VIII

It is possible to infer that the politicians' assessment of the popular mood played a role in their decision to support Grey, that the Foreign Office had been right in its belief that the strength of pacifism and neutralism was greatly overestimated, and that popular opinion was favourable to the idea of war, but is it possible to go further than inference? Any assessment of public attitudes must be tentative and impressionistic, but there are two ways in which the problem can be approached. One can examine the way people actually responded to the challenge of war, which gives retrospective insights into the nature of the pre-war mood; and one can assess the corpus of extant information available to late Victorian and Edwardian Englishmen, on the assumption that attitudes and opinions were formed largely from this source.

The response of the British people to the war was unequivocal. 'The whole of youth', wrote an observer, 'rushed with blind nobility, but with utter heedlessness of causes, into the arena of war at the first possible moment.'[37] Within weeks of the outbreak of war volunteers flocked to the recruiting booths at the rate of 100,000 a month for eighteen months. By 1916, Haldane's dream of a Hegelian army had been made flesh in Kitchener's three million volunteers, who, 'grimly baptised in the bloody waters of the Somme, deserved the title of Nation in Arms no less than those of Scharnhorst'.[38] Over six million British men were directly involved in the four-year war, showing themselves willing, unlike their French, Russian or German counterparts, to accept unbelievable suffering without being forced into mutiny or revolution.

The whole population showed itself willing to slave in mines and factories, to accept shortages and privations, loss of freedom and authoritarian government, and eventually to mobilise for total war with a continuing enthusiasm and resilience that was unmatched by any of the more overtly militaristic nations of Europe. Pacifists and anti-war propagandists found themselves an isolated and persecuted minority, in many cases forced to accept the necessity of war, if not the commitment of personal combat. It is difficult to believe that this enthusiasm for conflict and acceptance of militarism was born entirely out of the war itself.

Are we to conclude, therefore, that the Edwardian masses were 'howling for war'; and, if they were, how can we tell? Professor

Robbins is right to warn of the dangers inherent in any attempt to assess public opinion.[39] Even if we can establish a picture of the 'cultural climate' or the 'public mood', 'the precise connection with any particular policies is hard to establish', and it is indeed 'a far jump from the tracing of cultural influences to the formulation of public policy'. In this instance, however, we are dealing, to use A. J. P. Taylor's categories, with the foreign policy of 'action' rather than of 'talk': going to war requires the participation of the population, and it is this participation that must be explained.

Despite the insularity of the Foreign Office, officials were very aware of the limitations placed upon them by public tolerance. Grey's diplomacy was grounded firmly in the belief that, while 'public opinion may not be a great statesman', and should have little part in policy-making, no Foreign Secretary could afford to divorce himself from the public will, particularly in a decision to go to war. In total war the morale and unity of the masses is as important as that of the Army, and history is full of examples of disasters that befall regimes that undertake unpopular wars. Statesmen make wars, but the people fight them, and the historian must try to explain not only the diplomatic mechanics of Britain's entry into the First World War, but also the nation's ready acceptance of the decision: the popular will to fight without which international agreements and declarations of war would indeed be mere 'scraps of paper'.

It is one thing to analyse the body of information and argument available to Edwardians, but quite another to assess its impact on the Edwardian *Weltanschauung*. It is true that 'to pick on one volume as epitomising a general mood is a hazardous enterprise'. If we are to draw any conclusion about the national mood, it is not enough for the historian casually to mention Seeley or Kipling. His analysis must be spread across the whole spectrum of Edwardian and late-Victorian 'knowledge', examining not only books that historians have found 'influential' and articles in serious newspapers, but also the banal and more pervasive influence of the popular press, music-hall songs, school textbooks, childrens' books and comics, speech-day orations and examination questions. He must consider not only the philosophies and polemics of élitist opinion-formers, but also remember that fashionable ideas are diffused in a vulgarised and sloganised form through the popular press to the semi-educated, and even, *via* opinion leaders such as Robert Tressall's unsuccessful but archetypal hero, to the ignorant and the illiterate.[40]

To a large extent peoples' attitudes and opinions are dependent upon their knowledge. That knowledge is controlled by available information, and the analysis of that information by writers and journalists, politicians and pressure groups. People cannot form opinions about political issues in a void. What one can say with some confidence, is that the information and analysis available to most Britons in the Edwardian era was overwhelmingly imbued with the values of the political right rather than the left, or, expressed in terms of the earlier analysis, those of 'realism' rather than 'idealism'. The problem of whether the media reflected or stimulated these ideas is academic: either way, their pervasiveness in the media is evidence of their currency in the country.

While the serious press, those newspapers read by a few thousand educated people, was more equally divided between left and right than it is today, the popular press was overwhelmingly jingoistic, fascinated by military matters, and suspicious of German intentions. A profitable market existed for books dealing with war scares, invasion, and spies. The public schools were becoming increasingly militaristic both in their organisation and in the values that they sought to inculcate, while all schoolchildren were presented with a view of the world in which Britain's past military conquests were given pride of place. The many youth movements that flourished at this time were often overtly militaristic, and were certainly inimical to pacifism; it has been suggested that no fewer than 40 per cent of children and adolescents belonged to one of these movements in Edwardian times.[41] Both schools and youth gatherings welcomed representatives of the many pressure groups advocating conscription, naval expansion and military preparedness.

It would take many volumes and an army of historians to assess the predominant values of Edwardian society, but it is possible to suggest certain recurrent themes that have particular relevance to the popular response in August 1914: an attitude towards war that was tragically unrealistic; a belief that Britain had a special role in the history of the world; and what might be called the diffusion of the 'public-school ethic'.

The most important fact about the Edwardian attitude to war is that only a handful of people realised what a twentieth-century war would entail. Those few remarkably prescient writers, such as Bloch and Wells, who accurately foretold its nature were swamped by the optimistic images of the popular media. A future war, the people were told, would either be a spectacular naval contest culminating in a 'new Trafalgar' or a land war that would be brief and explosive; the 'spirit of the race' would at last test itself in a contest in which bravery, *élan* and physical superiority would be the deciding qualities. Much writing about war was couched in the vulgar terms of 'Social Darwinism', which presupposed the inevitability, and even the desirability, of conflict, and hinted that the 'logic of evolution' pointed to an eventual titanic contest between the two contending world giants, Britain and Germany. In brief, popular Edwardian writers and journalists projected an image of future war that was far from intimidating: the prospect of a historical culmination that was not only natural and inevitable, but also promised to be romantic, exhilarating and short.[42]

Another assumption that was implicit in much Edwardian popular writing was the idea that Britain had a unique mission in the history of the world. The superiority of British institutions, her unique development and her success as an imperial power had given her a special and elevated role to play in world affairs. This peculiarly moralistic patriotism was common to both idealists and realists. On the right it was expressed in terms of Britain's role as custodian of the *pax Britannica*; it was right that Britain should be strong, and if she was forced to exercise that strength it was acceptable, because she was a force for good in the world and had the interests of world harmony at heart. On the left there existed an equally powerful belief in Britain's special position, and a conviction that a 'just war' could be fought in pursuit of a sufficiently elevated cause. The Belgian issue proved to be a *Leitmotiv* which fused the moralistic and the custodial streams of British patriotism into a powerful crusading torrent.

A third, and perhaps the most significant, element in the pre-war climate of opinion was the popularisation and diffusion of the codes and values of the Victorian public school. Because they were identified with success, and with those heroes who had made Britain pre-eminent, it is possible to detect their influence at all levels of Edwardian society: they were expressed not only in the editorials of serious journals, but also in the popular press, in the textbooks of children at elementary school, in advertisements, in the rituals and literature of youth movements, and even in the codes governing the most proletarian of the new mass sports. The philosophy of the ruling class permeated down to the lowest levels of Edwardian society, where it mingled with the not dissimilar values of evangelical moralism.

The public schools by their very nature were closed institutions, and were organised along military lines, with strict rules of conduct, hierarchies and disciplines, and an emphasis on the inculcation of military values. By the early twentieth century, these tendencies had developed, as Haldane noted in 1907, into a more overt militarism. Speakers from the National Service League, the Imperial Maritime League and other propagandist organisations were frequent and welcome visitors, and the role that these institutions had always held as nurseries for the officer class was becoming more pronounced.[43]

There is little evidence, however, that the public schools were hotbeds of the sort of aggressive militarism that existed in Wilhelmine Germany, nor were such sentiments current in the country at large. The public-school values were those of militancy rather than militarism: the moral and historical role of their country was unique, and therefore demanded complete loyalty and, if necessary, self-sacrifice; if the cause was just, a man must do his duty with courage, discipline, and sportsmanship. There may have been excitement and anticipation of war as a unique stage upon which these values could be enacted, but there was little desire for conquest or world domination: these battles had already been won.

The realist tradition seems to have been far more decisive in moulding the values of Edwardian society, even at its lower levels, than the idealistic internationalism which influenced much Government policy in the areas of defence and foreign affairs. It was a philosophy that made it very difficult to go against one's government in time of crisis, and one which had a unique relevance in the testing years to come, in helping men not only to resist the slow torture of the trenches and fulfil the masochistic strategies of the generals, but also to bear with fortitude the austerities of total war. One can only speculate as to whether it would have allowed a government to introduce conscription or to enter into a full alliance with a continental power.

Now that some of 'the vast fog of information' that Churchill saw enveloping 'the fatal steps to Armageddon' has been dispelled, it may perhaps be time for historians to turn their energies towards penetrating the obscurities that surround the popular response to the war. The subject is elusive, but of crucial significance. The policymakers' assessment of public opinion, however mistaken, was an essential element in the structuring of Britain's diplomatic, strategic and military stance before the war. A belated realisation of the true nature of the popular mood seems to have been an important factor in the decision of the politicians to go to war. Above all, it was the values of Edwardian society and the will of the Edwardian masses that made it possible for the war to be fought and won; as Michael Howard suggests, in an image of great insight and evocative power, without 'that great reserve of enthusiasm and patriotism and endurance built up over a century of careful training . . . the military instruments of that will were as useless as empty suits of armour'.[44]

List of Abbreviations

AHR	*American Historical Review*
BJIS	*British Journal of International Studies*
BD	*British Documents on the Origins of the War, 1898–1914*, ed. G. P. Gooch and H. Temperley, 11 vols (1926–38)
BL	British Library
EcHR	*Economic History Review*
EHR	*English Historical Review*
HJ	*Historical Journal*
HWJ	*History Workshop Journal*
IHS	*Irish Historical Studies*
IRSH	*International Review of Social History*
JASS	*Journal of American Statistical Society*
JBS	*Journal of British Studies*
JCH	*Journal of Contemporary History*
JLE	*Journal of Law and Economics*
JRSS	*Journal of the Royal Statistical Society*
NR	*National Review*
OH	*Oral History*
P & P	*Past and Present*
PD	*Parliamentary Debates*
PP	*Parliamentary Papers*
PRO	Public Record Office
QR	*Quarterly Review*
TRHS	*Transactions of the Royal Historical Society*
VS	*Victorian Studies*
YBESR	*Yorkshire Bulletin of Economic and Social Research*

Bibliographical Notes

Note: For books, place of publication is London unless otherwise stated.

1. THE STANDARD OF LIVING, 1890–1914

At the national level, the reports of the Board of Trade provide a great deal of the necessary statistical material. Of particular interest are *Changes in Rates of Wages and Hours of Labour* and *Standard Time Rates of Wages*. The major findings are summarised in the *Annual Abstract of Labour Statistics*. Equally indispensable are the reports on working-class conditions *Memorandum on the Consumption of Food and the Cost-of-Living of the Working Classes in Urban Districts, 1903* (*PP*, 1903, LXVII), and *1904* (*PP*, 1905, LXXXIV), and the *Board of Trade Inquiry into Working-Class Rents, Housing, and Retail Prices, 1905* (*PP*, 1908, CVII) and *1912* (*PP*, 1913, LXVI). Some of the most important series have also been assembled in B. R. Mitchell and P. Deane, *Abstract of British Historical Statistics* (Cambridge, 1962); and C. H. Feinstein, *National Income, Expenditure, and Output of the United Kingdom, 1855–1965* (Cambridge, 1972). The 'received view' of the period is derived from those who have used and added to the following material: G. H. wood, 'Real Wages and the Standard of Comfort Since 1850', *JRSS*, LXXIII (1909), repr. in E. M. Carus-Wilson (ed.), *Essays in Economic History*, vol. III (1962); A. L. Bowley, *Wages and Income in the United Kingdom since 1860* (Cambridge, 1937); and, more recently, E. H. Phelps Brown and M. Browne, *A Century of Pay* (1968). A further variant is offered by J: Kuczynski, in *A Short History of Labour Conditions Under Industrial Capitalism*, vol. I (1942). A brief but useful summary of the economic explanation of the check to real wages can be found in W. A. Lewis, *Growth and Fluctuations, 1870–1913* (1978). The regional and local evidence is frustratingly thin, but E. H. Hunt, *Regional Wage Variations in Britain, 1850–1914* (Oxford, 1973) is essential reading. For London there is Frances Wood, 'The Course of Real Wages in London, 1900–12', *JRSS*, LXXVII (1913); and, for Sheffield, S. Pollard, 'Wages and Earnings in the Sheffield Trades, 1851–1914', *YBESR*, VI (1954). At the industrial level, J. W. F. Rowe, *Wages in Practice and Theory* (1928), contains valuable information on five industries as well as important caveats for would-be users of the data. There is also much useful material in K. Burgess, *The Origins of British Industrial Relations* (1975). Further reading on coal should include A. Slaven, 'Earnings and Productivity in the Scottish Coal-mining Industry during the Nineteenth-Century: The Dixon Enterprises', in P. L. Payne (ed.), *Studies in Scottish Business History* (1967); and R. Walters, 'Labour Productivity in the South Wales Steam-coal Industry, 1870–1914', *EcHR*, XXVIII (1975). Finally, for a more general introduction to the subject, with a broader perspective, there is little to beat A. J. P. Taylor's chapter 'The Economy' in S. Nowell-Smith (ed.), *Edwardian England, 1901–1914* (1964). E. H. Phelps

Brown, *The Growth of British Industrial Relations* (1959) remains a useful source, and W. Ashworth, *An Economic History of England, 1870–1939* (1960), and S. Pollard and D. W. Crossley, *The Wealth of Britain 1085–1966* (1968) may also be consulted, although the latter's use of Kuczynski is sometimes confusing. Of the wealth of writing on the working class during the period, the following appear to offer the most important insights: G. Stedman Jones, *Outcast London* (Oxford, 1971) – although the analysis is really confined to the nineteenth century; P. N. Stearns, *Lives of Labour: Work in a Maturing Industrial Society* (1975); P. Thompson, *The Edwardians: The Remaking of British Society* (1975) – although the remarks on the standard of living are rather bland; and S. Meacham, *A Life Apart: The English Working Class 1890–1914* (1977).

2. POLITICAL ECONOMY IN EDWARDIAN ENGLAND:
THE TARIFF-REFORM CONTROVERSY

The contemporary literature on the economic issues involved in the tariff-reform campaign has so far received very little scholarly attention. Some of the more notable contributions are indicated in notes 13 and 15 to this chapter, but there is a wealth of easily accessible material not only in books and pamphlets but also in journals such as the *Contemporary Review*, the *National Review* and the *Economic Journal*. The best recent work on the theoretical side of the debate is W. A. Coats, 'Political Economy and the Tariff Reform Campaign of 1903', *JLE*, xi (1968). The best book on the movement as a whole is still B. Semmell's *Imperialism and Social Reform, 1895–1914* (1960), although it is somewhat lacking both on the wider economic background to tariff reform and on the substantive economic issues in the debate itself. In the circumstances É. Halévy's great *History of the English People in the Nineteenth Century* (revised edn, 1961), vols v and vi, is still very well worth reading. There is also an excellent short selection of materials relating to the economic arguments about free trade and protection in W. H. B. Court, *British Economic History 1870–1914: Commentary and Documents* (Cambridge, 1965), ch.9. The economic arguments about tariffs in relation to the budgetary strategy of the Liberal Government has been dealt with by H. V. Emy in 'The Impact of Financial Policy on English Party Politics before 1914', *HJ*, xv (1972). The connexion between the tariff debate and Empire is still expressed most clearly in the fiercely partisan but brilliant work of R. Jebb, *The Imperial Conferences* (1911), and the more judicious but equally stimulating work of W. K. Hancock in the *Survey of British Commonwealth Affairs* (Oxford, 1940), vol. ii, pt i, ch. i. S. H. Zebel's article 'The Genesis of Joseph Chamberlain's Tariff Reform Campaign of 1903', *JBS*, vii (1967), is useful in outlining Chamberlain's links with the earlier 'fair trade' and 'imperial federation' movements. For an assessment of the strengths and weaknesses of protectionist and preferentialist arguments in relation to Britain's international trade position, see S. B. Saul, *Studies in British Overseas Trade, 1870–1914* (Liverpool, 1960), especially chs 3 and 6. There is a useful summary of Saul's work in F. Crouzet, 'Trade and Empire: The British Experience from the Establishment of Free Trade until the First World War', in B. M. Ratcliffe (ed.), *Great Britain and her World, 1750–1914: Essays in Honour of W. O. Henderson* (Manchester, 1975).

R. J. S. Hoffman's *Great Britain and the German Trade Rivalry, 1875–1914* (1933) gives a fascinating account of the connection between protectionism and anti-Germanism in England. The politics of tariff reform are rather more thoroughly documented. Halévy and Semmell give useful accounts and there is some solid material in political biographies, especially P. Fraser's *Joseph Chamberlain* (1966) and D. Judd's *Balfour and the Empire: A Study in Imperial Evolution, 1874–1932* (1968). Julian Amery's *Life of Joseph Chamberlain*, vols v and vi (1951 and 1968) is also indispensable for source materials on Chamberlain's attitudes. The fortunes of the tariff-reformers within the Conservative Party after 1903 have been charted by P. Fraser, 'Unionism and Tariff Reform. The Crisis of 1906', *HJ*, v, no. 2 (1962); R. A. Rempel, *Unionists Divided: Arthur Balfour, Joseph Chamberlain and the Unionist Free Traders* (Newton Abbot, 1973); N. Blewett 'Free Fooders, Whole Hoggers, Balfourists: Factionalism within the Unionist Party, 1906–10', *HJ*, xi, no. 1 (1968); and R. J. Scally, *The Origins of the Lloyd George Coalition: The Politics of Social Imperialism, 1900–1918* (Princeton, NJ, 1975). The electoral fortunes of the tariff-reformers have also been thoroughly treated by A. K. Russell, *Liberal Landslide: The General Election of 1906* (Newton Abbot, 1973) and N. Blewett, *The Peers, the Parties and the People: The General Elections of 1910* (1972). There is also a good deal of useful information about free trade, protectionism and Liberalism in P. F. Clarke, *Lancashire and the New Liberalism* (Cambridge, 1971) and the same author's 'The End of Laissez-Faire and the Politics of Cotton', *HJ*, xv, no. 3 (1972).

3.   EDWARDIAN POLITICS: TURBULENT SPRING
OR INDIAN SUMMER?

Any brief survey of books on Edwardian politics must of necessity be highly selective. The classic account remains the two-volume 'Epilogue' to E. Halévy's *History of the English People in the Nineteenth Century*, first written in the 1920s (revised edn, 1961): *Imperialism and the Rise of Labour, 1895–1905* and *The Rule of Democracy, 1905–1914*, trans. E. I. Watkin (revised edn, 1951). Also still relevant are Sir Robert Ensor's volume in the Oxford History of England series, *England, 1870–1914* (1936) and A. Briggs's 'The Political Scene' in S. Nowell-Smith (ed.), *Edwardian England, 1901–1914* (1964).

The two most valuable books on politics at the constituency as well as the parliamentary level are A. K. Russell, *Liberal Landslide: The General Election of 1906* (Newton Abbot, 1973) and N. Blewett, *The Peers, the Parties, and the People: The General Elections of 1910* (1972). Neither volume confines its attention to just a single year. Blewett's article, 'The Franchise in the United Kingdom, 1885–1918', *P & P* (Dec. 1965), remains central to our understanding of the electoral framework. Several of the essays in H. Pelling's *Popular Politics and Society in Late Victorian Britain* (1968) are equally relevant for Edwardian developments, as is the same author's *Social Geography of British Elections, 1885–1910* (1968) and P. F. Clarke's 'Electoral Sociology of Modern Britain', *History* (1972). M. Kinnear's *The British Voter: An Atlas and Survey Since 1885* (1968), and D. Butler and J. Freeman's *British Political Facts, 1900–1975* (4th edn 1975), provide detailed election results. Chris Cook illuminates local election trends in

'Labour and the Downfall of the Liberal Party, 1906–14', in A. Sked and C. Cook (eds), *Crisis and Controversy: Essays in Honour of A. J. P. Taylor* (1976). Two other relevant essay collections are A. J. A. Morris (ed.), *Edwardian Radicalism, 1900–1914* (1974) and K. D. Brown (ed.), *Essays in Anti-Labour History* (1974). Important monographs devoted to specific geographical regions include K. O. Morgan, *Wales in British Politics, 1868–1922* (Cardiff, 1963); P. Thompson, *Socialists, Liberals, and Labour: The Struggle for London, 1885–1914* (1967); and P. F. Clarke, *Lancashire and the New Liberalism* (1971). Thompson minimises and Clarke emphasises the vitality of pre-1914 Liberalism. In *Nonconformity in Modern British Politics* (1975), Stephen E. Koss reminds us of the importance of religion as well as social class in Edwardian politics. R. Blake's *The Conservative Party from Peel to Churchill* (1970), R. Douglas's *History of the Liberal Party, 1895–1970* (1971), and vol. 1 of R. R. James, *The British Revolution, 1880–1939*, 2 vols (1976), include numerous sage observations on the era's political leaders. So do the biographies of the leading actors: K. Young, *Arthur James Balfour* (1963); S. H. Zebel, *Balfour: A Political Biography* (1973); J. Wilson, *CB: A Life of Sir Henry Campbell-Bannerman* (1973); R. Jenkins, *Asquith* (1964); S. E. Koss, *Asquith* (1976); K. O. Morgan, *Lloyd George* (1974); D. M. Creiger, *The Bounder from Wales: Lloyd George Before the War* (1976); and R. S. Churchill, *Winston S. Churchill: The Young Statesman, 1901–1914* (1967).

Specific political episodes are illuminated in F. Bealey and H. Pelling, *Labour and Politics, 1900–1906* (1958); A. M. Gollin, *Balfour's Burden: Arthur Balfour and Imperial Preference* (1965); R. A. Rempel, *Unionists Divided: Arthur Balfour, Joseph Chamberlain, and the Unionist Free Traders* (Newton Abbot, 1972); D. Morgan, *Suffragists and Liberals: The Politics of Woman Suffrage in England* (Oxford, 1975); and R. Jenkins, *Mr Balfour's Poodle* (1954), a lively account of the struggle between the Asquith Government and the House of Lords, 1909–1911. Further removed from day-to-day politics are studies of political ideas such as H. V. Emy, *Liberals, Radicals, and Social Politics, 1892–1914* (Cambridge, 1973); and M. Freeden, *The New Liberalism: An Ideology of Social Reform* (Oxford, 1978). Books such as B. Semmel, *Imperialism and Social Reform: English Social-Imperial Thought, 1895–1914* (1960) and G. R. Searle, *The Quest for National Efficiency: A Study in British Politics and Political Thought, 1899–1914* (Oxford, 1971) remind us that some issues transcended partisan political divisions altogether.

4. CRITICS OF EDWARDIAN SOCIETY:
    THE CASE OF THE RADICAL RIGHT

Little has been written about the Radical Right as such, apart from the stimulating essay by J. R. Jones, 'England', in H. Rogger and E. Webber (eds), *The European Right – A Historical Profile* (Berkeley and Los Angeles, Cal., 1965). But there has recently been a reissue of *Efficiency and Empire* by Arnold White, a prominent protagonist of Radical Right views, with an introductory essay by G. R. Searle (Brighton, 1973). We still await a full-dress biography of Leopold Maxse and a modern assessment of the diehard movement; but the Belloc–Chesterton circle has been described in R. Speaight's *Hilaire Belloc* (1957) and in M. Ward's *Gilbert Keith Chesterton* (1944). It is also well worth going back to source and reading H. Belloc and C. Chesterton's *The Party System* (1910). The muck-raking activities of this group and of other more typical members of the Radical Right make an appearance in F. Donaldson's *The Marconi Scandal* (1962), which provides an admirably clear and enjoyable analysis of the scandal itself but fails to place the subject in a sufficiently wide context.

Historians have taken greater interest in the related topics of social imperialism and national efficiency. B. Semmel's important study *Imperialism and Social Reform* (1960) is still essential reading; see too G. R. Searle's *The Quest for National Efficiency: A Study in British Politics and Political Thought, 1899–1914* (Oxford, 1971) and R. J. Scally's *The Origins of the Lloyd George Coalition: The Politics of Social Imperialism, 1900–1918* (Princeton, NJ, 1975), though Scally's book is marred by factual errors and by a lack of proportion. There is much valuable discussion of these issues, and also of Opposition politics generally, in two biographical studies by A. M. Gollin, *The Observer and J. L. Garvin, 1908–1914* (Oxford, 1960) and *Proconsul in Politics: A Study of Lord Milner in Opposition and in Power* (1964).

Edwardian patriotism, militarism and xenophobia in their many manifestations have recently aroused much historical interest. The following articles and monographs are all worth consulting: S. Hynes, 'The Decline and Fall of Tory England', ch. 2 of his *The Edwardian Turn of Mind* (Princeton, NJ, 1968); A. Summers, 'Militarism in Britan Before the Great War', in *HWJ*; II (1976); J. O. Springhall, *Youth, Empire and Society* (1977); and B. Gainer, *The Alien Invasion: The Origins of the Aliens Act of 1905* (1972). C. Holmes's *Anti-Semitism in Britain, 1876–1939* is due to be published later in the year, as is a study of anti-semitism in Britain by Gisella Lebzelter.

5. THE CHARACTER OF THE EARLY LABOUR PARTY 1900–14

There is a variety of good, general surveys of Labour history, the best of which are P. Poirier, *The Advent of the Labour Party* (1954); H. Pelling, *A Short History of the Labour Party* (1961); and, most recently, R. Moore, *The Emergence of the Labour Party, 1880–1924* (1978). Significantly, this latest study puts much emphasis on Labour politics at local level. The outstanding book on the early years remains H. Pelling's *Origins of the Labour Party, 1880–1900* (2nd edn, Oxford, 1965). Trade-union attitudes to independent political action are well covered in H. Clegg, A. Fox, A. F. Thompson, *A History of British Trade Unionism since 1889* (Oxford, 1964). R. Gregory, *The Miners and British Politics, 1906–1914* (Oxford, 1968) is a model study of the attitude of a particular union. Two very substantial biographies have been produced in recent years, K. O. Morgan's *Keir Hardie, Radical and Socialist* (1975), which puts him firmly in the progressive tradition; and D. Marquand's *Ramsay MacDonald* (1977). On the opening years of the Labour Representation Committee, particularly the MacDonald–Gladstone pact, F. Bealey and H. Pelling, *Labour and Politics, 1900–1906* (1958) is recommended. R. Barker, *Education and Politics, 1900–51* (Oxford, 1972) is a much wider book than the title suggests and in the first chapter there is a strong defence of the progressive rather than the socialist nature of the Labour Party. Finally, three very different and thought-provoking books are E. J. Hobsbawm, *Labouring Men* (1964), R. Milliband, *Parliamentary Socialism* (1961) and the collection by H. Pelling, *Popular Politics and Society in late Victorian Britain* (1969). P. Thompson has produced a good regional study, *Socialists, Liberal and Labour: The Struggle for London, 1885–1914* (1967). Finally, Robert Tressell's fascinating novel *The Ragged Trousered Philanthropists*, written in 1906, is available in paperback (1978).

6. IRISH HOME RULE AND LIBERALISM

The literature on Wales is not voluminous, but she is well served by K. O. Morgan's *Wales in British Politics, 1868–1922* (Cardiff, 1963) and now D. Howell's *The Land and the People in Nineteenth Century Wales* (1968). Nationalism in Scotland can be viewed though H. J. Hanham's *Scottish Nationalism* (1969). Ireland has an extensive literature, though much of it should be approached with caution. F. S. L. Lyons, *The Irish Parliamentary Party, 1890–1910* (1951) and *John Dillon* (1968) offer good traditional interpretations of official nationalism. The best study of the 1912–14 crisis remains A. T. Q. Stewart's *The Ulster Crisis* (1967). More generally, Unionism is effectively treated by P. Buckland in *Irish Unionism*, vols I and II (Dublin, 1972 and 1973) and in his pamphlet published by the Historical Association, *Southern Irish Unionism* (1974). A recent biography by J. V. O'Brien, *William O'Brien and the Course of Irish Politics, 1881–1918* (Berkeley, Cal., 1976), tells the story of an explosive nationalist figure, and D. Gwynn's *The Life of John Redmond* (1932) remains the standard life of the Irish-party leader. D. Miller's *Church, State and Nation* (Dublin, 1974) considers the shifts in the political attitudes of some members of the Irish Roman Catholic hierarchy during the period. Ruth Dudley Edwards provides a highly interpretative account of the fortunes of potential and real extremists in *Patrick Pearse* (1977), while Leon Ó Broin's *Revolutionary Underground* (Dublin, 1976) also looks in this direction. His *The Chief Secretary* (1970) is a favourable portrait of A. Birrell, the long-serving minister for Ireland in Liberal and coalition governments. F. Prill's *Ireland, Britain and Germany, 1870–1914* (Dublin, 1976) and A. J. Ward's *Ireland and Anglo-American Relations, 1899–1921* (1969) are important accounts of how Ireland impinged on other countries: the former is especially noteworthy in showing the problem in a European context. G. Dangerfield's *The Strange Death of Liberal England, 1910–14* (1935) attempts to place the Irish crisis in an English context and remains a classic account of the ills of the late Edwardian years. His *The Damnable Question* (1977), however, does not advance new insights resulting from an additional forty years' reflection. More general treatments are numerous, and J. Lee's *The Modernization of Irish Society, 1848–1918* (Dublin, 1973), F. S. L. Lyons's *Ireland Since the Famine* (1971) and O. MacDonagh's *Ireland* (British edn, 1977) merit particular notice. *Irish Historical Studies*, which is not always easily accessible, contains many articles on the period.

7. THE FAMILY AND THE ROLE OF WOMEN

Two very helpful introductions to the sociology and historiography of the family can be found in M. Anderson's *Family Structure in Nineteenth Century Lan-*

cashire (Cambridge, 1971) and in L. Stone's *The Family, Sex and Marriage in England, 1500–1800* (1977). Also useful is the editorial introduction in A. Wohl (ed.), *The Victorian Family: Structure and Stresses* (1978).

Particularly enlightening for the working-class Edwardian family are S. Meacham's *A Life Apart: The English Working Class, 1890–1914* (1977), and P. Thompson's *The Edwardians: The Remaking of British Society* (1975). Both, but especially the latter, make extensive use of the materials in the archives for the project 'Family Life and Work Before 1918' at the University of Essex. Both also contain helpful bibliographies on contemporary and secondary materials pertaining to the family. An interesting comparison of the Edwardian working class with its continental counterparts is provided in P. N. Stearns, *Lives of Labour: Work in a Maturing Industrial Society* (1975).

There are few analytical works on the upper- and middle-class families. Most of the studies, with the exceptions of P. Thompson's *The Edwardians* and M. Laski's 'Domestic Life', in S. Nowell-Smith (ed.) *Edwardian England, 1901–1914* (1964) are anecdotal. However, information about the family structure in these classes, as well as in the working class, can be gleaned from recent studies on children and women.

Thea Vigne uses oral-history techniques in 'Parents and Children, 1890–1918: Distance and Dependence', *OH* (Autumn 1975). In fact, this entire issue of *Oral History* is on the family. J. Gillis's *Youth and History: Tradition and Change in European Age Relations, 1770–Present* (1974) incorporates much recent scholarship to present a stimulating explanation of educational changes.

In addition to the materials cited in the text and footnotes, descriptive citations of works about women can be found in two excellent bibliographical aids: *OH* (Autumn 1977); and B. Kanner, 'The Women of England in a Century of Social Change, 1815–1914', in M. Vicinus (ed.) *A Widening Sphere*, (Bloomington, 1977). Recent issues of *History Workshop Journal* also contain a number of pertinent articles.

8. EDWARDIAN ENGLAND AND THE COMING OF THE FIRST WORLD WAR

A good starting point for those who are unfamiliar with the origins of the First World War is L. Lafore *The Long Fuse* (1966). A useful collection of essays from diverse sources is H. W. Koch (ed.), *The Origins of the First World War* (1972). Perhaps the best detailed study of this vast subject is L. Albertini, *The Origins of the War of 1914* (1965), and for those who wish to examine the original documents the most comprehensive and accessible collection is G. P. Gooch and H. Temperly (eds), *British Documents on the Origin of the War, 1898–1914* (1926–38).

A recent and massive work is F. H. Hinsley, *The Foreign Policy of Sir Edward Grey* (Cambridge, 1977), which gathers together the research of many scholars in dealing with every aspect of British policy before and during the war. This volume also contains a most up-to-date and comprehensive bibliography. S. R. Williamson has written an important study, *The Politics of Grand Strategy* (Cambridge, Mass., 1969), which explores the ambiguous diplomatic relationship between Britain and France in the years after 1904.

For those who wish to examine the frameworks which governed the making of foreign policy, M. E. Howard, 'Reflections on the First World War', in *Studies in War and Peace* (1971), and J. Joll, 'The Unspoken Assumptions', in Koch, *Origins of the First World War*, provide a brilliant and provocative introduction. The book that bridges the gap between diplomatic, social and political history most effectively is Z. S. Steiner, *Britain and the Origins of the First World War* (1977). This lucid synthesis is essential reading for any student of the First World War, or, indeed, for those who are interested in Edwardian England in general: it charts the course through the maze of facts and arguments with remarkable clarity of expression and organisation.

Every aspect of the British reaction to the Sarajevo assassination has now been exhaustively examined. C. Hazlehurst's *Politicians at War: July 1914–May 1915* (1971) is a stimulating study that uses many original sources to explode some of the myths that the subsequent justifications of the politicians generated about the decision to go to war. M. Ekstein, 'Sir Edward Grey and Imperial Germany in 1914', *JCH*, vi (1971), charts the Foreign Secretary's reactions to the collapse of his diplomatic position. C. Howard, 'MacDonald, Henderson and the Outbreak of War in 1914', *HJ*, xx, no. 4 (1977), and K. Wilson, 'The British Cabinet's Decision for War', *BJIS*, i (1975) explore some of the party political pressures bearing on the decision-makers.

For the influence of the Radical idealist group, A. J. Dorey's work 'Radical Liberal Criticism of British Foreign Policy, 1906–1914' (Oxford, D. Phil., 1966), which unfortunately is as yet unpublished, has been a seminal work. A. J. P. Taylor's *The Trouble Makers* (1957) is full of provocative and stimulating insights, while A. J. A. Morris, *Radicalism against War, 1906–1914* (1972), is a useful synthesis. Two articles by H. Weinroth throw much light on the convolutions of Radical ideology in the years before the war: 'The British Radicals and the Balance of Power 1902–14', *HJ*, xiii, no. 4 (1970), and 'Norman Angell and "The Great Illusion"', *HJ*, xvii, no. 3 (1974). An interesting recent work on this subject is M. E. Howard, *War and the Liberal Conscience* (1978).

The elusive subject of public opinion is approached by S. Hynes in *The Edwardian Turn of Mind* (Princeton, NJ, 1968), and other useful studies in this area that might be mentioned are G. Best, 'Militarism and the Victorian Public School' in B. Simon and I. Bradley, *The Victorian Public School* (1975); J. Gooch, 'Victorian and Edwardian Attitudes to War', in B. Bond and I. Roy (eds), *War and Society*, vol. i (1975); and J. Springhall, *Youth, Empire and Society* (1977). Interesting work is at present in progress on such subjects as the Edwardian press, the content of early twentieth-century history textbooks, and the influence of pressure groups such as the conscriptionist National Service League. With the publication of these studies we may expect further insights into the more subtle influences that affected the making of Edwardian foreign policy.

Notes and References

For abbreviations used here, see p. 169 above.

I. THE STANDARD OF LIVING, 1890–1914 *T. R. Gourvish*

1. C. H. Feinstein, *National Income, Expenditure, and Output of the United Kingdom, 1855–1965* (Cambridge, 1972) Table 42.
2. Lady Florence Bell, *At the Works* (1907); A. L. Bowley and A. R. Burnett-Hurst, *Livelihood and Poverty* (1915).
3. A. L. Bowley, *Wages and Income in the United Kingdom since 1860* (Cambridge, 1937) p. 30.
4. P. Snowden, *The Living Wage* (1912) pp. 61 and 64; G. R. Askwith, 'The Present Unrest in the Labour World', draft paper, 25 July 1911, CAB 37/107/70, PRO. My thanks to Roy Hay for this reference.
5. E. H. Phelps Brown and M. Browne, *A Century of Pay* (1968) pp. 444–5.
6. A. J. Taylor, 'The Economy', in S. Nowell-Smith (ed.), *Edwardian England, 1901–1914* (1964) pp. 131–2; S. Pollard and D. W. Crossley, *The Wealth of Britain 1085–1966* (1968) p. 235.
7. Feinstein, *National Income, Expenditure, and Output*, Table 5 (GNP from income data) and Tables 54–5.
8. Ibid., Tables 54–5.
9. L. G. Chiozza Money, *Riches and Poverty, 1910* (1911) p. 50.
10. *Report of an Enquiry by the Board of Trade into Working Class Rents, Housing, Retail Prices, and Standard Rate of Wages in the United Kingdom* (PP 1908, CVII) p. vii and Appendix I. Cf. the analysis of G. S. Jones, *Outcast London* (1971) pp. 215–18.
11. See Bowley, *Wages and Income*, pp. 3–7.
12 Census data, taken from the *17th Annual Abstract of Labour Statistics of the United Kingdom* (PP, 1914–16, LXI). A more sophisticated analysis of British white-collar employees (males only) reveals growth of 72 per cent over the period 1891–1911, as compared with 33 per cent for the total occupied male labour force. See G. Crossick, 'The Emergence of the Lower Middle Class in Britain: A Discussion', in G. Crossick (ed.), *The Lower Middle Class in Britain 1870–1914* (1977) p. 19.
13. J. Kuczynski, *A Short History of Labour Conditions Under Industrial Capitalism*, vol. I (1942) pp. 72, 74–7 and 113.
14. E. H. Hunt, *Regional Wage Variations in Britain, 1850–1914* (Oxford, 1973) p. 357.
15. Ibid., p. 104.
16. F. Wood, 'The Course of Real Wages in London, 1900–12', *JRSS*, LXXVII (1913) 37; R. S. Tucker, 'Real Wages of Artisans in London, 1729–1935', *JASS*, XXXI (1936) 80.

17. S. Pollard, 'Wages and Earnings in the Sheffield Trades, 1851–1914', *YBESR*, VI (1954) 63; Phelps Brown and Browne, *A Century of Pay*, pp. 444–5. Note that Pollard excluded data for weeks affected by strikes and lock-outs.

18. G. J. Barnsby, 'The Standard of Living in the Black Country during the Nineteenth Century', *EcHR*, XXIV (1971) 220–39; E. Hopkins, 'Small Town Aristocrats of Labour and Their Standard of Living, 1840–1914', *EcHR*, XXVIII (1975) 222–42; E. Roberts, 'Working-Class Standards of Living in Barrow and Lancaster, 1890–1914', *EcHR*, XXX (1977) 306–21.

19. Derived from Hopkins, in *EcHR*, XXVIII, 237, 239 and 242.

20. Roberts, ibid., XXX, 309, 313 and 320.

21. Calculated from Barnsby, ibid., XXIV, 238.

22. Wood, in *JRSS*, LXXVII, 14.

23. Roberts, in *EcHR*, XXX, 319.

24. Hunt, *Regional Wage Variations*, p. 104.

25. Kuczynski, *Short History of Labour Conditions*, pp. 72–3, 87.

26. G. L. Anderson, 'The Social Economy of Late-Victorian Clerks', in Crossick, *The Lower Middle Class*, pp. 131–2. See also his *Victorian Clerks* (Manchester, 1976) esp. ch. 4.

27. D. Lockwood, *The Blackcoated Worker* (1958) pp. 26–7, 42–4; Anderson, in Crossick, *The Lower Middle Class*, pp. 113–29.

28. Ibid., p. 25; B. Supple, *The Royal Exchange Assurance* (Cambridge, 1970) p. 380.

29. Bowley, *Wages and Income*, pp. 7–9; K. Burgess, *The Origins of British Industrial Relations* (1975) p. 243.

30. R. Walters, 'Labour Productivity in the South Wales Steam-Coal Industry, 1870–1914', *EcHR*, XXVIII (1975) 300.

31. Taylor, in Nowell-Smith, *Edwardian England*, p. 131.

32. J. W. F. Rowe, *Wages in Practice and Theory* (1928) pp. 2–5; and see also Hunt, *Regional Wage Variations*, p. 74.

33. Walters, in *EcHR*, XXVIII, 284; and A. Slaven, 'Earnings and Productivity in the Scottish Coal-mining Industry during the Nineteenth-Century: The Dixon Enterprises', in P. L. Payne (ed.), *Studies in Scottish Business History* (1967) p. 247.

34. Cf. Walters, in *EcHR*, XXVIII, 291–4, 303; Slaven, in Payne, *Scottish Business History*, p. 229; and Burgess, *Origins of British Industrial Relations*, pp. 207–8.

35. Slaven, in Payne, *Scottish Business History*, p. 234.

36. *17th Annual Abstract of Labour Statistics*, p. 66; Rowe, *Wages in Practice and Theory*, pp. 6 and 257–9; Pollard and Crossley, *The Wealth of Britain*, p. 237.

37. *Board of Trade (Department of Labour Statistics) Report on Changes in Rates of Wages and Hours of Labour in the UK in 1913* (*PP*, 1914–16, LXI) p. iii.

38. South Eastern Railway Staff Book (Bricklayers' Arms), RAIL 635/302, PRO.

39. Rowe, *Wages in Practice and Theory*, pp. 13, 56–63 and 243–8; *Board of Trade Report*, p. 38; Bowley, *Wages and Income*, p. 30.

40. Pollard, in *YBESR*; VI, 63; Bowley, *Wages and Income*, p. 30; *Board of Trade Report*, p. 38.

41. Taylor, in Nowell-Smith, *Edwardian England*, p. 130; Pollard and Crossley, *The Wealth of Britain*, pp. 238–9; P. Thompson, *The Edwardians: The Remaking of British Society* (1975) pp. 292–6.

180 THE EDWARDIAN AGE

42. Cf. P. N. Stearns, *Lives of Labour: Work in a Maturing Industrial Society* (1975) pp. 193–211; and S. Meacham, *A Life Apart: The English Working Class, 1890–1914* (1977) pp. 129–30, 140–3 and 208ff.
43. In this context, see, *inter alia*, Bowley, *Wages and Income*, pp. 14, 25–6; Snowden, *The Living Wage*, pp. 62–3; J. H. Porter, 'Wage Bargaining under Conciliation Agreements, 1860–1914', *EcHR*, XXIII (1970) 474–5; G. Alderman, 'The National Free Labour Association', *IRSH*, XXI (1976) 309–36.
44. St Pancras Borough Council Minutes, 30 June 1920, Local History Library, Swiss Cottage.
45. T. McKeown, R. G. Record, and R. D. Turner, 'An Interpretation of the Decline of Mortality in England and Wales during the Twentieth Century', *Population Studies*, XXIX (1975) 417.
46. G. B. Wilson, *Alcohol and the Nation* (1940) p. 333.
47. Snowden, *The Living Wage*, pp. 64–5; Taylor, in Nowell-Smith, *Edwardian England*, pp. 127–8; W. Ashworth, *An Economic History of England, 1870–1939* (1960) pp. 252–3.
48. Pollard and Crossley, *The Wealth of Britain*, pp. 242–3.
49. South Eastern and Chatham Railway Staff Register (goods department), RAIL 633/359, PRO.

2. POLITICAL ECONOMY IN EDWARDIAN ENGLAND: THE TARIFF-REFORM CONTROVERSY   *Peter Cain*

1. F. E. Smith, *Speeches, 1906–9* (Liverpool, 1910) pp. 275–6.
2. W. A. Lewis, 'International Competition in Manufactures', *American Economic Review. Papers and Proceedings*, XLVII (1957) 579.
3. P. Deane and W. A. Cole, *British Economic Growth, 1688–1959* (Cambridge, 1964) p. 31.
4. E. J. Hobsbawm, *Industry and Empire: An Economic History of Britain since 1750* (1968) p. 121.
5. D. H. Aldcroft (ed.), *The Development of British Industry and Foreign Competition, 1875–1914* (1968) p. 13.
6. Deane and Cole, *British Economic Growth*, p. 33. The figure for manufactured imports in 1880 contains unallocated items which may not all be attributable to manufactures. The later figures also contain a 'miscellaneous' element.
7. P. L. Payne, 'Iron and Steel Manufactures', in Aldcroft, *Development of British Industry*, p. 75.
8. Calculated from B. R. Mitchell and P. Deane, *Abstract of British Historical Statistics* (Cambridge, 1962) pp. 283 and 304–5.
9. On the relationship between increasing economic competition and hostility to Germany, see R. J. S. Hoffman, *Great Britain and the German Trade Rivalry, 1875–1914* (1933).
10. G. R. Searle, *The Quest for National Efficiency: A Study in British Politics and British Political Thought, 1899–1914* (Oxford, 1971).
11. General accounts of Chamberlain's conversion to a preferentialist

strategy include: J. Amery, *Life of Joseph Chamberlain*, vols v and vi (1951 and 1968); P. Fraser, *Joseph Chamberlain* (1966) esp. chs. 10–12; E. Halévy, *History of the English People in the Nineteenth Century*, v (revised edn, 1961) pp. 285–331; S. H. Zebel, Joseph Chamberlain and the Genesis of the Tariff Reform Campaign', *JBS*, vii (1967); W. K. Hancock, *Survey of British Commonwealth Affairs* (Oxford, 1940), vol. ii, pt i, pp. 72ff.

12. For some of the propaganda of Chamberlain's pressure group, the Tariff-Reform League, see B. Semmell, *Imperialism and Social Reform 1895–1914* (1960) ch. 5; and D. Read, *Documents from Edwardian England 1901–15* (1973), pp. 156–7.

13. This and the next paragraph are largely based on the following sources: W. J. Ashley, *The Tariff Problem* (1903); W. A. S. Hewins, *Apologia of an Imperialist: Forty Years of Empire Policy* (1929) vol. i, esp. chs 2 and 3; C. S. Vince, *Mr. Chamberlain's Proposals: What They Mean and What We Shall Gain by Them* (Birmingham, 1903); N. Cunningham, *The Case Against Free Trade* (1911); H. J. Mackinder, 'Man-Power as Means of National and Imperial Strength', *National Review*, xlv (1905) 136–43. Informative material from political spokesmen for tariff reform can be found in J. Chamberlain, *Speeches* (1914), vol. ii; A. Bonar Law, *The Fiscal Question* (1908); Viscount Milner, *The Nation and the Empire* (1913); Smith, *Speeches*, pp. 275–307; L. S. Amery, *Union and Strength* (1912) chs 11 and 12; R. Jebb, *The Imperial Conference* (1911) pp. 191–263.

14. There are useful extracts from Balfour's *Notes* in W. H. B. Court, *British Economic History, 1870–1914: Commentary and Documents* (Cambridge, 1965) pp. 452–9.

15. This and the next two paragraphs are based on 'Professors of Economics and the Tariff Question', *The Times*, 15 Aug. 1903, p. 4 (on which see W. A. Coats, 'Political Economy and the Tariff Reform Campaign of 1903', *JLE*, xi (1968); A. Marshall, 'Memorandum on the Fiscal Policy of International Trade', in his *Official Papers* (Cambridge 1926); J. A. Hobson, *International Trade* (1904); Cobden Club, *The Cobden Club's Reply to Mr. Chamberlain* (1904); L. G. Chiozza Money, *Through Preference to . . . Protection. An Examination of Mr. Chamberlain's Fiscal Proposals* (1903); W. S. Churchill, *The People's Rights* (1909; repr. 1970); R. B. Haldane, Introduction to P. Ashley, *Modern Tariff History* (1904); P. Snowden, *Mr. Chamberlain's Bubble* (1903). There are extracts from Marshall's *Memorandum* in Court, *British Economic History*, pp. 459–68.

16. The main influences on the reasoning in the rest of this section are R. Gilpin, *U.S. Power and the Multinational Corporation: The Political Economy of Direct Foreign Investment* (1976) ch. 3; W. D. Rubenstein, 'The Victorian Middle Classes: Wealth, Occupation and Geography', *EcHR*, xxx, no. 4, (1977); H. W. Richardson, 'Overcommitment in Britain before 1930', *Oxford Economic Papers*, xvii (1965), and 'Retardation in Britain's Industrial Growth, 1870–1913', *Scottish Journal of Political Economy*, xii (1965) – both reprinted in D. H. Aldcroft and H. W. Richardson, *The British Economy, 1870–1939* (1969); and W. P. Kennedy, 'Foreign Investment, Trade and Growth in the United Kingdom, 1870–1913', *Explorations in Economic History*, xi (1974), and 'Institutional Response to Economic Growth: Capital Markets in Britain to 1914', in L. Hannah (ed.), *Management Strategy and Business Development* (1976).

17. M. Simon, 'The Enterprise and Industrial Composition of New British

Portfolio Investment, 1865–1914', *Journal of Development Studies* (1967) Table 6, p. 289.

18. S. B. Saul, *Studies in British Overseas trade, 1870–1914* (Liverpool, 1960) ch. 6.

19. S. B. Saul, 'The Export Economy, 1870–1914', *YBESR* xvii (1965) p. 6.

20. On this issue see D. C. M. Platt, *Latin America and British Trade 1806–1914* (1972) pp. 103–35.

21. Saul, *Studies in British Overseas Trade*, chs 3 and 9; F. Crouzet, 'Trade and Empire: The British Experience from the Establishment of Free Trade until the First World War', in B. M. Radcliffe (ed.), *Great Britain and her World, 1750–1914: Essays in Honour of W. O. Henderson* (Manchester, 1975) esp. pp. 224–8.

22. See the extract from Crowe's memorandum in Court, *British Economic History*, pp. 468–70.

23. Hoffman, *Great Britain and the German Trade Rivalry*, p. 285.

24. Semmell, *Imperialism and Social Reform*, p. 97.

25. R. A. Rempel, *Unionists Divided. Arthur Balfour, Joseph Chamberlain and the Unionist Free Traders* (Newton Abbot, 1972) pp. 94–5.

26. Rempel, *Unionists Divided, passim*; P. Fraser, 'Unionism and Tariff Reform: The Crisis of 1906', *HJ*, v, no. 2 (1962).

27. A. K. Russell, *Liberal Landslide: The General Election of 1906* (Newton Abbot, 1973) pp. 65–73,.80, 83–91, 172ff. For the tariff-reformers' attempts to woo the working class, and their failure, see Semmell, *Imperialism and Social Reform*, pp. 106ff.; and K. D. Brown, 'The Trade Union Tariff Reform Association', *JBS*, xi (1970).

28. This paragraph and the two following are based upon N. Blewett, 'Free Fooders, Balfourites, Whole Hoggers: Factionalism within the Unionist Party, 1906–10', *HJ*, xi, no. 1 (1968). For the more strictly Chamberlainite and Empire-minded amongst the Whole Hogger element, see R. J. Scally, *The Origins of the Lloyd George Coalition: The Politics of Social Imperialism, 1900–1918* (Princeton, NJ, 1975) Introduction and chs 4 and 5.

29. H. V. Emy, 'The Impact of Financial Policy on English Party Politics before 1914', *HJ*, xv, no. 1 (1972).

30. N. Blewett, *The Peers, the Parties and the People: The General Elections of 1910* (1972) ch. 6 and pp. 320–2.

31. Ibid., chs 7–10.

32. Figures are from ibid., p. 381. This paragraph has also benefited from Blewett's general analysis of the elections, ibid., pp. 395ff., and from J. A. Hobson, 'The General Election: A Sociological Interpretation', *Sociological Review*, iii (1910); and also W. D. Rubenstein, 'Wealth, Elites and the Class Structure of Modern Britain', *P & P* (Aug 1977) esp. pp. 117ff.

33. P. F. Clarke, 'The End of Laissez-Faire and the Politics of Cotton', *HJ* xv, no. 3 (1972).

34. Semmell, *Imperialism and Social Reform*, pp. 124–7.

3. EDWARDIAN POLITICS: TURBULENT SPRING OR INDIAN SUMMER? *Walter L. Arnstein*

1. K. O. Morgan, *Lloyd George* (1974).

2. M. Kinnear, *The British Voter: An Atlas and Survey since 1885* (1968) p. 26.

3. Cf. H. Pelling, *Social Geography of British Elections, 1885–1910* (1967) pp. 431–2; J. P. Conford, 'The Transformation of Conservatism', *VS*, VII 54–5.

4. N. Blewett, 'The Franchise in the United Kingdom, 1885–1918', *P & P* (Dec 1965) 30 and 33–4.

5. Ibid., 31–42. See also A. K. Russell, *Liberal Landslide, The General Election of 1906* (Newton Abbot, 1973) pp. 15–21. It is worth keeping in mind that, though four males in ten were therefore practically disenfranchised at any given election, less than one male in ten was necessarily disenfranchised for a lifetime.

6. Blewett, in *P & P* (Dec 1965) 44–51; Russell, *Liberal Landslide*, pp. 18–19; N. Blewett, *The Peers, the Parties and the People: The General Elections of 1910* (1972) p. 365.

7. Cf. Russell, *Liberal Landslide*, pp. 125–7; Blewett, *The Peers, the Parties and the People*, p. 372.

8. Cf. G. R. Searle, *The Quest for National Efficiency. A Study in British Politics and Political Thought, 1899–1914* (Oxford, 1971).

9. *QR* (Apr.1906) 576.

10. *Hansard*, 4th ser., CXLI (14 Feb 1905) col. 128.

11. Cited in Russell, *Liberal Landslide*, p. 56.

12. Russell, *Liberal Landslide*, pp. 44, 61–3. Blewett provides a closely analogous analysis for 1910 in *The Peers, the Parties and the People*, pp. 228–30.

13. See, for example, the introduction by Jeremy Thorpe to Roy Douglas, *The History of the Liberal Party, 1895–1970* (1971) p. xii.

14. H. Pelling, 'Labour and the Downfall of Liberalism', in his *Popular Politics and Society in Late Victorian Britain* (1968). See also F. Bealey and H. Pelling, *Labour and Politics, 1900–1906* (1958) chs 5 and 6.

15. A. Havighurst, *Twentieth-Century Britain*, 2nd edn (New York, 1966) p. 85.

16. Russell, *Liberal Landslide*, p. 65.

17. Cited ibid., p. 76.

18. Cited ibid., pp. 64 and 115, and in Pelling, *Popular Politics*, p. 9, respectively.

19. 'The Political Situation', *QR* (Apr 1906) pp. 572–3.

20. Ibid., pp. 574–5.

21. Russell, *Liberal Landslide*, pp. 175 and 176.

22. Ibid., pp. 40, 41 and 176.

23. Ibid., pp. 182–94, 138, 206 and 132.

24. D. Butler and J. Freeman (eds), *British Political Facts, 1900–1960* (1963) p. 122.

25. B. Gilbert, 'David Lloyd George: Land, the Budget and Social Reform', *AHR*, LXXXI (1976) 1060–71.

26. Cited in J. Wilson, *CB: A Life of Sir Henry Campbell-Bannerman* (1973) p. 563, and S. E. Koss, *Asquith* (1976) p. 106, respectively.

27. Butler and Freeman, *British Political Facts*, p. 127; *Nation* cited in Blewett, *The Peers, the Parties and the People*, p. 49.

28. Gilbert, in *AHR*, LXXXI, 1058.

29. Blewett, *The Peers, the Parties and the People*, pp. 51, 61 and 63–4; Koss, *Asquith*, p. 103.

30. Blewett, *The Peers, the Parties and the People*, pp. 68–9; Gilbert, in *AHR*, LXXXI, 1063–4.

31. Cited in Koss, *Asquith*, p. 116, and Blewett, *The Peers, the Parties and the People*, p. 99.

32. Ibid., pp. 87, 107–9, 113, 276, 290 and 301–12.

et. Ibid., pp. 116 and 317.

33. C. C. Weston, 'The Liberal Leadership and the Lords' Veto, 1907–1910', *HJ*, XI (1968) 508–37.

34. Blewett, *The Peers, the Parties and the People*, pp. 105 and 312.

35. Ibid., pp. 107, 101, 116, 317, 312 and 323.

36. Ibid., pp. 126–7.

37. Cited in Koss, *Asquith*, p. 118.

38. 'I cannot become another Peel in my party', Balfour explained. (Cited ibid., p. 123.) Roy Jenkins provides a reliable survey of the conference in *Mr. Balfour's Poodle* (1954) pp. 101–17.

39. Cf. Blewett, *The Peers, the Parties and the People*, p. 379.

40. Ibid., pp. 169–94, 170 and 326.

41. Kinnear, *Atlas*, pp. 31–2.

42. Cited in Koss, *Asquith*, p. 126.

43. The prime champion of the thesis that the 1910 Liberals had become, to a great degree, the political party of the working class, is P. F. Clarke. 'There is no inconsistency', he writes, 'between the reformist politics and the development of a trade union consciousness among the working class. The reformist Liberal party was in principle perfectly capable of expressing working class interests of this kind' – 'Electoral Sociology of Modern Britain', *History*, LVII (1972) 49. The thesis was first elaborated by Clarke in *Lancashire and the New Liberalism* (Cambridge, 1971).

44. Blewett, *The Peers, the Parties and the People*, pp. 109 and 389–95.

45. B. Webb, *Our Partnership* (1948) p. 465, cited in Blewett, *The Peers, the Parties and the People*, p. 408.

46. See Pelling, *Popular Politics*, pp. 117–18 and 149; and P. Thompson, *Socialists, Liberals and Labour: The Struggle for London, 1885–1914* (1967) p. 296.

47. Butler and Freeman, *British Political Facts*, pp. 127–8. 'After 1910,' writes P. F. Clarke, 'the Labour Party seems to have run out of steam' – 'The Electoral Position of the Liberal and Labour Parties, 1910–14', *EHR*, XC (1975) 828–36. As Chris Cook has shown, the situation in local government was similar: 'Outside a very few heavily industrialised wards of major cities, Labour's municipal advance prior to 1914 was either negative or non-existent' – in A. Sked and C. Cook (eds), *Crisis and Controversy: Essays in Honour of A. J. P. Taylor* (1976) p. 58.

48. G. Dangerfield, *The Strange Death of Liberal England, 1910–14* (1935) p. 370. In the final volume of his *History of the English People in the Nineteenth Century*, Élie Halévy had labelled the era one of 'domestic anarchy'.

49. Cf. S. Meacham, '"The Sense of an Impending Clash": English Work-

ing Class Unrest before the First World War', *AHR*, LXXVII (1972) 1343–64.

50. Cf. Pelling, 'The Working Class and the Origins of the Welfare State' and 'The Labour Unrest, 1911–1914', in his *Popular Politics*.

51. Cf. Sked and Cook, *Crisis and Controversy*, p. 63.

4. CRITICS OF EDWARDIAN SOCIETY: THE CASE OF THE RADICAL RIGHT *G. R. Searle*

1. In 1895 the Liberal Unionists joined Lord Salisbury's Conservative administration. From then on the two parties were usually called by contemporaries 'the Unionist Party', i.e. the party that stood for the maintenance of the Act of Union of 1800 which bound Ireland to Great Britain, so forming the United Kingdom. I have frequently employed the terms 'Unionist Party' and 'Unionism' in their Edwardian usage.

2. G. R. Searle, *The Quest for National Efficiency, 1899–1914: A Study in British Politics and Political Thought, 1899–1914* (Oxford, 1971); R. J. Scally, *The Origins of the Lloyd George Coalition: The Politics of Social Imperialism, 1900–1918* (Princeton, NJ, 1975).

3. Searle, *Quest*, ch. 6; Scally, *Origins of the Lloyd George Coalition*, ch. 7.

4. *NR*, LVI (1911) 719; House of Lords Record Office Wargrave MSS., Maxse to Goulding, 19 Dec 1910.

5. *The Times*, 6 and 19 Oct 1910; *NR*, LVI (1911) 713–14.

6. See G. R. Searle, Introduction to Arnold White, *Efficiency and Empire* (Brighton, 1973) pp. vii–xxix.

7. For a general discussion of the phenomenon of populism, see G. Ionescu and E. Gellner, *Populism: Its Meanings and National Characteristics* (1969).

8. *NR*, LIX (1912) 566–7.

9. West Sussex Record Office, Maxse MSS., 466, Willoughby de Broke to Maxse, 16 June 1912.

10. K. D. Brown, 'The Anti-Socialist Union, 1908–49', in K. D. Brown (ed.), *Essays in Anti-Labour History* (1974) p. 243.

11. A. White, 'A Committee of Public Safety', in *The Throne*, 13 Mar 1912.

12. *NR*, LIX (1912) 602–5. But this editorial, incidentally, is based upon a speech recently delivered by Bonar Law at Glasgow.

13. Bodleian, Selborne MSS., 74, fo. 182, Willoughby de Broke to Selborne, 17 Aug 1911.

14. House of Lords Record Office, Bonar Law MSS., 24/4/92, Page Croft to Bonar Law, 30 Nov 1911.

15. For example, Arnold White in the *Daily Express*, 2 June 1913.

16. For example, *NR*, LVIII (1911) 176 and 197.

17. West Sussex Record Office, Maxse MSS., 468, Willoughby de Broke to Maxse, 31 Aug 1913.

18. For example, *NR*, LVI (1910) 374–9. See also Arnold White, in *Daily Express*, 8 Dec 1913.

19. *NR*, LXII (1914) 916–19. Alfred Harmsworth, Lord Northcliffe, owned a chain of newspapers, including *The Times* and the *Daily Mail*. His brother, Harold, had a controlling interest in a number of provincial Liberal newspapers.

20. House of Lords Record Office, Strachey MSS., S/10/9/18, Strachey to Maxse, 20 Sep 1911.

21. *NR*, LVII (1911) 383.

22. Speech at Tunbridge Wells, 16 May 1914, reported in *The Times*, 18 May 1914.

23. *The Outlook*, 8 Feb 1913, 171.

24. H. J. Hanham, 'The Sale of Honours in Late Victorian England', *VS*, III (1960) 284–9.

25. *Hansard*, 4th ser., 189, cols 1289–90, 28 May 1908.

26. *New Witness*, 24 July and 30 Oct 1913. Arnold White was on the council of the League.

27. This episode has been well treated in Frances Donaldson, *The Marconi Scandal* (1962).

28. For example, *The Outlook*, 31 May 1913, 741–2; 7 June 1913, 780–1.

29. S. E. Koss, *Sir John Brunner: Radical Plutocrat, 1842–1919* (Cambridge, 1970) p. 238, note 1.

30. National Maritime Museum, Arnold White MSS., file 112; West Sussex Record Office, Maxse MSS., *passim*.

31. Another characteristic of Radical Right propaganda was the frequency with which not only the Irish (nationalists), but also the Welsh and the Scots, were attacked – apparently because of the strength of Liberalism in the Celtic fringes and the high proportion of ministers who were in some way connected with Wales and Scotland. The Radical Right raucously claimed that it stood for an *English* patriotism (see, for example, Arnold White, in *Daily Express*, 6 Oct 1913).

32. House of Lords Record Office, Willoughby de Broke MSS., WB/3/44, Lord Lovat to de Broke, 17 Aug 1911.

33. Searle, Introduction to White, *Efficiency and Empire*, pp. xix–xxv.

34. Arnold White, in *Daily Express*, 7 July 1913, and in *The Referee*, 31 May 1908.

35. *The Referee*, 5 July 1908. See also David French, 'Spy Fever in Britain, 1900–1915', in *HJ*, XXI (1978) 355–70. On the popularity of invasion-scare stories, see I. F. Clarke, *Voices Prophesying War, 1763–1984* (1966).

36. G. Crossick, 'The Emergence of the Lower Middle Class in Britain', in G. Crossick (ed.), *The Lower Middle Class in Britain, 1870–1914* (1977) pp. 41–6.

37. In its most undiluted form in Maxse's *National Review*; but also in Arnold White's weekly column in *The Referee* and, starting in 1913, in the *Daily Express*. See also the periodicals *The Outlook* and *The Throne*. *The Eye-Witness* (later renamed the *New Witness*), the organ of Belloc and the Chestertons, though highly idiosyncratic and eccentric, was in this tradition, as, perhaps, was Horatio Bottomley's *John Bull*. But Radical Right comment appeared sporadically in most of the popular Unionist newspapers and journals, and even in Radical Liberal ones, though less frequently.

38. For example, *Daily Express*, 8 Dec 1913.

39. For examples of Radical Right propaganda in war time, see S. E. Koss, *Lord Haldane: Scapegoat for Liberalism* (New York and London, 1969) chs 5 and 6.

5. THE CHARACTER OF THE EARLY LABOUR PARTY, 1900–14   *Dennis Dean*

1. P. Fraser, *Joseph Chamberlain* (1966) p. 230.
2. G. Dangerfield, *The Strange Death of Liberal England, 1910–14* (1935).
3. J. H. Thomas and J. Chynes, *My Story. Memoirs* (1937).
4. P. Snowden, *An Autobiography* (1934), vol. i, p. 81.
5. G. D. Cole and R. Postgate, *The Common People* (1938) p. 433.
6. Sir Robert Ensor, *England, 1870–1914* (1936) p. ix.
7. H. Clegg, A. Fox and A. Thompson, *A History of British Trade Unionism since 1889* (1964) vol i.
8. K. D. Brown, *Labour and Unemployment* (Newton Abbot, 1974); R. Barker, *Education and Politics* (Oxford, 1972); and B. Porter, *Critics of Empire* (1968).
9. Barker, *Education and Politics*, ch. 2.
10. B. Pimlott, *Labour in the Thirties* (Cambridge, 1977); and D. Howell, *British Social Democracy* (1976).
11. W. Kendall, *The Revolutionary Movement in Britain, 1900–21* (1969).
12. R. D. Challinor, *British Bolsheviks* (1977).
13. R. Moore, *The Emergence of the Labour Party, 1880–1924* (1978) p. 76.
14. R. V. Clements, 'British Trade Unions and the Popular Economy', *EcHR*, xiv (1961).
15. T. R. Tholfsen, *Working Class Radicalism in Mid-Victorian England* (1976).
16. P. Thompson, *The Edwardians: The Remaking of British Society* (1974); and S. Meacham, 'The Sense of an Impending Clash: English Working Class Unrest before the First World War', *AHR*, lxxvii (1972), 1343–64.
17. G. Crossick, *The Lower Middle Class in Late Victorian Britain* (1977) ch. 1.
18. J. Saville, 'Trade Unions and Free Labour', in A. Briggs and J. Saville (eds), *Essays in Labour History* (1960), vol. i.
19. N. Blewett, 'The Franchise in the United Kingdom, 1885–1918', *P & P* (Dec 1965).
20. H. Pelling, 'The Working Class and the Origins of the Welfare State', in his *Popular Politics and Society in Late Victorian Britain* (1969).
21. K. O. Morgan and I. Maclean both produced Lives of Keir Hardie in 1975.
22. F. Bealey and H. Pelling, *Labour and Politics* (1958).
23. C. Cook, 'Labour and the Downfall of the Liberal Party', in A. Sked and C. Cook (eds), *Crisis and Controversy: Essays in Honour of A. J. P. Taylor* (1976).

6. IRISH HOME RULE AND LIBERALISM   *Alan O'Day*

1. *PD*, I, iv (15 March 1898), 1732.
2. Balfour at Ipswich, *The Times*, 7 Jan 1910.
3. Cited in H. J. Hanham, *Scottish Nationalism* (1969) p. 98.
4. Ibid., p. 97.

5. Ibid.; and K. O. Morgan, *Wales in British Politics, 1868–1922* (Cardiff, 1963).

6. Cited in F. W. Hirst, *Early Life and Letters of John Morley* (1927) vol. I, p. 213.

7. Cited in Hanham, *Scottish Nationalism*, p. 41.

8. Cited in Morgan, *Wales in British Politics*, pp. 91–2.

9. Cited in D. Gywnn, *The Life of John Redmond* (1932) p. 102.

10. *South Wales Daily News*, 18 Jan 1895, cited in T. J. McCarry, 'Lloyd George and Irish Home Rule, 1886–1914' (University of Bristol, M. Litt., 1975) p. 118.

11. H. W. McCready, 'Home Rule and the Liberal Party, 1899–1906', *IHS*, XIII (Sep 1963) 316–48.

12. Cited in Arthur Mitchell, *Labour in Irish Politics, 1890–1930* (Dublin, 1974) p. 30.

13. Bodleian, Bryce MSS., J. Bryce to Goldwin Smith, 26 Jan 1905.

14. BL, Add. MS. 45,994, Asquith to H. Gladstone, 22 Oct 1905.

15. BL, Add. MS. 41,213, Lord Crewe to Campbell Bannerman, 19 Nov 1905; National Library of Ireland, Bryce MSS., 11011, Bryce to A. V. Dicey, 3 Feb 1905.

16. Cited in A. C. Hepburn, 'Liberal Policies and Nationalist Politics in Ireland, 1905–10' (University of Kent, Ph. D., 1968) vol. I, p. 110. This is a remarkably full thesis, which, however, offers a very different interpretation from that offered here.

17. At Stirling, *The Times*, 24 Nov 1905.

18. 13 Feb 1905, cited in McCready, in *IHS*, XIII, 341.

19. BL, Add. MS. 41,217, Campbell-Bannerman to H. Gladstone, 20 Nov 1905.

20. At Liverpool, 11 Nov 1906, in *Weekly Freeman's Journal*, 17 Nov 1906, cited in Hepburn, 'Liberal Policies', vol. I, p. 171.

21. BL, Add. MS. 41,211, Bryce to Campbell-Bannerman, 8 Oct 1906.

22. Foreign Office, Grey MSS., Bryce to Sir Edward Grey, 6 July 1907, cited in Hepburn, 'Liberal Policies', vol. I, p. 291.

23. Ibid., p. 268.

24. BL, Add. MS. 41,240, A. Birrell to Campbell-Bannerman, 30 Oct 1907.

25. At Sheffield, *The Times*, 3 Dec 1907.

7. THE FAMILY AND THE ROLE OF
    WOMEN *Suzann Buckley*

1. Hannah Mitchell, *The Hard Way Up*, ed. G. Mitchell (1968) p. 130.

2. Gerda Lerner, 'Placing Women in History', *Feminist Studies*, III (1975) 5–13.

3. *Census of England and Wales, 1911* (*PP*, 1917–18, **xxv**), *passim*, for these figures and other statistical data.

4. Lee Holcombe, *Victorian Ladies at Work* (1973), provides detailed information on middle-class women in the workforce from 1850 to 1914.

5. *Census, 1911*, p. 161.

6. Anna Davin, 'Imperialism and Motherhood', *HWJ*, v (1978) 9–64.
7. P. Thompson, *The Edwardians* (1975) p. 103.
8. Unless otherwise indicated, the material for working-class women is drawn from S. Meacham, *A Life Apart: The English Working Class, 1890–1914* (1977); P. N. Stearns, 'The Working Class Women in Britain 1890–1914', in M. Vicinus (ed.), *Suffer and Be Still* (1973) pp. 100–20; and P. Knight, 'Women and Abortion in Victorian and Edwardian England', *HWJ*, IV (1977) 57–69.
9. Meacham, *A Life Apart*, pp. 174–5.
10. E. Roberts, 'Working-class Women in the North West', *OH*, v (1977) 22.
11. Duncan Crow, *The Edwardian Woman* (1978) p. 15.
12. Constance Rover, *Love, Morals and the Feminists* (1970) p. 145.
13. Holcombe, *Victorian Ladies at Work, passim*.
14. Andrew Rosen, *Rise Up, Women!* (1974) pp. 58–60.
15. *PD* (Commons), XCII, 28 Mar 1917, col. 471. See also Martin Pugh, 'Politicians and the Women's Vote', *History*, LIX (1974) 358–74.

8. EDWARDIAN ENGLAND AND THE COMING OF THE FIRST WORLD WAR *Colin Nicolson*

1. A. J. P. Taylor, *Rumours of Wars* (1952) p. 75.
2. Speech of Sir Edward Grey, *PD* (Commons) cols 1609–1827.
3. *BD*,X, no 283.
4. Ibid., no.369, memorandum by Crowe, 31 July 1914.
5. W. S. Churchill, *The World Crisis, 1911–1918* (1923).
6. D. C. Watt, 'The British Reactions to the Assassination at Sarajevo', *European Studies Review*, I, no. 3 (1971) 238.
7. J. Steinberg, 'The German Background to Anglo-German Relations', in F. H. Hinsley (ed.), *The Foreign Policy of Sir Edward Grey* (Cambridge, 1977) p. 189
8. P. M. Kennedy, 'Idealists and Realists: British Views of Germany, 1864–1939', *TRHS*, 5th ser., XXV (1975), and 'The Tradition of Appeasement in British Foreign Policy', *BJIS*, II, no. 3, (1976).
9. I. C. Willis, *How We Went into the War* (1918) p. iii.
10. A. J. A. Morris, *Radicalism against War, 1906–1914* (1972) p. 94.
11. Z. S. Steiner, *Britain and the Origins of the First World War* (1977) p. 150.
12. A. J. P. Taylor, *The Trouble Makers* (1957) p. 114.
13. K. G. Robbins, *Sir Edward Grey* (1971) p. 301.
14. H. Nicolson, *Lord Carnock* (1930) pp. 402–3.
15. Burns Papers, BL, Add. MS. 46,336, Burns's appointment diary, 29 July 1914.
16. Harcourt to Pease, 31 July 1914, cited in C. Hazlehurst *Politicians at War: July 1914–May 1915* (1971) p. 85.
17. Asquith to Venetia Stanley, 2 Aug 1914, cited ibid.
18. H. Weinroth, 'Norman Angell and "The Great Illusion"', *HJ*, XVII, no. 3 (1974). See also M. E. Howard, *War and the Liberal Conscience* (1978).
19. H. Weinroth, 'The British Radicals and the Balance of Power, 1902–14', *HJ*, XIII, no. 3 (1974) 676.

20. O. Anderson, 'The Growth of Christian Militarism in Mid-Victorian Britain', *EHR*, LXXXVI (Jan 1971).

21. M. Ekstein, 'Sir Edward Grey and Imperial Germany in 1914', *JCH*, VI (1971).

22. Churchill, *The World Crisis*, p. 114.

23. Burns Papers, diary, 27 July 1914.

24. For an analysis of Cabinet opinion, see Hazlehurst, *Politicians at War*, pp. 54–65.

25. Lord Riddell, *War Diary* (1933) p. 6.

26. Churchill to Lloyd George, cited in Hazlehurst, *Politicians at War*, p. 66.

27. I. Geiss, *July 1914: Outbreak of the First World War – Selected Documents*, document no. 130.

28. Frances Lloyd George, *The Years that are Lost* (1967) pp. 73–4.

29. F. Fischer, *War of Illusions: German Policies from 1911 to 1914* (1975).

30. Hazlehurst, *Politicians at War*. See also A. Mayer, 'Domestic Causes of the First World War', in L. Krieger and F. Stern (eds), *The Responsibility of Power* (New York, 1967), and the reply by D. Lammers, 'Arno Mayer and the British Decision for War', *JBS*, XII, no. 2 (1973).

31. C. Trebilcock, 'Legends of the British Armaments Industry 1890–1914: A Revision', *JCH*, V (1970).

32. Z. S. Steiner, *The Foreign Office and Foreign Policy, 1898–1914* (Cambridge, 1969).

33. *BD*, III, appendix A.

34. R. Langhorne, review article 'The Foreign Office before 1914', *HJ*, XVI, no. 4 (1973).

35. C. Howard, 'MacDonald, Henderson and the Outbreak of War in 1914', *HJ*, XX, no. 4 (1977). See also K. Wilson, 'The British Cabinet's Decision for War', *BJIS*, I (1975).

36. Steiner, *Britain and the Origins of the First World War*, p. 232.

37. C. E. Playne, *The Pre-War Mind in Britain* (1928).

38. M. E. Howard, *Haldane and the Territorial Army* (1966) p. 14.

39. K. G. Robbins, 'Public Opinion, Press and Pressure Groups', in Hinsley, *The Foreign Policy of Grey*, pp. 75ff.

40. R. Tressall, *The Ragged Trousered Philanthropists* (1914).

41. P. Wilkinson, 'English Youth Movements, 1908–30', *JCH*, II (1969). See also J. Springhall, 'Boy Scouts, Class and Militarism, 1908–30', *IRSH*, XVI, pt 2 (1971).

42. J. Gooch, 'Victorian and Edwardian Attitudes to War', in B. Bond and I. Roy (eds), *War and Society*, I (1975).

43. G. Best, 'Militarism and the Victorian Public School', in B. Simon and I. Bradley (eds), *The Victorian Public School* (1975).

44. M. E. Howard, 'Reflections on the First World War', in *Studies in War and Peace* (1970).

Notes on Contributors

WALTER L. ARNSTEIN, Professor of History, University of Illinois at Urbana-Champaign. He received his Ph. D. from Northwestern University. He is the author of numerous articles and his books include *The Bradlaugh Case: Britain Yesterday and Today*; he collaborated with W. B. Willcox on the third edition of *The Age of Aristocracy*.

SUZANN BUCKLEY, Associate Professor of History, State University of New York at Plattsburgh. She received her Ph. D. from Duke University. She has published articles on British imperial and military policy and on British and Canadian feminists.

PETER CAIN, Senior Lecturer in Economic History, University of Birmingham. He was educated at Oxford. Author of numerous articles on British railways, one being awarded the T. S. Ashton Prize by the Economic History Society in 1972. His current work is on British economic imperialism and the imperial thought of J. A. Hobson.

DENNIS DEAN, Lecturer in History, Institute of Education, University of London. MA, Cambridge; M. Phil., Ph. D., London. He has published several articles and is currently researching on the historiography of the labour movement for Britain and the United States and also writing a book on the history of education.

T. R. GOURVISH, Senior Lecturer in Economic History, University of East Anglia. BA, Ph. D., London. He has published numerous articles on the standard of living and on British railway management and is the author of *Mark Huish and the London and North Western Railway*. At present he is working on a study of Sir Edward Watkin and James Staats Forbes.

COLIN NICOLSON, Senior Lecturer in History, Polytechnic of North London. He was educated at the University of Birmingham and has written several articles and a book on immigrants. He did research on public opinion and foreign policy in the Edwardian period at the Centre for Contemporary Culture, University of Birmingham.

ALAN O'DAY, Senior Lecturer in History, Polytechnic of North London. He received his BA and MA from American universities and then took a Ph. D. at the University of London. He has taught for British, German and American universities and wrote *The English Face of Irish Nationalism*. He is completing a study of Irish home rule.

G. R. SEARLE, Lecturer in History, University of East Anglia. MA, Ph. D.,

Cambridge. His books are *The Quest for National Efficiency* and *Eugenics and Politics in Britain, 1900–1914*. He is at present preparing a further study of the critics of Edwardian society.

Index

abortion 138
Admiralty 148–9
Afrikaaners 63
Agadir crisis (1911) 151–2
Aldcroft, D. 37
aliens 91–2
Aliens Act, 1905 70
Amery, J. 155
Anderson, G. L. 23
Anderson, M. 134
Angell, N. 155–6
Anglo-German Friendship League 160
Anti-alien 85
anti-feminists 140, 142
anti-German 51
anti-parliamentary ideas 93–4
Anti-Socialist Union 86
'appeasement' 152
Army 145–6, 148–9
Army Chiefs of Staff 150
Army ineptitude 63–4
Army reform 83
Arms Race 152
Askwith, G. R. 15
Asquith, H. H. 10, 60, 70–2, 74, 76, 90, 99, 112, 114, 123–4, 130, 142, 152–3, 155, 158–60, 162
Association of Railway Servants 101
Australia 48, 86
Austria 115, 146

balance of power 154, 156
balance of trade 38, 46, 47
Balfour, A. J. 44, 53–5, 57–8, 60, 64–5, 70–5, 80–8, 96, 107, 113, 119–20
Balfour, G. 120

Balfour Government 65, 68, 90, 123
Balkan Wars 152
Barker, R. 100
Barnsby, G. 20–1
Belgium 146, 149, 151, 156, 159, 162, 166
Bell, R. 101, 104
Belloc, H. 88, 90–1
Beresford, Admiral C. 85
Beveridge, W. 5
Birrell, A. 126–8
birth control 135, 137
Blake, Lord 9, 114
Blatchford, R. 74, 85, 108
Block, M. 165
blue-collar workers 22, 24–5, 29
Board of Trade 14, 16–17, 21, 27–8
Boer War 37, 40, 61, 63–4, 80, 82, 146, 154
Booth, C. 4, 13
Booth, W. 107
Bowley, A. L. 13–23, 25–8
British Expeditionary Force (BEF) 148–9, 153, 155
de Broke, W. 84, 86, 89, 95
Broadhurst, H. 101
Browne, M. 13–16, 20
Brunner, Sir J. 92
Bryce, J. 68, 123, 125–6
Bryce Memorandum 1886 161
budget (1909) 54–5, 60, 71–3, 81, 111
Burgess, K. 25
Burns, J. 73, 100, 110, 155, 157
by-elections (1902–3) 106; (1906–10) 71; (1910–14) 78, 111

Cabinet Committee on Foreign Affairs 152
Cadbury, G. 89
Cambon, J. 147, 152–3
Campbell-Bannerman, Sir H. 63, 65, 68, 71, 124, 128, 153
Canada 40, 41, 48–9, 115
Carlton Club 82
Cawdor Programme (1904) 150
Caxton Hall agreement 106
Chemicals 49
census of 1911 136
Challinor, R. D. 100
Chamberlain, J. 5, 38, 40–41, 44, 52–5, 57–9, 65, 69–72, 75, 80, 83, 97, 110, 146
Championites 107
Chesterton brothers 88, 90–1
Chinese labourer/slavery 54, 63, 68–9
Church disestablishment 105
Church influence in Ireland 126–7
Churchill, W. S. 55, 70, 72, 77, 81, 97, 100, 107, 111, 115, 157, 150, 155, 157, 159, 167
Civil Service 93, 151
civil war threat 113
class polarisation 57, 58
Clagg, Fix, and Thompson 99
Clements, R. V. 101
Clynes, J. 98, 112
coal industry 38, 46, 49
Cobden, R. 150
Cole, W. A. 39, 47
Colonial Conference (1897) 41; (1907) 55
Collinson, W. 104
Committee on Imperial Defence 64, 148, 160
The Common People 98
conscription 149, 153, 160, 165, 167
Conservative Governments/Cabinets 41, 60–1, 63, 65, 68, 80
Conservative party/Unionist party/conservatism 2, 7–9, 58–9, 61–3, 65–6, 68, 70, 78–87, 93, 95, 105, 107, 109–12, 113–15, 117, 119–23, 125, 130, 162

conspiracy theories 93
Constitutional Conference 74–5, 83–4
constitutional crisis 56–7, 81–2, 87, 111, 129
Constitution, The 116, 125, 130
constitutional reform 109
constructive conservatism 120–2
continental socialist congresses 109
cotton industry 37, 45, 48, 50, 53
county seats 62
courts and trade unions 104
craft unions 102
Creighton, Mrs 133–4, 143
Crossick, G. 103
Crowe, Eyre 51, 147, 154
cultural revival in Ireland 122–3
Curtis, L. P. 119–20

Daily News 89
Daily Mail 73–4
Dangerfield, G. 1–2, 4, 7–10, 77–8, 98–100, 113–14, 131, 134, 140
Davin, A. 136
Deane, P. 39, 47
defence 75, 111
defence expenditure 58, 80
devolution crisis (1904) 123
Devonshire, duke of 69
diehards 84, 87–8, 93
Diet 138
Dilke, Sir C. 104
Dillon, J. 116, 123–5, 131
diversionary war 160–1
divorce 139–41
dock strike (1889) 103
domestic servants 137
double sexual standard 140
Dreyfus supported 92
drink question 83; (local option 105–6)
Dunraven, earl of 122

economic difficulties 35–7, 58–9, 131
Education Act (1870) 103
Education (Act of 1902) 54, 64, 68–9, 83, 103, 110, 125

Edward VII   74, 92, 139, 144
eight-hour day   103, 105
elections (uncontested)   60, 70, 75
Elgin Commission   (1903)   63
Elibank, Master of   91
Empire   40–46, 49–51, 54, 59,
   64–5, 74, 92–3, 100, 136–7,
   140, 147, 154
Employers Federation of Engineers
   Association   103
Emy, H. V.   114
engineering   27
Ensor, Sir R.   99
Entente, the   147, 152, 156
Eugenics Education Society   85
Europe   37–8, 42, 46, 50, 149, 154,
   156–58, 161, 163
export of capital   45, 48, 57

Fabians   101, 106–7
family   10, 133–9, 141, 143
Far East markets   50
fatherhood (manhood)   132, 137
Feinstein, C. H.   16
feminists   2, 9–10, 141–2
Firestone, O. J.   40
fiscal reform   51–2, 57–8
fiscal retrenchment   68
Fischer, Professor   160–1
Fisher, Admiral   85
foreign competition   19, 23
Foreign Office personnel   161
France   146–53, 155–6, 158–9, 163
franchise (women)   9–10, 133–4,
   136, 140–2
Fraser, D.   5
Fraser, P.   97
free trade   6, 38, 40–5, 48–51,
   53–8, 65, 68–71, 73, 95, 109,
   111

Gaelic League   123
Garvin, J. L.   83
General elections (1906)   54, 56,
   70, 76; (1910)   55, 81, 111,
   129; (January 1910)   55, 72–6;
   (December 1910)   57, 75–6
General unions   99
George V   74, 159

George, H.   71
German navalism   51, 74, 81
Germanophiles   92
Germany   9, 36, 38, 40, 44, 51, 53,
   64, 74, 80, 85, 92, 94–6, 115,
   136, 145–52, 154–61, 163, 165–7
Gilbert, B.   5, 71
Gladstone, H.   66–7, 110–11, 121,
   124
Gladstone–MacDonald pact   110–
   11
Gladstone, W. E.   8, 52, 61, 72–3,
   79, 101, 109, 117–21, 124, 150
Gladstonian   8, 9, 11, 145, 151–2
government by managerial elite
   82–3
Grayson, V.   109
Grey, Sir E.   1, 70, 74, 80, 146–55,
   157–64

Haldane, R. B.   51, 64, 68, 70, 153,
   163, 167
Halévy, E.   99
Hanham, H. J.   115
Harmsworth brothers   89
Harcourt, L.   152, 155
Harcourt, Sir W.   118, 121
Hardie, K.   98, 100–1, 104, 106–
   10, 112, 60, 67
Harris, J.   5
Havighurst, A.   67
Hay, J. R.   5
Healy, T. M.   127
Henderson, A.   67, 98, 106, 112
Hepburn, A. C.   127
'Herr Dumper'   73
high society's failings   93
Hobsbawm, E. J.   100
Hobson, J. A.   155
Hoffman, R. J. S.   51
Home Rule all-round   131
honours system   90–1
Hopkins, E.   20–1
House of Commons   70–3, 75, 77,
   113, 124–5, 129–30, 141, 152–5,
   157
House of Lords   56–7, 71–2, 74–5,
   81, 83, 111, 114, 117, 125
Howard, M.   167–8

Howell, D.   100
Hudson, Sir R.   72
Hunt, E. H.   19, 22
Hyde, D.   122
Hyndman, H. H.   102, 107, 109

idealism   145, 150–6, 158–60, 162,
    166–7
immigrants   139
Imperial Maritime League   95,
    167
imperial federalism   115
Imperial unity   5, 41, 52–3, 59
Imperialism   61, 156
imports   37–8, 41, 45–6, 55, 57
Independent Labour Party (ILP)
    101, 107–9, 142
industrial efficiency   36
industrial disputes   29, 77, 86, 98
India   46
infant welfare   30, 136, 138
insurance earnings   38, 47
Ireland   7, 63, 65, 68, 77, 83–4,
    94–5, 113–18, 120–28, 130–1,
    145, 156–7, 160
Irish-Americans   93
Irish in Britain   70, 75
Irish Councils bill   125–9
Irish home rule   2, 7–8, 53, 57, 61,
    65, 68, 73–5, 77, 86, 89, 93,
    105, 113–18 120–9, 131–32
Irish home rule bill (1912)   90
Government of Ireland Bill   114–
    15
Irish Land Bill (1909)   125
Irish party   56–7, 70, 74, 76, 81,
    90, 93, 116, 120, 122–8
Irish Worker   122
iron and steel industry   36–8, 42,
    45–6, 50–1, 53
Isaacs, R.   91
Italy   146

Jews   70, 92, 95

Kaiser   161
Kendall, W.   100
Key, E.   133, 141

Kipling, R.   90, 164
Kuczynski, J.   18, 19, 22

Labour Government (1931)   98,
    100
labour mobility   18
Labour movement   11, 121
Labour party   54, 56–7, 59, 60, 63,
    67, 69–72, 74, 76–9, 81, 87, 97–
    101, 108, 110, 111–12, 121–2,
    162
labour relations   27
Labour Representation Committee
    66, 97, 101, 104, 106
labour unrest   15, 145, 156, 160
labourers' cottages bill (Ire.)   125
Lansdowne, Lord   80
landed interest   3, 51, 54, 56
Latin America   47, 49
Law, B.   58, 81, 88–90
Lee, J.   122
Lerner, G.   135
Lesbians   140
Liberal Government   4, 8, 29, 60,
    71–2, 74, 81–2, 84, 86–7, 89–91,
    93, 95, 100, 115, 124–5, 127,
    130, 144–5, 150–59, 162
Liberal ideology/state   3, 6–10, 67,
    79, 95
Liberal imperialists   51
Liberal League   154
Liberal party   7–8, 10–11, 52–5,
    57, 59, 61–81, 84, 86–7, 97,
    101, 104–12, 117–21, 123–24,
    127–31, 151, 155, 159, 160
Liberal Publications Department
    68
Liberal Unionists   52–3, 62, 79
Licensing Act (1904)   64
Liddington, J & J. Norris   134
Little Englanders   45
Lloyd George   55–6, 70, 72–3, 77,
    81, 83–4, 91, 99, 100, 109, 111–
    12, 120–1, 129, 156, 162
lower middle class   23, 103
Lyons, F. S. L.   117

McCready, H.   121

MacDonald, R. 66–7, 98, 104, 106, 109–12
MacDowell, Sir A. 126
McKibbin, R. 11
Manchester Guardian 153, 158
Mann, T. 102, 105
Marconi scandal 91, 96
Married Women's Property Act (1882) 142
Marquand, D. 108
Marx, K. 71
Masterman, C. 13
Maxse, L. 85–90, 92
Meacham, S. 102
military preparations 144, 146–50, 154, 165
Milner, Lord 83–4, 98, 110, 154
miners' strike (1912) 86
miners' union 99, 105–6, 111
miners' wages 26–8
Mitchell, H. 134, 139, 141
monarchy 93
Money, C. 13, 15–16
Moore, R. 101
Morgan, D. 133
Morgan, K. O. 60, 98, 100, 108, 115
Morley, J. 118, 124
Morris, A. J. A. 100
Morris, W. 108
Mosley, O. 7, 89
most-favoured-nation treaties 44–5
motherhood 136–8
mutual preferences 41–5, 48–51, 54–6, 58–9

Nation, The 71
national efficiency 38, 64, 82–3, 98
National Free Church Council 69
National Free Labour Association 103
National Government 83; (coalition, 1910) 129
national insurance 5, 29; (National Insurance Act, 1911) 78
National League for Clean Government 91

national regeneration 89
National Review 85–7, 92
National Service League 85, 95, 167
National Union of Railwaymen 102
National Union of Women's Suffrage Societies 142
naval strategy 150
naval strength 35; (race) 150, 165
naval war 149–50, 154
Navy 83
Navy League 85, 154
naval panic 81
New Liberalism 100, 112
New Zealand 86
newspapers 63, 89, 165–6
Nicolson, A. 154–5
Nonconformists 54, 61, 71, 108

The Observer 75
O'Brien, W. 122–3, 127
O'Connell, D. 117
O'Connor, T. P. 124–5
Oliver, F. S. 83
organic state 118–22, 124, 129, 131
Osborne Judgement 74

pacifists 80, 84, 145, 151, 155–6, 158, 163, 165
Palmerston, Lord 150
Pan-German League 94
Pankhurst, C. 140, 142
Pankhurst, E. 10
Parliament 3, 41, 109–10, 149, 154
Parliament Act (1911) 77, 82, 84
Parliamentary Committee of TUC 106
parliamentary supremacy 116, 130
Parnell, C. S. 117
party strife 162
Payne, P. L. 37
peace through trade 45, 50–1
Pearse, P. 117, 131
Pelling, H. 67, 77–8, 99, 105, 107
Phelps Brown, E. 13–17, 20

Pimlott, B. 100
Playfair, L. 119
Plunkett, Sir H. 122
Plural voting 62
pluralist state 118–24, 129, 131
political lawyers 88
Pollard, S. 20
Ponsonby, Sir A. 13, 155
Portugal 152
poverty 4, 13, 29, 31
prices 14–16, 18–21, 23–4, 43–4, 55
Primat der Aussenpolitik 145, 161
Primat der Innenpolitik 161
progressives 100, 111
propaganda 164–7
prostitution 140–1
protection 5–6, 40–2, 44–5, 48–53, 55, 57–9, 65, 68, 71, 92
protection in USA/Germany 36–7, 40, 42, 44
pro-war opinion 145, 161–7
public school ethic 165–7

Quarterly Review 64, 68–9
Queen Victoria 38

Radicals 62, 85, 87, 90, 92, 106–7, 111–12, 145, 150–3, 155–6, 160–1
railways 23–4, 27–8, 31
realism 145, 150–1, 154, 156–61, 166–7
Redmond, J. 75, 93, 116–17, 120, 124–9, 131
Referendum (on tariff) 57; (plan) 75, 86
Reform Act (1884) and Redistribution Act (1885) 61–3, 116
regional wage/price variations 19–22
registration (voting) rules 62, 105
religious liberty 106
rents 16–19 21
    retaliationist(s) 44, 48–9, 53–4, 65; (against Britain) 50
Reveille movement 84, 89
Robbins, K. G. 164
Roberts, E. 20–1

Roberts, Lord 94
Rosebery, Lord 64–5, 107, 119, 121
Rosen, A. 134, 141
Rousseaux's index 14
Rover, C. 133
Rowe, J. W. F. 26, 28
Rowntree, S. 4, 13
Royal Commission on Divorce, etc. 139
Royal family 151
Royal Navy 148–9, 154, 158
Ruskin, J. 108
Russell, A. K. 66
Russia 146, 151–2, 158, 163

Sackville-West, V. 139
Salisbury Government 104
Salisbury, Lord 61, 64, 80
Sauerbeck–*Statist* index 14
Saville, J. 103
Schlieffen Plan 148, 150
Scholte, W. 50
Scotland 61, 113–16, 119, 121–2
Seeley, Sir J. 164
Serbian Crisis 157
sex war 140
Shipbuilding 45, 48, 53
shipping 38, 47
Sinn Fein 128
Slaven, T. 27
Smith, F. L. 34
Snowden, P. 15, 98, 108, 112
Social Darwinism 94, 166
Social Democratic Federation 100–2, 106–7
social imperialists 59
social purity 140
social reform 51–4, 57–8, 61, 63, 65, 67, 70–1, 75, 78, 81, 83, 87, 100, 105, 107, 109, 111–12
socialism 55–6, 59, 73, 81, 85, 87, 97, 100–1, 105–8, 111
Socialist Labour Party 100
South Africa 63, 68, 97
'spy mania' 94
standard of living 3–4, 16, 19, 21, 24, 29, 31, 42, 98, 103, 137
    intangible improvements 29, 30

Steinberg, J. 150
Strachey, R. 133
Suffragettes 9, 77–8, 140, 143, 157
Syndicalists 78, 112
Synge, J. M. 122

Taff Vale 68–9, 104
tariffs 40, 54, 59
tariff reform 5–7, 34, 38, 41–3, 50–2, 54–9, 69, 71, 73, 75, 80, 83, 86–7, 97, 110
Tariff Reform League 53
tariff warfare 51
taxes 71–2
Taylor, A. J. P. 1, 146, 164
temperance 68–70
textiles 37, 46, 50
Tholfsen, T. R. 101
Thomas, J. H. 98, 112
Thompson, P. 77, 102, 114
Thorne, C. 102
Times, The 83
Tone, W. 117
total war 144, 163–4, 167
trade (overseas) 36–8, 42, 46, 57
trade revival 45–6, 57
Trade Unions 2, 29, 30, 54, 66, 69, 77, 81, 97, 100–1, 103–7, 111–12
Trades Union Congress (TUC) 101
Tressall, R. 164
trial marriages 140
Triple Alliance 146
Tucker, R. 19
Turkey 151

Ulster Unionists 2, 77, 88, 114, 117, 130
ultra-Tories 84
underdeveloped world 37
unemployment 16, 21, 28, 45, 49, 54–5
Unionist party, see Conservative party
USA 36–8, 40–44, 48, 50, 67, 104, 115, 126, 136
universal military training 94

university seats 62

Victorian Studies 60
Vincent, J. R. 118–19
visible income 38, 42, 46–7
voluntary societies 138
voting (disqualifications) 61–2

wage levels 13–40, 41, 44, 46, 54–6
wage variations skilled/unskilled 22
Wales 57, 61, 110, 113–16, 118–19, 121–3
Walters, R. 26
War Office 148
war's impact 144, 154–5
Webb, S. & B. 64, 77, 107
Weber, E. 120
Weber, M. 131
welfare state/legislation 4–6, 9, 11, 30–1, 43, 55–6
Wells, H. G. 139, 165
Westminster, archbishop of 125
White, A. 84, 86, 90, 92–3, 95
white-collar workers 18, 22–3, 29
'Whole Hogger' 55, 57, 75
widows 135–6
Wiebe, R. 120
Wilson, General H. 149, 153, 158, 161
woollen industry 38, 48, 50
women 133–5, 137–43;
(employment) 135–6;
(unmarried) 135–6, 140–1;
(working class) 134, 137–8, 141–2
Women's Liberal Federation 70
Women's Social & Political Union (WSPU) 134, 142
womens' wages 22, 141
Wood, F. 19, 21
working class 4, 52, 55, 59, 66, 85–6, 97–8, 102, 103
Wyndham, G. 120
Wyndham Land Act (1903) 64–5, 120

Yeats, W. B. 122
youth movements 138, 165–6